UNPREDICTABLE
JOURNEY

UNPREDICTABLE
JOURNEY
A Memoir

ERNLÉ W.D. YOUNG

iUniverse®

UNPREDICTABLE JOURNEY
A MEMOIR

Scripture taken from the New King James Version®. Copyright © 1982 by Thomas Nelson. Used by permission. All rights reserved.

New Revised Standard Version Bible, copyright © 1989 National Council of the Churches of Christ in the United States of America. Used by permission. All rights reserved worldwide. http://nrsvbibles.org

THE HOLY BIBLE, NEW INTERNATIONAL VERSION®, NIV® Copyright © 1973, 1978, 1984, 2011 by Biblica, Inc.® Used by permission. All rights reserved worldwide.

iUniverse books may be ordered through booksellers or by contacting:

*iUniverse
1663 Liberty Drive
Bloomington, IN 47403
www.iuniverse.com
1-800-Authors (1-800-288-4677)*

*ISBN: 978-1-5320-3276-9 (sc)
ISBN: 978-1-5320-3278-3 (hc)
ISBN: 978-1-5320-3277-6 (e)*

Library of Congress Control Number: 2017918520

Print information available on the last page.

iUniverse rev. date: 12/21/2017

For Margaret, my beloved wife and life's companion,
who with unfailing love has believed in me and stood
by me in the best of times and in the worst of times

Foreword

1. Welcome

If you are a family member or a friend of Ernlé Young, you come to this memoir out of love, admiration, or appreciation for this man, or all three; as well as with a curiosity to learn more of his life story. Your times with Ernlé have usually left you feeling better. You have experienced his acceptance, his caring for your spirit, his wit and laughter, his attention to detail in speech and deeds, his love of learning new things, his passionate transparency, his wisdom. Your times together have left you feeling more alive, if not always more comfortable.

If you are not a family member or friend, perhaps you are a reader some of Ernlé's many books and articles on ethical topics in medicine and health care. You are interested in learning more about this man who writes with such clarity, bringing reason to his analyses of difficult and emotionally turbulent ethical challenges in neonatal intensive care, genetics (is a fertilized egg a person?), or the uses and misuses of technology at the end of a patient's life. You may have been a student or resident in one of Ernlé's courses in the medical school at Stanford, or a member of the congregation during one or more of Ernlé's Sunday sermons at Stanford Memorial or one of the nearby churches.

If you belong to Ernlé's family, you'll quickly see that this memoir is meant as a gift to you. He has researched and populated branches and limbs of your family trees, providing colorful details and lights about some of your relatives that may give you smiles of recognition and insight, like seeing an old photograph of a cousin as a child, and noticing the subtle yet telltale smirk that you saw so often that you stopped noticing. Context is there, too: geography and culture. He gives you in his memoir glimpses of the times, some of the cultural and political events—local, national, and professional—that formed the context of the events in his and his family's life that he recounts. He also gives the gift of transparency, letting you see what he was feeling and thinking as he lived, moved, studied, and worked in so many settings in South Africa and the United States.

I see Ernlé's memoir as a love story, a story of his love for his strong and beautiful bride of 58 years, Margaret, for his children, Heather, Andrew, Jenny, and Tim, for his mother, Peggy, for Margaret's parents and her brother, Ken, and his wife; and for his grandchildren and their progeny. Following his marriage, Ernlé's priority concern became and remains his family's well-being. Daughter Heather's beautiful note in the memoir shows that his love is deeply felt and reciprocated.

If you are among Ernlé's friends and colleagues in South Africa, Britain, Australia, and the United States, you'll easily find the part of his story that intersects with yours, whether briefly or over a long span of time. You'll read Ernlé's memoir because you're thankful for his presence in your life, for the times you've shared, and because you've sometimes wondered what makes this guy tick—what moved him to work, play, and sometimes even fist-fight with others.

2. First meeting

I have been Ernlé's friend and colleague for more than 40 years. I first met him in 1974, when he was 42, more than halfway through his still continuing "unpredictable journey." At that time Ernlé was Chaplain to the Stanford University

Medical Center, the Associate Minister at Stanford Memorial Church, and a member of the Faculty of Stanford's Medical School as Senior Lecturer in Medical Ethics.

I met Ernlé in his office on the main floor of the Medical Center. I was nervous. Why? As an Assistant Professor of Religious Studies at Santa Clara University, I had confided in a faculty colleague, Stuart McLean, that I felt that my approach to teaching about suffering and death in Religious Studies courses had become too academic. I asked him for suggestions about how I might tether my teaching more closely to the experiences of persons living with critical illnesses. Stuart offered to ask Ernlé, his friend and colleague at Stanford, if he would be willing to mentor me or point me in the direction of someone who might.

So there I was, in the midst of an enormous medical center that felt like a giant beehive to me compared to my natural habitat of a quiet college campus. I was encountering for the first time a tall guy with a reddish beard, an easy gait, and a fetching accent, who, I hoped, would be open to letting me try to improve my teaching by helping and learning from hospitalized patients and their families. I was surprised to feel so immediately at ease. This tall guy, who was doing such important and well-recognized work at Stanford University and Memorial Church, ambled into his office in the middle of a busy day and gave me, a total stranger, his full attention. Thirty minutes later, after his listening and gentle questioning helped me realize and organize what I wanted from him, we arranged to meet again so that he could give me a tour of the hospital and agree on how I might begin trying to learn by helping others. He conveyed his support and his genuine interest in sharing my journey. He looked me straight in the eyes the whole time, spoke with the clarity of a mountain stream, and connected with me professional to professional, and behind and through that professional connection, man to man.

That first meeting was life-changing for me. I had found

a mentor who would over time become both a professional colleague and a good friend. I drove home from Palo Alto to Santa Clara that afternoon, still nervous about beginning in the Intensive Care Unit's family waiting area in a few days, yet also glowing with hope from Ernlé's encouragement to begin a new adventure—one which would lead me away from the "ivory tower" of university teaching into consulting and teaching in clinical health care ethics, a professional life which I continue into my mid-seventies.

Like kindred planets in a solar system, our orbits would continue to overlap and intersect from time to time over the years, and then diverge again for long periods before converging again, with interpersonal exchanges adding dimensions to our professional camaraderie. We became friends, and are friends still.

3. Reading Ernlé's Memoir

As I read through this memoir, I enjoyed its structure and clarity. Ernlé organizes it geographically, telling stories about the places where he was living, going to school, trekking, sailing, playing, and working. I learned much about the man, some of which are things that I had noticed and wondered about over the years. For example, I learned how he became so good at playing tennis, which I first experienced at first-hand after we played a set on a court in Menlo Park one day. He stood cool at his end of the court, returning every one of my shots with ease, forcing me to race back and forth, up and back, breathless and sweating, smiling compassionately as I lost every point. I also learned in reading his memoir why he spent so much time in his workshop, making beautiful pieces of furniture. I learned how he came to his way of preparing his sermons and lectures, which had always amazed me with their clarity of thought and sentiment. I learned why he seemed to thrust himself with such passion into his singing, whether a popular ditty or a hymn. I learned why, when he finally let go of "working for a living"—when he left his work at NASA's Ames Research Center—he set himself to learning to play the piano, practicing diligently for hours each day.

I learned that his Dad had enkindled his first serious enquiry into philosophy, by impressing on young Ernlé the importance of character, and a curiosity about what character is that sent his son into reading Greek philosophers on train trip commutes back and forth from work to find answers. I learned how he came to be so crazy about Cornish pasties, and why he seems to love talking about cars so much.

(The photo on the cover of the memoir is of a fit young man of 21 about to sail off for many months of hiking and hitchhiking through Britain and Europe, returning afterwards to divinity studies at Rhodes and preaching excursions to cities and towns in Eastern South Africa, sometimes borrowing a car, sometimes thumbing rides, aching with longing for his own car and for the freedom and independence that came with it. When he finally came to climb into a car of his own, he learned all he could about motors, and frequently enough used that knowledge to diagnose engine problems and keep his cars on the road.)

Mostly, though, I learned in reading his memoir that his story is a tale of rich and lasting friendships—both with his own friends and those he shares with Margaret. He could have told his story as one of prodigious professional accomplishments: his lectures, his articles and books in medical ethics, his creation of the Stanford Center for Biomedical Ethics, his consulting relationships with biomedical companies and health systems (the Palo Alto, Fresno, and San Francisco Veterans Administration medical centers).

While he provides glimpses of all these in his memoir, my overwhelming impression of my friend from this tale, as I said before, is of the wealth and quality of his friendships. In tender of friendships, Ernlé is the richest man I know. Key friendships for him, in this life story, have been like stepping stones and bridges upon which he has made his way, through and across the currents and the turning points of his life. His many friendships, in each of which he invests his heart and soul, are among his greatest treasures in his memoir and in his life through the present.

4. From the memoir to the man.

Ernlé is a good friend. By that I mean the usual things with friends who stay friends over long periods of time: love and understanding, shared interests (in our case, graduate degrees in theology, professional careers in Clinical Ethics, single malt Scotch), travel to Britain and through Europe, joy at the thought of getting together with each other. Ernlé's allowing himself the freedom to be himself gives his friends unlimited breathing space, the freedom to be themselves.

Ernlé loves to talk, to share thoughts and stories. Even more, he loves to listen. From time to time in long, almost timeless conversations, out of the blue, he laughs, and exclaims, "I love you, man!" He is with you, mind, heart, soul, and imp.

Ernlé's memoir shines the light on those with whom he is sharing time, sometimes more than it reveals him. More than most autobiographies I know, the light and focus in Ernlé's memoir is most often upon others in his life—with whomever is sharing his table, his church, his congregation, his classroom, his roadway, his campsite, or even his vehicle. Like Ernlé in person, his memoir reveals himself more, in many of its sections, in the background over time, as he pays attention to others. There are few "selfies" in this story.

In many other sections he does reveal himself, of course: how he felt about his studies, his teachers, his bosses, his colleagues, his mentors. He recounts several choices that he made that have hurt people that he loves and led him to feel deep sadness, shame, guilt, and regret. He must have felt that he owes it to his family and friends to be transparent about those painful aspects of his life as well as the labors, joys, and accomplishments that he relates. I winced a bit during those sections of the memoir—not so much at his descriptions, but imagining the angst I might feel if I invited my Mr. Hyde into the spotlight in view of family, friends, and strangers. At the same time I appreciated and admired Ernlé's courage in being honest in print, as he is in life. I don't know many people who can truly say that their lives are an open book.

A person's character consists, I believe, mostly in what that person loves. Ernlé's memoir is a love story, a story of his loves. His foundational love, the bedrock of his story, is his love of and for his family. Next is his love for his friends. Then comes his love of fairness, sometimes calling out injustice in public spaces, sometimes helping to make things better for the vulnerable ones, the have-nots in the communities in which he participates. He loves striving for excellence or quality in everything he does in work and play. He delights in bringing joy to his family and his friends. I know that his bubbling presence and his friendship bring tastes of the eternal—abundant and memorable life and joy— to those who know and love him. He calls some of these loves and delights "gifts," and credits his family:

> "Looking back on the story thus far, I can see how significantly my upbringing shaped my life. Being willing to go from the security of the known to the uncertainty of the unknown was part of my heritage. My love for the game of tennis, my delight in singing, playing the piano, and listening to music, and my sense of being at home in the great outdoors were gifts my family gave me."

His family, friends, and colleagues, of course, know the character that is Ernlé Young, the richly human character of a passionate guy whose scratches, scars and flaws on the surface add character to the burnished gold at the core, what he cares for and about. His memoir reflects both the scratches and the core.

5.

I enjoyed reading Ernlé's brief personal creed at the end of his memoir, and the samples of his sermons that he provides. Pascal observed that the heart has its reasons, which reason does not know. Ernlé is a man of both heart and reason. His professed convictions and values have a religious flavor, but they are not dry, and they don't read like rote recitations or high-sounding pious platitudes. They emerge out of the memoir and they ring true. They rise up from within the preceding story as a kind of prayer. The reader can, when Ernlé names them, recognize them as ingredients giving taste and texture throughout the whole loaf of the memoir. This is a man, as I felt in our very first meeting, who practices transparency with compassion, who leads with his vulnerability more than his strength, and who has forged his integrity in a life lived and being lived deeply and with passion. I believe that those who read his memoir will see what I mean.

Daniel Dugan, PhD
Modesto, CA, USA
July 2017

Preface

After an accident (described in chapter 10) that left me unable to walk and in a wheelchair for more than two months—and then not long afterward with my left arm immobilized for another two months—I continued writing in earnest, first with both hands and then with just one, what I had started earlier and worked on in desultory fashion: the story of my life's journey. I wanted to do this for our children and grandchildren so that they would better know their Dad and Dad-dad, their Mom and Granny. It was also important to me to record for a wider audience our experience of the inhumanity of South African apartheid, our small part in resisting and working to end it, and the consequences. The autobiographies of Mason Willrich, Herant Katchadourian, and Rod Derbyshire collectively served as an inspiration.

Having now completed this record of the unpredictable road I have traveled, I must acknowledge an immeasurable debt of appreciation and gratitude to several friends and family members who have helped with the book's eventual birthing process. Herant Katchadourian read and made invaluable editorial comments on two earlier versions of the manuscript. Daniel Dugan not only read it three times but also graciously undertook the writing and then the re-writing of the foreword. Margaret, my wife, and Heather, our daughter, each cast a critical eye on sections of what I had written and nudged me from time to time to make changes in emphasis. John Anton and Coralie Farnham each offered wise editorial suggestions after reading several chapters. Johann Maree read chapter 8 and made useful critical comments. Heather assembled the photographs and drew up the genealogical table included in the book. I am deeply grateful to them all for giving me so much of their time and for their astute insights. Andrew hand-drew the two maps, doing the lettering in his beautiful architectural script. Surely two of life's greatest blessings are those of a loving family and cherished friends. In both, I am abundantly blessed.

Ernlé W. D. Young
Talent, Oregon
March 2017

PART 1

Beginnings

1

Forebears

From Northumberland and London, England, and Cork, Ireland, to Judith's Paarl, Johannesburg, South Africa

Tracing my lineage is somewhat confusing because my mother's maiden name was Young and she married a Young. They were not related. All my grandparents and uncles were Youngs, as are all my male cousins. My grandmothers, aunts, and female cousins took the names of the men they married. Those were the days before the rise of feminism.

My mother's parents, Thomas Young and Jane Young (neé Cairns), were "Geordies," a common nickname for Northumbrians. Northumberland is the northeasternmost of the forty-eight counties that comprise England. It is bordered on the east by the North Sea (Newcastle-Upon-Tyne is its most well-known and major coal-exporting port from which the phrase "carrying coals to Newcastle" takes its origin), by Hadrian's Wall to the south, by the Cheviot Range to the west, and by Scotland to the north. Alnwick, on the River Aln, is its premier market town and is the seat of Percy, Duke of Northumberland, whose majestic castle overlooks both the river and the countryside to the north and the town to the south.[1]

My grandfather was born on January 31, 1856. He was a man of many parts: farmer, stonemason, publican, sheepdog trainer, and skilled veterinarian, though without any formal training in any of these arts. His father, my great-grandfather, Richard Young, had been an "agricultural laborer," and his wife's father, my great-grandfather, John Wilkins Cairns, was a shepherd.[2]

Sometime in the latter part of the nineteenth century (probably in the 1870s) he emigrated from Northumberland to South Africa, still a bachelor. The north of England has always been poorer than the south, and in consequence, many in England and Scotland were seeking better lives in the colonies. He bought the farm "Orange Springs" near Klokolaan, about thirty miles from Ladybrand, in the Orange Free State, and began various enterprises in addition to farming. The Orange Free State was one of three former Boer Republics, the others being Natalia and the Transvaal.

*

---

[1] George MacDonald, the Scottish poet (1824–1905), wrote these lines about Northumberland in his poem "A Book of Strife in the Form of The Diary of an Old Soul":
All things seem rushing into the dark
But the dark still is God. I would not give
The smallest silver piece to turn the rush
Backward or sideways. Am I not a spark
  Of him who is the light?—Fair hope doth flush
  My east.—Divine success—Oh, hush and hark!

[2] I am indebted to my cousin Gillian and her husband, Nic, for sending me copies of our grandfather's birth certificate and his and our Gran's marriage certificate.

Family Tree

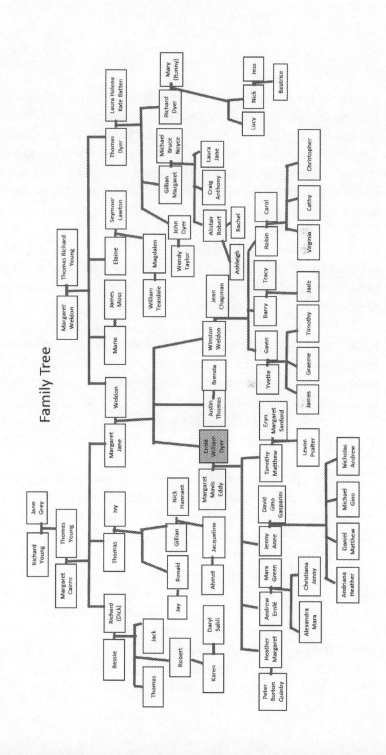

Under the leadership of the intrepid Dutchman Jan van Riebeeck, the first Europeans to arrive in southern Africa settled in the Cape of Good Hope in 1652 and established a refueling station for the ships of the Dutch East India Company. A small number of individual Huguenot refugees joined them in the Cape then or shortly afterward—the first Huguenot to set foot on the southernmost tip of Africa was Maria de la Quellerie, Jan van Riebeeck's wife. A larger number of French refugees began to arrive in the Cape in 1688 and 1689 after the Edict of Fontainebleau revoked the Edict of Nantes, which had granted religious tolerance to Protestants, ushering in a period of intense religious persecution.

With its Mediterranean climate, the Cape was ideally suited to the cultivation of citrus trees, fruits, vegetables, and grapes—fresh produce essential for preventing scurvy in those sailors making the long journey from Europe to Asia two centuries before the Suez Canal was completed in 1869. The Huguenots brought with them their skills as vintners and at Franschoek and Stellenbosch began to produce superb white and red wines. The tradition continues to this day.

At the time, the indigenous people in the area were the nomadic Khoisan (Bushmen). The Africans (as I shall refer to the indigenous tribal Bantu, a generic African word meaning "people") were moving steadily south from the north. It was not long before the British set covetous eyes on the Cape refueling station, seeing it as ideal for their own East India Company. They overran the Dutch and gained control of the Cape. In addition to the Khoisan who had been hunted almost to extinction "as vermin" (as they were then described) and the Dutch, the Cape by then had a population of mixed-race people, part Dutch, part Huguenot, and part Malay (for the Dutch had brought back to the Cape slaves from Malaysia), subsequently known as "coloreds."[3] The Afrikaans language[4] evolved from Dutch, with German, French, and Malay words thrown in for good measure.

After the British freed all slaves in the Cape in 1833, the Boers, not about to live on equal terms with the Khoisan and the coloreds, began what is known as "the Great Trek," an epic journey by the self-styled *voortrekkers* over the Hex mountains and the coastal range (including the Drakensberg[5]) into the interior, on the way fighting and conquering the African tribes that were migrating south. They established three Boer Republics independent of Britain—the Orange Free State on the northern side of the great Orange River (the boundary of the Cape), the Transvaal between the Orange and Vaal rivers (*vaal* means gray in Afrikaans; the Vaal is the major tributary of the Orange), and Natalia on southern Africa's east coast after conquering the Zulu and Xhosa tribes that had settled there before their arrival.

Natalia, renamed Natal after its invasion and annexation by the British in 1843, has a tropical climate ideally suited to the cultivation of pineapples, bananas, and sugarcane. The major port, Durban, so named after Sir Benjamin D'Urban, first English governor of the territory formerly held by the Boers, was the gateway to the east coast of Africa. To work

---

[3] Since this word for mixed-race people has endured for more than four centuries, it will be used henceforth without quotation marks.

[4] The word *Afrikaans* is spelled with two a's. The word *Afrikaner,* describing those who descended from the Dutch, the Huguenots, and others mentioned in the text, is spelled with one a. This is probably because in Afrikaans the a in Afrikaner is pronounced aa, that is it a long a. Afrikaners are also called *Boers,* an Afrikaans word meaning *farmer.* Afrikaans was and is also primarily the language of the Cape's colored population.

[5] The Drakensberg—Dragon Mountains—are a magnificent part of the coastal range, in places fourteen thousand feet above sea level. The interior of South Africa, known as the Highveld, has an average elevation of six thousand feet above sea level.

the sugarcane fields, the British imported indentured workers from India, thus contributing a sizeable number of Indians to southern Africa's burgeoning population.[6]

After diamonds were discovered in the Orange Free State in the Kimberley area, the British again conquered a republic established by the Boer voortrekkers. They did the same once gold was found in the Transvaal. This led to the first Anglo-Boer war (December 16, 1880–March 23, 1881), also known as the Transvaal War, in which the Boers were victorious. In the second Anglo-Boer war (October 11, 1900–May 31, 1902) the eventual defeat of the Boers by the British was accomplished only at enormous cost in both Boer and British lives.[7]

In 1910 the four provinces, the Cape, Natal, the Orange Free State, and Transvaal, were reconciled into one country, the Union of South Africa, and became a member of the British Commonwealth of nations. It is important to note that the foundations of the subsequent political system of apartheid were laid in 1910. The Constitution of the new country specified that white people only would have the franchise; Africans and coloreds would have white representatives in parliament but were permanently disenfranchised. It is also significant that the Afrikaners in 1918 began working through a secret society known initially as Jonge Zuid Afrika and after 1920 as the

---

[6] In 1893, Mohandas Gandhi, a trained lawyer and labor organizer, was among the thousands of Indians who arrived in Natal. He spent twenty-one years in South Africa working for civil rights, leaving in 1914. In Johannesburg, he went to a worship service at the Methodist Central Hall, but was turned away at the door because of the color of his skin.

[7] The best contemporary history of the two Anglo-Boer wars is Candice Millard's *Hero of the Empire: The Boer War, a Daring Escape, and the Making of Winston Churchill* (New York, Doubleday, 2016).

Broederbond (the band of brothers) to wrest political power from the British.[8]

English and Afrikaans were declared the official languages, and all South Africans were expected to become proficient in both. Additionally, Africans were fluent in two or more of the fourteen Bantu languages, while whites seldom knew one, and even fewer mastered more than one—with the exception of those who worked in the mines where good communication meant the difference between life and death. All working in the mines learned the basic lingua franca, *Fanagalo*, with a vocabulary of a mere two hundred words.

---

[8] For those interested in learning more about the history of South Africa, there is no better source than the two-volume *Oxford History of South Africa,* edited by Monica Wilson and Leonard Thompson (Oxford: Clarendon Press, 1969). The South African edition was published with four hundred blank pages. These pages include material documenting the appalling injustices of apartheid and critiques of this cruel system by both South African and overseas commentators. They had been banned by the censorship board of the South African government. My two volumes were purchased in and sent to me from England. They contain the four hundred pages left blank in the South African edition. A particularly ludicrous example of the work of the censorship board was the banning of the novel *Black Beauty*—probably without having read it. Not realizing that it was a story about a horse, they surmised that it was about an African beauty queen and proscribed it. Other examples of their diligence were the banning of the Beatles' music because John Lennon had said they were more popular than Jesus Christ (probably true), and of Martin Luther King Jr.'s speeches (see chapter 8).

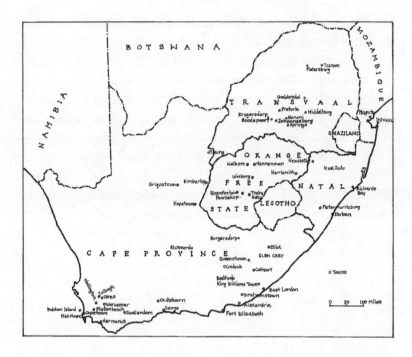

In addition to farming, my grandfather trained sheepdogs, served as the local veterinarian, later started the cheese factory in Ladybrand, and built the beautiful little Anglican Church in Ladybrand out of dressed sandstone without mortar—as was the practice in the north of England. He is buried in the church graveyard. In 1973, his son (my Uncle Tom), my mom, Peggy his daughter, Margaret my wife, and I found his tombstone and buried the ashes of his older son (my Uncle Dick) in the same grave as his father.

Later, while in Bloemfontein, I took note of the fact that the walls of the huts of the native Africans in that part of the Orange Free State are all built of dressed stone—without mortar. This is atypical. Throughout the rest of Southern Africa, the walls are constructed of lathe and mud. I often speculate whether this innovation was due to my grandfather's teaching and example.

In 1880, the first of two Anglo-Boer wars broke out, followed in 1899 by the second, more extensive conflict made famous by the heroic and dramatic escapades of the British journalist, Winston Spencer Churchill. During this second protracted series of battles between the Boers and the British, my grandfather found himself fixed on the horns of a dilemma. He could not fight against the Boers—many of whom had become his friends—or turn against his own people, the British. He solved the problem by returning to Alnwick for the duration of the war.

Back in Alnwick, Richard Young became a publican. British pubs typically were and still are at the center of British social and community life. A young eighteen-year-old girl from Morpeth, six or so miles to the south of Alnwick, by the name of Jane (Jeanie) Cairns, blessed with a beautiful (though untrained) singing voice, performed regularly in the pub and my grandfather, then in his early forties, fell in love with her. They were married on May 29, 1902, when he was forty-six years of age and she just twenty-three. When the Boer War ended in 1902, he took his young bride back with him to Orange Springs, Klokolaan, where their three children were born: Richard Thomas (Dick) Young (1903), Margaret Jane (Peggy) Young, my mother (1904), and Thomas (Tom) Young (1914).

It would have been at this time that my grandfather established the cheese factory and built the church. Prior to the church being erected, the few Anglicans in that part of the Orange Free State worshipped in a little cave on a hill just outside Ladybrand. To this day, every Easter morning, the early congregation crowds into that tiny chapel in a cave to rejoice in the message of transformation and commemorate their humble beginnings.

On one of his many visits to London, my Uncle Tom researched the Geordie side of my Young family history at Somerset House. As far as I know, he never wrote anything down, but I remember him telling us that one of "Gran's" forbears (we always called my maternal grandmother Gran) was the product of an extramarital liaison between the Duke of Northumberland and one of his chambermaids. Several others in the family had been hanged for stealing sheep and cattle across the border between Northumberland and Scotland. Gran's mother Jane Young (neé Gray) lived to the age of ninety-six (I can still remember a black-and-white photograph of the stern-looking old lady that hung in Gran's and then my mother's home).

Another of the black-and-white photographs on one of the walls in my parents' home was of my mother at the age of three riding an enormous mule at Orange Springs, her little legs barely stretching across the animal's back and her feet at least two or three feet above the stirrups. Peggy became an accomplished horsewoman, and later this was her primary means of getting to and fro from the farm into Ladybrand, the nearest town. Whenever supplies had to be bought, Mom and Gran took their little horse and buggy.

I often imagine, with amazement at her courage, what it must have been like for Gran to move as a young woman from the relative safety of the moors of Northumberland to the veld of the Orange Free State. Wildlife in southern Africa was abundant in those days; Gran would tell of encountering lions on the farm as well as venomous snakes. Taking it all in her stride, she adapted with a resilience that seems characteristic of our family.

My mother's formal education ended in standard four,[9] perhaps because there was no middle or high school in Klokolaan. However, she, like Gran, was a gifted musician. The two of them, it seems, were constantly singing, harmonizing with one another entirely by ear. They would tell of not daring to sing while in the horse-drawn buggy if they were at all late; the horse would invariably slow down at the sound of their melodious voices. Soon after leaving school, she began to work toward the Licenciate in Music from Trinity College of Music, London (the LTCL), practicing the piano for up to eight hours

---

[9] Standard four in South Africa is the equivalent of the sixth grade in the United States.

a day with the horse listening through the upper half of the kitchen door, taking correspondence courses, and sitting for the examinations in Bloemfontein. Later, she began studying to be a pianist with a music teacher, probably in Ladybrand. By the age of nineteen, she was awarded the LTCL degree and began her own career as a professional musician.

Mom would ride on horseback the thirty miles from Orange Springs to Ladybrand, first for her piano lessons and then later to teach. She also went into Ladybrand (or stayed there once her lessons for the day were over) to play the piano in the one cinema in town. Those were the days of silent movies, and the pianist had to improvise accompanying music to match the mood of each scene. It must have been extremely demanding— but also invaluable for her musical career.

My mother had a sixth sense, as did Gran. Two anecdotes, one about each of them, became part of our family lore. One day, my mother was teaching in Ladybrand when she had a premonition that her father was dying. Instead of staying over until the next day and riding back in broad daylight, she instinctively knew that she needed to get home immediately. It was a moonless night, yet she told of a "light" shining in front of her horse that safely led her back to Orange Springs. She got home just in time to be with her father as he died.

After my grandfather's death, Gran had to have an emergency appendectomy. This operation could not be performed in Ladybrand, and she had to be taken to the national hospital in Bloemfontein, about eighty miles away, leaving young Tom, still a child, in the care of my <u>Mom</u> and Uncle Dick. While recuperating in the hospital in Bloemfontein, Gran distinctly heard Dick yelling at his younger brother one night: "For God's sake, Tom, get that candle away from the curtains; you'll set the house alight!" When she returned to Orange Springs, she asked about this incident. Both Uncle Dick and my Mom confirmed that young Tom had indeed carelessly placed a candle under the drapes in the living room of the farmhouse, and Dick had shouted out his warning just in time to avert a conflagration.

After my grandfather's death, money was in short supply. Gran was compelled to leave the farm and her youngest child in the care of Dick (who became a farmer, about which I will say more later) and my mother, while she went to Naivasha, Kenya, to serve as the governess of the children of a wealthy family named Grant, sending money home for the upkeep of her little family. At some point, when my Mom would have been in her early twenties, that position terminated, and Gran returned to South Africa. Shortly afterward, she decided to sell the farm and move to Johannesburg.[10] Gran bought a little house in Judith's Paarl[11] where she, my Mom, and Uncle Tom lived. Uncle Dick was later appointed the manager of an enormous cattle ranch, "West End Ranch," in what was then the British protectorate of Bechuanaland (renamed Botswana after achieving independence in 1966 but remaining within the British Commonwealth). The nearest towns were Mafeking and Maritsani, and the closest village was Setlagoli.

In Johannesburg, Peggy resumed her career as a piano

[10] The origin of the name Johannesburg is uncertain. Johannes is a common Dutch name. There are three possible contenders for the honor of having the city named after him. Johann Rissik was the first clerk in the office of the surveyor-general, established after gold had been discovered on the Witwatersrand. Rissik Street in Johannesburg is named after him. Christoph Johannes Joubert was the temporary head of the office of the surveyor-general. Joubert Street and Joubert Park in Johannesburg bear his name. And Johannes Meyer was the veldkornet, the first Transvaal government official appointed to oversee this area.

[11] Judith's Paarl was a middle-class suburb, one of scores of suburbs in the rapidly expanding gold mining town that became the economic hub of South Africa. These suburbs were from the beginning for whites only. Africans and coloreds working in urban areas were compelled to live in segregated townships usually on barren land on the outskirts of South Africa's major cities.

teacher. It was also there that Gran met William Clay, a widower and an engineer with the Proudfoot Civil Engineering Company. They were married, and after his retirement "Pop" (from the time we first knew him, William Clay wanted us children to call him Pop) they bought a small farm named "Trekdrift" not far from Zeerust in the Northern Transvaal. It was at Trekdrift at the age of five that I had the first of several close encounters with one of Africa's many deadly venomous snakes,[12] a puff adder. Adult puff adders are comparatively short, typically about three feet long, but their girth is disproportionally large, often three inches in diameter in the middle section of their bodies. They appear fairly sluggish and don't move rapidly across the veld as do mambas, for example. Their danger lies in the fact that when anything treads on or near them, they strike backward with lightning speed, and unless antivenom serum is injected within minutes, the bite is fatal.

I was pushing my twin brothers, then about two years old, around the farmyard in an old wheelbarrow. We came to the farm's outhouse, the only available toilet, which had corrugated iron siding, painted red. On the sunny side of the outhouse, where the siding met the ground, I saw what looked like a gorgeous brightly colored trouser suspender. Putting the wheelbarrow down, I went forward to pick it up. As my shadow

---

[12] Two other incidents are etched in my memory. At our home in Befordview, we had a large birdcage on the front veranda, in which we had a melodious blue budgerigar. One morning, we came out to the veranda—and the budgerigar was gone. In its place, lying on the bottom of the cage and unable to crawl back out through the wire netting because of an enormous bulge in its abdomen, was a small cobra. Later, when Margaret and I had married and had three children, we went to a friend's vacation cabin at Hibberdene, Natal, overlooking the Indian Ocean. Being a tropical climate, papayas grew in abundance. We bought one and left it on the kitchen table overnight. The next morning, a neat hole had been drilled through the papaya. We looked up and saw a black mamba between the kitchen wall and the ceiling.

fell over it, the puff adder moved. Instinctively I knew it was a snake, drew back, and then shouted for Pop. Pop came at once and dispatched it with a gunshot. The last thing any of us needed was a puff adder in or around our outhouse!

Gran and Pop did not stay long at Trekdrift. Pop was not cut out to be a farmer. So they sold their little farm and bought a house in the suburb of Kensington, Johannesburg—number 64 York Road—with a tennis court. Pop was the only grandfather I knew, and the tennis court at York Road, where family and friends gathered every Sunday, was where I first learned at the age of six to play and love tennis. One memorable feature of those Sunday afternoons was Gran's delicious granadilla[13] cake, which we children looked forward to more than anything else,

In the late 1920s, my Mom met and fell in love with William Weldon Young, another resident of Judith's Paarl whose lineage will be traced later in this chapter. Uncle Dick, at West End Ranch, met and married an Afrikaner woman, Bessie (I did not know her surname). They had three boys: Thomas, Robert, and Jack. Thomas worked on the (then) Rhodesian Railroads. Robert and Jack became printers. I have childhood memories of all three, but only Robert ("Robbie"), his daughter Karen, and her husband Daryl and I have connected personally in later life. I was able to correspond with Jack after Karen gave me his address. Unfortunately, Jack died in 2014. Later, Uncle Tom married Ivy Jacobsen (a Scot). They, in turn, gave birth to my cousins Ronald and Gillian. I have maintained contact with Ron and Gillian across the years and over the miles that separate us.

Moving forward in time to reflect on uncles Dick and Tom and their influence on my life, I must break the chronological flow of this narrative. My earliest memories as a young boy are

---

[13] Granadilla is perhaps better known in the United States and elsewhere as passion fruit. The icing between the two layers of Gran's sponge cake, on the top, and on the sides was made with squeezed-out granadillas, sugar, and fresh whipped cream.

of spending school vacations with Uncle Dick and Aunt Bessie at West End Ranch. The ranch had no electricity other than that provided for lighting and heating each night by a stack of two dozen or more car batteries wired together in series and charged with a small diesel engine. Once the adults decided to go to bed, the engine was switched off. We spent the rest of the night in complete darkness—quite a frightening experience for a young child. Next to the room where the batteries and small engine were located was another room on the walls of which Uncle Dick had hung the skins of the scores if not hundreds of snakes he had killed on the ranch. Among them was the twenty-foot skin of a python—extremely impressive to my young mind.

At West End, as a seven year old, I can remember going with Uncle Dick to Setlagoli across dirt farm roads in his new 1939 Plymouth Coupe. It was at Setlagoli that he bought and gave me my first pocketknife—an enormous treasure for a young lad to be entrusted with. And it was at Setlagoli that Uncle Dick, who went there to shop and socialize, had too much to drink and then announced, as we were going back to West End, that he wanted to see whether his Plymouth could do one hundred miles per hour (on torturous dirt roads!). I was literally terrified and started to cry. While driving very fast, Uncle Dick turned on me sternly with the rebuke, "Youngs don't cry!" That brought my protest to a sudden stop. On a more positive note, I remember Uncle Dick inviting me to accompany him and a small group of men from Mafeking who went to hunt wildebeest (they shot six) and actually allowing me to carry a couple of their rifles as we trekked across the veld. At nightfall, Uncle Dick shot a small duiker for our dinner, and then lassoed a dead tree, bringing it down to provide us with fuel for our duiker barbeque and for the fire that burned all night to ward off marauding lions. We slept around the fire, which he stoked constantly, and we could hear the lions roaring some (not-too-safe) distance away.

Another anecdote reveals how Uncle Dick displayed many of

his father's skills as an amateur veterinarian. On the front lawn of the West End farmstead, there was a large birdbath. Often a whole troop of baboons would gather around the birdbath seeking water to drink. When the dogs, of which there were several, including one small fox terrier, saw them, they would dash out yelping and barking to chase away the baboons. As if in slow motion, I was watching this drama unfold one morning. The largest baboon, probably the alpha male, stopped running away from the dogs, turned around, opened his massive jaws, and then clamped them shut across the top of the fox terrier's back. The baboon's jaw was so large that the upper teeth penetrated the terrier's rib cage and lung on the one side of his body, and the lower jaw punctured his chest and lung on the other. The wounded little dog was left dying, with blood spurting out of his body on both sides. Undeterred, Uncle Dick ran to get the tar he always used to put on the heads of his cattle after they had been dehorned and stuffed tar into the puncture wounds on the terrier's sides. His remedy saved the little dog's life. The bleeding stopped. And the terrier eventually made a complete recovery.

I idolized my Uncle Tom. Later, I will relate his influence on my initial choice of a career. Here I must mention his talent as a pianist, playing entirely by ear. In Gran's Kensington home and then in our Kensington and Bedfordview homes, we had musical evenings once or twice a month. Uncle Tom was always the life and soul of the party. He would accompany Gran as she sang "Jerusalem" or harmonize with her as they sang ballads such as "Just a Song at Twilight," Scottish and Irish folk songs, as well as those of Stephen Foster, and of course "Sarie Marais" an Afrikaans "volk's lied" (folk song) from the Boer War. He would lead us all in singing around the piano and then play for us as we started dancing. Music was in his blood, untrained though he was.[14] To return to chronology, I was not yet on the horizon. My parents must first move onto center stage.

~

Tracing my lineage on my father's side is made easier by a somewhat humorous incident. Some years ago, when we were living in California, I received a letter, the first of several, from a firm of solicitors in Durban, South Africa, informing me that my Aunt Marie (my father's sister) had died. She and her husband, James Moss, had no children. The entirety of her estate, I was told, was to be divided among her nieces and nephews. This first letter was followed by others asking me to validate my status as Aunt Marie's oldest nephew—and also asking me to furnish details about my twin brothers. Winston and Justin had both died by then. Months, maybe even years, went by, and I had forgotten about the bequest completely. Then a letter arrived from the same firm of solicitors informing me that the estate had finally been wound up and that my inheritance was the munificent sum of twenty dollars. They asked me how I wanted the money to be sent. I instructed the solicitors to give the twenty dollars to a children's charity in South Africa. However, the greatest gift Aunt Marie bequeathed me through this firm was a complete list of the names and addresses of all my paternal cousins who were now living literally on three

---

[14] Later, when I tried to emulate Uncle Tom by playing the piano by ear, he would invite me over every week to his and Aunty Ivy's home in Rosettenville for an evening of working at chords and chord progressions. "Play something you are busy with," he would begin. I would tentatively play a tune that had caught my ear. Then he would start to dissect the piece and enrich the chords. I would practice what he had taught me until the following week, when again, he would listen to what I had come up with. Only after he was satisfied that I had got the full depth of expressive meaning out of the tune that I had elected to play would we move on to the next.

different continents. While my Mom was alive, she had kept in touch with my father's side of the family. After her death, being the only surviving son, this self-imposed duty was mine. With the solicitors' list in hand, I immediately began corresponding with and later visiting each of my cousins.[15]

When Margaret and I were with cousin Richard and his lovely wife Bunny in Perth and Margaret River (where they have a second home) early in 2009, Richard gave me copies of our grandfather's obituary notice, and also a thirty-six-page history of my father's mother's side of the family, written by Aunt Marie after the death of her mother, my paternal grandmother. These documents provide me with most of the factual information I have about my father's side of the family.

My father's grandfather was William A. Young, the manager of the Farringdon Street Station, Great Northern Railway, in London. He was the son of a London coach builder. His wife was Emma Dyer. Emma's father was a wool merchant in Yorkshire. William and Emma had a family of seven; three died young. Those who survived were Thomas Dyer the oldest son, my grandfather, William (Willie), his twin brother, Alice, and Ada. Thomas Dyer became a banker working for the Standard Bank.[16] The bank transferred him to South Africa in 1894 first to Johannesburg, then, in 1899, to Durban. In 1896, he met and married my grandmother, Margaret Mary Weldon, about

---

[15] On my father's side, my cousins are John (who died on April 29, 2017) whose widow is Wendy and lives in their home in Hampshire, UK; Gillian (married to Michael Noyce) and still in South Africa; and Richard and Bunny in Perth, Australia. Aunt Elaine and Seymour Laughton's only child was Magdalen, widow of William Teasdale, who lives in Hampshire, UK.

[16] With Barclay's, one of the two of South Africa's largest banks until 1948 when the Nationalist government came to power, they established several "Afrikaner" banks to which all government contracts and accounts were assigned. Economic power invariably follows political power.

whom more will be said in due course. Since Thomas Dyer was an Anglican and Margaret Mary a Roman Catholic, their marriage was performed in the registry office. Later, Margaret prevailed on him to have a religious wedding service in the Roman Catholic Church.

Thomas Dyer and Margaret Mary Young rented a house on Cowie Road where their four children were born: Elaine, Marie, William (my father), and his twin brother, Thomas.[17] In 1901, while my grandmother was in England with the young Elaine and Marie meeting for the first time and getting to know her parents-in-law, word came that her husband had been stricken with what was thought to be dengue (but later turned out to be enteric) fever, and that she should return at once to South Africa. Her husband, who had been delighted that she had gotten on so well with his parents, unexpectedly died at the age of thirty-one shortly after her return. The Obituary in the *Natal Mercury* (of which Richard gave me a copy), concludes as follows:

> [Mr. Thomas Dyer Young] was removed to the Sanatorium ... Hope was expressed till the last that he would pull through, but, in spite of everything that could be done, he passed peacefully away at 3:30 on Tuesday afternoon. The late Mr. Thomas Dyer Young was the possessor of a fine baritone voice, and was well known in musical circles. He leaves a wife and four children. To them as well as to his sorrowing parents and relatives, great sympathy is extended. His death is all the more sad, as he

---

[17] Their dates of birth are: Elaine Margaret (born on March 12, 1898), Marie Emma (born on June 24, 1899), and twin boys born on July 15, 1901—Thomas Dyer (my uncle) and William Weldon (my father).

was contemplating a trip to England early next
year, to visit his people, whom he had not seen
for nearly seven years. The funeral took place
yesterday afternoon, and was largely attended.
Owing to the death of Mr. T. D. Young, of the
Standard Bank, the cricket match arranged
between the Wheeler Theatrical Company and
the United Banks for yesterday was postponed.

My father was barely four months old when his father died.
It now fell to Margaret Mary Young to support and bring up
her four young children. Some details about the background
of this remarkable woman are therefore necessary. This is my
summary of what I obtained from my cousin Richard.

Margaret Mary Weldon's great-grandfather on her father's
side was Flood Weldon, a widower, whose second wife was
a Miss Costello of Spain. They and their six sons and one
daughter emigrated from Cork, Ireland, to South Africa in
1846. He was a farmer, and they settled in Kragga Komma,
near Grahamstown in the Eastern Cape. John, the eldest son,
my grandmother's father, became a blacksmith. His smithy was
in Port Elizabeth where he met his future wife, a woman also of
Irish descent, Mary Ann Acton. They were married in 1865. The
Acton family's roots in South Africa go back to 1722 when Dr.
Acton, a ship's surgeon, jumped ship and established a medical
practice in Port Elizabeth. John and Mary Ann Weldon (neé
Acton), who had moved from Port Elizabeth to King William's
Town to set up their new home, had six sons and six daughters
between 1865 and 1881. My grandmother, Margaret Mary, was
the oldest—born on August 10, 1866.

Margaret (or Maggie, as her fellow students called her),
like her mother Mary before her, had begun her education at
the age of seven as a boarder at the Grahamstown Convent. At
the age of twelve, practical difficulties compelled the family to
summon Margaret home to King William's Town to help care for

her many siblings. In King William's Town, her parents enrolled her in the convent as a day scholar, a school she was to attend for the next three years. When she left King Williams's Town Convent (again for financial reasons) she was, in the words of Aunt Marie, "a well-poised, tall young woman ... able to read music and play accompaniments for those who wished to sing."

John Weldon, her blacksmith father, was becoming restless in the small village of King William's Town. He needed to be better able to support his large family, which now included twelve children. His imagination was stirred by accounts of gold in the Transvaal. By the end of 1881, John had made up his mind: he and his family would leave King William's Town (their home since 1865) to seek their fortune in the gold fields of the Witwatersrand (white waters' ridge). The journey, by oxcart, took many months in the face of daily dangers. They arrived in 1886, penniless, with their large family and few prospects. John became a speculator, and the economic pattern in his household became, to quote Aunt Marie's history, was "Here today, gone tomorrow." John Weldon died of pulmonary disease in 1908. At the time, my grandmother was teaching music at Koedoeslaagte, near Potchefstroom, in the Transvaal. Returning to Johannesburg, Grandma Margaret rode her bicycle to teach students in Wanderer's View, Doornfontein, and Jeppe (three of Johannesburg's far-flung suburbs)—at fifteen shillings a pupil.

In a large family like the Weldons, many friends gathered to enjoy musical evenings. Among the visitors to their home was my grandfather, Thomas Dyer Young, the banker who had arrived two years earlier. He was six years younger than Margaret, but they were attracted to one another by their mutual love of music. As mentioned earlier, they were married in 1896 in the registry office in Johannesburg.

After my grandfather Thomas Dyer's death, the Standard Bank gave my grandmother three hundred pounds to pay for his funeral expenses, and his parents sent her five pounds a month to live on. She saved the money, and she used it to buy her first home in Judith's Paarl in 1915, where the family lived until 1928 when she bought a property in Forest Town (where I, at the age of three, first remember her). After studying by night she earned her high school matriculation certificate and trained as a school-teacher (obtaining her teacher's certificate in 1908). She supported her family by teaching, giving piano lessons, and occasionally working as a governess. She retired in 1926 because of poor health. She died in Knysna at the home of Elaine (her older daughter) and Elaine's husband, Seymour Laughton on May 22, 1936.

Unlike Aunt Elaine, who had obtained her PhD in botany at the University of Wisconsin, Madison and Uncle Dyer, who had been awarded a law degree at the University of the Witwatersrand, Johannesburg (working by day in the government's Department of Native Affairs and enrolling in night classes at the university), my father did not attend university. In 1915, by stating that his age was eighteen rather than fifteen, he had managed to enlist in the South African Defense Force and entered World War I as a bugle boy. After the war, he studied and eventually became a Fellow of the Chartered Institute of Secretaries, his only academic qualification, and worked as a company secretary and as an accountant.

———

It was in Judith's Paarl, where both were living, that my father (William Weldon Young) would have met and fallen in love with my mother (Margaret Jane Young, always known as Peggy) — probably in 1928. The Great Depression had begun, my father was out of work, and being employed was a precondition for their being able to marry. Sometime in 1928, he left South Africa for New Zealand where he was able to find employment as a salesman in Christchurch. Once on his feet financially, he sent for my mother, and they were married on January 31, 1929, in the Roman Catholic cathedral. Because my mother was an Anglican, they had to promise to raise their children as Catholics if they were to be married in the Roman church—a promise they kept in my case but forgot by the time my younger twin brothers, Winston Weldon and Justin Thomas, were born on August 16, 1936. There were four people at their wedding: my Mom and Dad, the officiating priest, and the lady who owned the boardinghouse where my father had been staying who served as witness to the ceremony.[18]

Times were hard, and for this reason—as well as because they both loved traveling—they moved around a great deal, living in Wellington and Auckland as well as Christchurch, and eventually leaving New Zealand for Australia, where my father found work in Sydney. The Sydney Harbour Bridge,[19] a moonlit oil painting of which hung above the fireplace in my parents' home in Bedfordview, was opened in March 1932. I must have been conceived in April 1932. Sometime after that, my father received a cable saying that his mother was dying and that they should return (by ship, since there were no airlines in those days) to South Africa immediately. I was born on December 14, 1932, back in Johannesburg. My grandmother lived another four years. But for that cable, I would have been an Australian rather than a South African.

At the beginning of my story and the end of this chapter, I must say something about my names: Ernlé William Dyer. William and Dyer are straightforward. They are my father's first name William and the middle name of his twin brother, my uncle Dyer and also a family name going back to Emma Dyer. It is the Ernlé (pronounced Ern-lay) that I have had to explain for most of my life. My mother was a tremendous admirer of

---

[18] When Margaret and I were in New Zealand in 2003, we went to the cathedral and obtained a photocopy of my parents' marriage certificate.

[19] This is the official name of the bridge. The word "Harbour" is spelled with a "u" in British English, unlike "Harbor" as in American English.

Winston Churchill.[20] It happened that one of Churchill's senior aides had the improbable full title: Admiral the Honorable Sir Reginald Aylmer Ranfurly Plunkett-Ernlé-Erle-Drax, KCB, DSO, JP, DL (August 28, 1880–October 16, 1967). My mother read of his exploits in the *London Illustrated News* while in the hospital after giving birth to me. The name Ernlé (which goes back to the fifteenth century in British history) took her fancy, and I was registered and later christened with it. When I became a citizen of the United States, I was given the opportunity, routinely part of the process of naturalization, to change my name. I declined the offer. By the age of forty-five, it was part of my identity—and I had come to appreciate it, if not as unique, certainly as altogether out of the ordinary.

Looking back on the story thus far, I can see how significantly my upbringing shaped my life. Being willing to go from the security of the known to the uncertainty of the unknown was part of my heritage. My love for the game of tennis, my delight in singing, playing the piano, and listening to music, and my sense of being at home in the great outdoors were gifts my family gave me. I also saw, from an early age, that religious values not professed in glib or easy words were operative in the lives of Gran, my mother, and my uncles Dick and Tom. Genetic factors undoubtedly contributed to who I was to become, but the unconscious influence of those who surrounded me in my childhood and youth were equally important. We are never fully cognizant of the extent to which who we are and what we do affects those who come after us. I was fortunate that those who helped shape my own life did this in positive, creative ways. Many are not so blessed.

---

[20] My one younger brother, Winston Weldon, was named after Winston Churchill (Weldon—also a family name—was my father's middle name). His twin, junior by about five minutes, was given the names Justin Thomas, I suppose, because Justin rhymed with Winston and Thomas was Uncle Dyer's first name.

2

Growing Up: Judith's Paarl, Kensington, Bedfordview—Johannesburg

On their return from Australia, it would have been natural for my parents to settle in Judith's Paarl, a modest, middle-class suburb of Johannesburg. My father's mother lived there (before buying the house in Forest Town). My mother's mother (Gran) lived there as well.

The first house I remember living in was on Albermarle Street, Judith's Paarl (I think it was #5). It was on Albermarle Street, when I was three, that my father announced that he was taking the training wheels off my little bicycle and then sent me off down the fairly steep street to learn to ride on two wheels only. Somehow I managed both to ride and survive. It was also in the Albermarle Street house that I had my first traumatic experience of helplessness. I would have been two years old (because I was three years older than my twin brothers who were born in 1936). Between my birth and that of the twins, Mom was in her second pregnancy, and close to full term. It was a Sunday morning. She was alone at home, in bed. My father was at the Jeppe Quondam Club, playing tennis, hockey, or cricket (he had not yet taken up golf). I can remember my Mom urgently sending me to get help from a neighbor. I vaguely recall standing in the neighbor's front doorway: pathetically knocking (the #3 on the door and that it was green stays in my mind). I have no recollection of whether the neighbor came or not. What I do know is that my Mom lost the baby, a little girl, who must have been stillborn. I think this was also the moment when she began to have doubts about the man she had married. My father, always a selfish man, was not there at her side when she needed him most.

When I was two or three years old, I managed to cause my Mom to risk serious injury, if not her life. My parents owned a little Morris sedan. In those days before seat belts and child seats, I was simply left to occupy the rear bench-seat of the car. The doors on that car were hinged at the back, not the front. The door latch was at the front of the doors, just below the window. As we were driving along at about forty miles per hour, I fiddled with the door latch—and the door opened slightly. The wind caught it and swung it wide open. I tumbled out, but because I must have been completely relaxed as I fell, I was unhurt.

Mom was sitting in the passenger seat next to my Dad, in front of me, and as soon as she felt the rush of wind and saw me fall out of the car, she instinctively dove out after me in a vain attempt to rescue me. She was anything but relaxed and landed hard on the shoulder of the road, suffering extensive abrasions, cuts, and bruises. Thankfully, she had no broken bones. That was the first time she tried to save my life. The second time she actually did save me. I will come to that later.

～

It was perhaps because the Albermarle Street house now had sad memories that my parents sold it soon after the miscarriage and bought a house in Kensington—154 Highland Road. We were living there when my twin brothers, Winston Weldon and Justin Thomas, were born on August 16, 1936. They were the third set of identical twins in our family—my father and Uncle Dyer and his father and Uncle Will were the second and first.

I loved this home, where I was to live for the next eight years. A little way up the street there was a "castle," a house designed and built out of stone exactly like the sort of turreted castle one sees in picture books (or nowadays at Disney theme parks). I never saw the interior, but it always made my road seem incredibly special, like none other I had ever known. On the other side of the street from our house was a *koppie,* a hill, with steps leading down to Robert's Avenue where the trams ran. My school-friend Paul Fisk and I never tired of playing cowboys and Indians on that koppie. And outside our back gate was a huge open field, part of the Hellenic School grounds. The Hellenic School, as the name implies, must have been built by the Greek community. At the time it was leased by the Transvaal Education District (TED). The school occupied a magnificent building, a facsimile of the Parthenon, on top of a hill. It was at Hellenic that I would eventually enter the third grade.

But before this, I was enrolled at the age of three in the Oak Tree Kindergarten, run by Mrs. Bennett (a gracious lady whose funeral service I conducted more than thirty years later). I think the reason I was sent to school so young was that I was constantly trying to take the twins out of their baby carriage to play with them. This, of course, could not be allowed. So off to school I went. My mother would walk me down to the tram stop on Roberts Avenue, and off I would go on the tram—I loved sitting on the upper deck and looking down at the houses and traffic below—to be met by Mrs. Bennett at the other end and taken to her little school. Although the epitome of kindness, she was also a strict disciplinarian. I can remember her washing my mouth out with soap for having used a "bad word." In the afternoons, the process would be reversed. Mrs. Bennett walked me to the tram, and Mom met me at the tram stop where I had to get off to escort me home. Eventually I was reckoned to be big enough to walk by myself to the tram in the morning, from the tram stop on to school, and then back to the Robert's Avenue tram after school, and then from the tram stop up the steep steps over the koppie to my home.

When I was about six, my parents took the three of us boys on a picnic to Robinson Lake, one of the many man-made dams that were invariably close to gold mines. As these mines were burrowed deeper and deeper into the ground, the mineshafts would become waterlogged. The water had to be pumped out into dams adjacent to them. The Robinson mine was old, and the dam was large. Close to the shore in the designated swimming area, the bottom of the dam had been lined with concrete until the water got to be about three feet deep. Then the concrete ended and the water became deeper. This brings me to the second time my Mom risked her life to save mine.

My Dad was teaching me to swim. We were in the shallow water, close to the shore. He would hold the upturned palm of his hand below my stomach while I kicked my legs and stroked the water with my arms. Gradually, as I gained confidence, he would remove his hand and let me swim on my own; walking beside me to lift me up should I go under. His method was effective, and by the age of six, I was fairly comfortable in the water. On this occasion, after spending twenty minutes or so working with me, he told me to stay where I was in the shallow end while he swam across the lake and back. Off he went, and as I saw him swimming away with powerful strokes, it looked so easy that—disobeying his instruction—I decided to follow him. I must have swum out about forty or fifty feet, well beyond the concrete bottom close to the shore. When I tried to rest by standing on the bottom, there was nothing to stand on. I must have panicked and started to drown. I remember sinking twice below the surface of the water and coming up, desperate for breath and blowing the water out of my mouth as I did.

Mom, sitting fully clothed on the grassy shore and taking care of the twins, saw me go under a third time. She dove in clothes and all, swam out to where I was, and brought me safely to shore where I was placed on my stomach. The water I had taken in was pumped out of my lungs. Twice in my short life I could have died—and twice my Mom was there to save me.

So good was Mrs. Bennett's preparation at Oak Tree that I skipped the first and second grades.[21] I vaguely remember having to do a test (probably the Stanford-Binet Intelligence Scale) and had tremendous fun answering all the questions.[22] After the results of the test came out, I started at Hellenic[23] in the third grade at the age of six, and went on to Jeppe High School when I was eleven. My Dad and Uncle Dyer had attended the same school. By the time the twins were ready to enter elementary school, the lease on the old Hellenic School building had expired. They started at Hillcrest School (as it was now named) in a brand-new building on an opposite hill a little further to the east.

The years in Kensington were happy. My father had a good job as secretary of the African Consolidated Theaters. This meant that we got free tickets to movies and concerts. Chernovsky Impressarios were part of the African Consolidated Theaters group and brought to South Africa world-famous artists such as Beniamino Gigli, Tito Gobbi, Elizabeth Schwartkopf, Claudio Arrau, Yehudi Menuhin, and Jüssi Bjorling. Thanks to the free tickets our family got through Dad, I heard them all, as well as many, many others, developing early a lifelong love of classical music. The little Morris had been replaced with a new Willy's car, and we went each year to the Natal south coast for our family holiday—usually to Scottborough or Margate.

---

[21] In South Africa, grades one through seven in elementary and middle school were called grades one and two in kindergarten and standards one through five in preparatory school. Grades eight through twelve in high school were called forms I through V in high school or secondary school as it was sometimes known.

[22] I never did find out my IQ score.

[23] Mr. Bovet, a kindly and dignified man, was the principal.

We listened to the hilarious radio program *Snoektown Calling* every Saturday night (there was no television in those days). And life at home was mostly tranquil.

I was also maturing as a five- or six-year old, gradually taking on more responsibilities. Highland Road was on top of a ridge. Down on the north side (the way I went to the Oak Tree Kindergarten and later to Jeppe High School for Boys) was the suburb of Kensington. The south side led from the fields around Hellenic down to the suburb of Malvern a mile and a half away, where there were the nearest shops. Among them, I remember Fotheringham's bakery, Mr. Grimes's jewelry store, the butcher, a Greek café, and a fish and chip shop.

At first, I accompanied my mother to the shops, but eventually, she would send me off on my own for a loaf of bread, some fish and chips, or more milk, and I would walk there and back by myself. I particularly enjoyed going for a loaf of fresh bread because it was always warm, right out of the oven, and I could nibble at one end on my way home. Going to the butcher with Mom was also something to look forward to. No matter what meat she ordered, the butcher always sliced off a piece of baloney and gave it to me as a treat. After I was given my first watch, a Swiss-made gold-plated Roamer, I would walk down to Mr. Grimes to have it adjusted or to have him punch a new hole in the strap. What I didn't fully appreciate at the time was that we who went to these shops and the shopkeepers themselves constituted a small community of which we were all members, with most people knowing each other's names and being interested in how each other was doing.

There was also a small cinema in Malvern, and on Saturday mornings, black-and-white serials would be shown for us children (admission was only a sixpence). Here, week by week, we would follow the adventures of *The Prisoner of Zenda, The Man in the Iron Mask, The Three Musketeers, The Count of Monte Cristo,* or *The Lone Ranger,* and I was deemed sufficiently responsible to go and come back by myself.

The nearest Roman Catholic Church was in Malvern as well, three quarters of a mile beyond the tram terminus. As mentioned earlier, a condition for my parents' marriage in the Roman Catholic cathedral in Christchurch, New Zealand, had been that they were to bring up their children in the Roman Catholic faith. I would be sent off (never taken, least of all by my father, the Roman Catholic in the marriage) early each Sunday morning. I would catch the tram at the shops in Malvern, ride to the terminus, then walk the three quarters of a mile to church, and reverse this sequence several hours later. It's interesting now to reflect that once I had been confirmed and had taken my First Holy Communion at the age of eight, my parents did not think it necessary to extend their promise to the religious upbringing of my younger brothers. As far as I know, the only time the twins went to church was when they got married. Perhaps my brothers' lives would have turned out differently had they had even a rudimentary religious upbringing. The church I went to was run by the Paulist Fathers, a religious order, and three things about it stand out in my memory.

First and foremost, the Paulist Fathers taught me how to box. There was a boxing ring in the basement of the church, and every Sunday morning before our catechism lessons, we boys were paired off according to size. We would have to put on boxing gloves, step into the ring, and face off against one another. Then the Fathers would instruct us not only in the techniques of boxing but also in the Queensberry rules. I must have been a quick learner because knowing how to box stood me in good stead time and time again whenever a bigger boy at school tried to bully me or one of my friends. Without my really being aware of it, the Paulist Fathers were building my self-confidence and giving me the courage to stand up for what I believed was right.

Second, after the excitement of the boxing ring, the catechism lessons were anticlimactic and incredibly boring. It was all rote learning, without any attempt by the instructors to impart understanding. A question would be posed in the catechism—what is the Holy Trinity?—and the answer would have to be memorized: The Holy Trinity is God the Father, God the Son, and God the Holy Ghost. I had no difficulty memorizing the answers, but without comprehension, the good that did me is questionable.

Third, even worse were the Sunday morning services. In those days, the Mass was in Latin. At the time, I knew not a word of it. I was only to learn Latin when I entered high school. I thus had no idea what the liturgy was all about. And the prayers involved kneeling on hard wooden kneelers, seemingly until one's knees were raw and one's back was agonizingly stiff. This was an ordeal to be endured rather than a celebration of God's amazing grace. Only the boxing lessons made it all worthwhile. I did get a reprieve one Sunday, however. I jumped off the tram shortly before it came to a stop and landed right in front of a car. The driver reacted in time to avoid what could have been a serious accident and was as shaken up as I was. He insisted on taking me home so that he could tell my parents what had happened. I remember being punished for my foolishness, but being allowed to stay home after the kind driver had left.

I have to say something now about tennis. How I came to love the game! My father was my first teacher. The practice board, to which he took me religiously each evening after he came home from work, was the smooth granite-faced wall at the back of Hellenic School. The ground beneath, on which we kids played marbles during school breaks, was anything but smooth; it was rocky and lumpy. Of course, from Dad's point of view, this was the best possible surface to practice on—one couldn't possibly anticipate the bounce of the ball and, therefore, one had always to be on one's toes.

When I was about six years old, Gran and Pop bought 64 York Road, Kensington There was a tennis court on the property. Thereafter, every Sunday, our extended family was at York Road playing tennis. I'll return to the subject of tennis in the following chapter.

———

For me, 1943 was a momentous year. My parents decided to sell the Highland Road house and buy a small, three-acre holding in peri-urban Bedfordview (later enlarged by the purchase of another three or four acres next door). In the same year, I moved on from Hellenic to the Jeppe High School for Boys,[24] where Mr. Grant was the principal, as a day scholar.

The small farm at Bedfordview, #10 Sugarbush Road, later given a name suggested by one of our Italian prisoners of war—"Bella Vista"—was a child's paradise. The farmhouse was snuggled high on a hill with a commanding view of our land and the river in the valley below (we called it a river, but it was in fact only a creek). We could see the dairy farm and brick works on the far side of the river. On the farm itself, we had fruit trees and vegetables. Eventually, my parents bought several cows to milk, and Mom had five horses that she and her friends would ride. We had a concrete irrigation dam next to the well that we used as a swimming pool. When algae started growing in the pool, it would be emptied onto the vegetable fields. One of my chores was then to scrub the inside of the pool until it was

---

[24] The school was named for the Right Honorable Julius Gottlieb Ferdinand Jeppe, OBE. Jeppe was born in Germany and emigrated at the age of eleven to the Transvaal with his parents in 1870. In 1886, the Jeppes moved from Pretoria to Johannesburg where they formed a syndicate that bought large areas of land known as Randjieslaagte and then Jeppestown. Julius Jeppe's older brother Carl was a founder of the Witwatersrand Council of Education, which set up the Jeppestown Grammar School, modeled on British public schools. After the Boer War, the school was reestablished as Jeppe High School. Julius Jeppe was elected to its first governing body and was its chair from 1918 until his death in 1929. He was knighted in 1922.

clean enough to be re-filled with fresh water.[25] I had trees to climb, a hill to roam and explore, a river to play in with my first Bedfordview friend, a black child my own age whom I knew only as Stanley,[26] a swimming pool, horses to ride occasionally (I was never an enthusiastic horseman), cows to milk, milk to separate, the separator to disassemble, wash, and reassemble each evening, butter to churn, buttermilk to drink, and a fruit orchard in which to gorge myself in summer with apricots, plums, peaches, figs, loquats, and pomegranates.

I entered Jeppe High School in the eighth grade. As mentioned earlier, my Dad and Uncle Dyer had been students at the same school. My brothers Winston and Justin would follow me there[27] as well. The school's motto was *Forti Nihil Difficilius*—Nothing is too Difficult for the Brave. I must have internalized this motto and made it my own, because I have never ever been afraid of taking on new challenges or new projects, always believing that if I set my mind to doing something, I could accomplish it.

I had either to walk four miles to catch the tram that ran past Jeppe High School for Boys and then walk home again from the tram terminus or, later, ride my bicycle all the way to school

---

[25] Another far less pleasant task assigned to me was periodically to get into the septic tank and clean it out thoroughly.

[26] Stanley taught me how to make a penetrating whistle with my fingers in my mouth. He did this by inviting me to put my fingers into his mouth so that I could feel the way be curled up his tongue and then by putting his fingers into my mouth to teach me properly to do the same. He patiently persevered with his instruction for many weeks, until I became as proficient a whistler as he was. Despite our innocent intimacy, at some unconscious level I felt a deep sadness about my friendship with Stanley but could not articulate at the time; it had to do with the dawning realization that in a segregated society we could not and would not remain friends as we grew older and began to inhabit completely different worlds.

[27] Winston's boys, Gavin, Barry, and Robin would also attend the Jeppe High School for Boys in later years.

and back. I did not do well in my first term, coming thirty-third in a class of thirty-four students. This was in stark contrast to my performance at Hellenic, where I was always either first or second in the class. Dismayed, my parents decided I needed the discipline of boarding school. So, at the age of eleven, and all too soon after our move to Bedfordview, I was enrolled as a boarder—to be allowed home for only one weekend a month.

Much as I hated it, the discipline of boarding school was probably the best thing that ever happened to me. I had to learn to survive bullying, regular canings by the house master, and the "fag" system similar to that of British boarding schools which required "new boys" to serve a prefect for a whole year, obeying slavishly his every command.[28] We had set hours for homework and study, rising and going to bed. We took ice cold showers at 6:00 a.m., and had hot baths only once a week, on a Saturday night. I had to learn to overcome my fear of ghosts without my mother's shoulder to cry on. I was in Tsessebe House—all eight houses at Jeppe were named after African antelope—and the other boardinghouse was Oribi. As a day scholar, I had been in Duiker; there were also Kudu, Impala, and Sable, Roan, and Steenbok houses. Each house had its prefects and monitors. The closest I came to exercising power in the school system was in my final year when I was made a monitor.[29]

The older of the two houses for boarders, Tsessebe, was reputedly haunted. In my second year at the school I was assigned to a dormitory of sixteen boys, eight lined up on either side of the room. The power of suggestion is such that I woke up one night convinced that I had seen the ghost of a young girl

---

[28] Among other things, I had to polish my prefect's shoes every day, shine the buttons on his cadet uniform, polish his "Sam Browne" uniform belt, and run endless errands for him.

[29] No one ever explained to me the duties of a monitor, and to this day, I still do not know what they were.

in a red cape sitting on the bottom of Johnson's bed (I was in the corner of the dormitory, then came Payne—who went on to become shot put champion at the Commonwealth Games—and then Johnson). I was terrified and started screaming. This brought the housemaster running into our dormitory and was followed by months of merciless teasing from my schoolmates. Fear of seeing Johnson's "girl in a red cape" was particularly difficult for me to overcome. For years, I slept with my head turned toward the wall. I couldn't bear to look out onto the dormitory in case I saw her again.

Certainly, whether it was because of the discipline of boarding school, or because I was beginning to find my way in the new curriculum, my grades steadily improved. By the time I matriculated from Jeppe with a university pass[30] at the age of fifteen, I was back to always being first or second in the class. Because of my improved grades, my parents relented and allowed me to finish my final year no longer as a boarder but once again as a day student.

It was in my early days at Tsessebe—without ever having heard the word let alone knowing what homosexuality was—that I had my first frightening encounter with a gay teacher. The dormitory we form one (eighth grade) boys slept in was small; there were fewer than a dozen of us assigned to it. One night after lights out, we had a pillow fight. We were jumping around on the beds, laying into one another with our pillows, and shouting and screaming with delight, when suddenly the lights went on and in strode "Mr. Lacey,"[31] our housemaster. Mr. Lacey grabbed the nearest boy who happened to be me and told me to go to his study and wait for him there. Shivering in my

---

[30] In South Africa at the time, one was only eligible to go on to university after graduating from high school if one's grades were sufficiently high (this was known as a university pass.) If they were not, the only option for higher education was a technical college where various practical skills were taught.

[31] Lacey is not his real name, and he is now deceased.

thin pajamas, I awaited my punishment. After giving the other boys a stern lecture, he came up to his study and told me he was going to give me four "cuts" with his cane. I was fairly used to being caned because after three infringements of the house rules in a week, one had to go to the headmaster to be punished. I was well-accustomed to bending down before Mr. Grant to get "six of the best."[32] But this time, it was very different. Mr. Lacey made me touch my toes, and then he whacked me on my bottom with his cane. But instead of getting it over with and giving me the next three, he had me stand up, put his arm around me, stroked my hair, and asked me how it felt. I felt horrified. Never had my punishment been meted out like this. It must have taken him twenty minutes to give me four "cuts," and between each one, there was this eerie fondling. It was only years later as an adult that I realized he must have been a pedophile.

I want to say a little about how Mom kept in touch with me during my four years as a boarder. One was through the vegetables, eggs, and butter from our farm. My mother had become friendly with the matron of Tsessebe, and had been given the contract to supply the house with weekly produce and provisions. Whenever she delivered these, Mom would try to see me if only for five minutes. The other way was through her work as an organist, playing for services in the chapels of Johannesburg's funeral homes. She no longer gave piano lessons to students (I think my refusal to practice and my insistence on playing the piano by ear, like Uncle Tom, was partly responsible for her turning away from teaching!). She had become primarily an organist, playing at various churches

---

[32] Mr. Grant, the headmaster, is now deceased. The last time I was sent to him to be caned was on August 15, 1945, VJ-day. As I was shown into his office, the news came over the radio that the Japanese had surrendered unconditionally. Mr. Grant was so overjoyed that he turned to me and said, "Young, on this occasion, I am going to let you off with a stern warning. Mend your ways, and don't let me ever see you here again."

and also, more lucratively, in the funeral homes and at the Braamfontein Crematorium. Whenever she was on duty for a funeral or cremation on an afternoon when I was not playing rugby, tennis, or cricket, she would let me know. I would stand outside the school to glimpse her little "Bluebird" (an old Austin 7 she herself had spray-painted blue) coming down Robert's Avenue. Again, we would have a few precious minutes together before we each went our separate ways. Incidentally, I never mentioned my encounter with Mr. Lacey to her or anyone else until I was married to Margaret; she was the first and only person I ever told.

It was also in these years that, at a tender age, I had my first direct experience of an untimely, brutal, senseless death. On the farm, we had three African workers. "Jack", a tall, gentle Rhodesian man, was our domestic servant, our chief cook, and one of my older friends and confidants; and "Dixon" and "Gabriel"[33] who labored in the fields under my father's direction and were less cultured and sensitive than Jack. The arrangement my parents had with these three men was that, on weekends, two would have their days off and the third would remain on the farm to help with such chores as milking the cows. They would rotate their weekend shifts so that none was deprived of a weekend break more than the others. One weekend it was Dixon's turn to remain on the farm while Jack and Gabriel had their days off. The morning before they left, Dixon and Gabriel had quarreled bitterly over breakfast. Evidently, Dixon carried a grudge against Gabriel the entire

---

[33] "Dixon" and "Gabriel" are pseudonyms. Both men are deceased. All Anglicized names of Africans that appear in this book for the first time are in quotation marks. This reflects the fact that few of us whites, myself included, were intimate enough to be entrusted with their true African names. In African culture, to reveal one's given name (always symbolic or indicative of some or other phenomenon surrounding one's birth) was the highest possible mark of trust. Few of us merited that level of acceptance.

time he was away, and his grievance was inflamed by smoking "dagga."[34] He waited impatiently for Gabriel to return to the farm and must have premeditated killing him, his weapon a sharpened steel knitting needle about fourteen inches long.

At dusk, one of the men came back up our driveway, but it was Jack—not Gabriel. Wanting to preserve the element of surprise and under the influence of dagga, Dixon did not wait to be certain that he was taking vengeance on the person who had aggrieved him. In the dim light, he ran the needle clean through the heart of the unsuspecting Jack. My father heard Jack's agonized scream and ran out of the house to our backyard, with me following closely behind. We found Jack on his back with blood spurting out of a tiny hole in his chest. Between us, Dad and I carried him into the kitchen and laid him on a blanket on the floor. Mom telephoned for an ambulance and called the police, but before they arrived, Jack's life slipped quietly away. Dixon was arrested and subsequently convicted of murder. As a result of this, I developed a lifelong aversion to cannabis, and I have never once been tempted to smoke or ingest it.

In 1944, while I was still a boarder at Jeppe High School, my parents arranged for Italian prisoners of World War II to live and work on our farm. This is a fascinating story. When Mussolini decided to invade and annex Abyssinia, Italian forces were deployed to carry out this mission. Almost universally, these men who had been conscripted had no heart for the war—least of all on the side of dictators like Hitler and Mussolini. South Africans, who were among the Allied soldiers fighting the Axis forces,[35] were sent north into Ethiopia and eventually into the

---

[34] "Dagga" was the South African name for a particularly potent variety of pot, cannabis, or marijuana, as it is known in the United States and elsewhere around the world. Though illegal, it was readily available if one knew where to look or whom to ask.

[35] The prime minister at the time was Field Marshall Jan Christiaan Smuts who had fought against the British in the Anglo-Boer Wars, had gone on to Cambridge University for graduate studies, and was

Saharan Desert where they fought under Montgomery against Rommel at El Alamein, and then into Italy itself.[36]

In Ethiopia, the Italians almost begged to be captured, laying down their weapons and waving their arms in friendly gestures. Thousands were taken prisoner and were transported back to huge prisoner-of-war camps in South Africa at Pietermaritzburg in Natal and Zonderwater (literally "without water") in the Transvaal. My parents qualified as farmers so were able to apply to take prisoners back to our farm to live with and work for us; in exchange for their labor, they were paid a nominal sum each day. So we came to have a succession of Italian prisoners staying with us—at one time as many as eleven. My father had them build the apartments on our property in which they lived, in addition to doing stone work, farm work, cabinet making, wrought iron work, and other fine crafts.

In one of these men, Attilio Bertucelli, a professional cabinetmaker from Viareggio, I serendipitously discovered a revered mentor and role model. My father had set him up with a small workshop. "Chilli," as we called him, made many of his tools himself, including a bench, several hand planes, a bow saw, a drill press, and a table saw. My final year at Jeppe was one of the happiest of my life. I was again a day scholar, able to live at home. I would come back from school, do my homework, and then sit for a couple of hours until dinner time on Chilli's workbench, learning by osmosis how properly to sharpen plane irons and chisels, how to plane wood with the grain, how to cut

---

by now an anglophile and leader of the United Party. The opposition was comprised of Afrikaners belonging to the Nationalist Party. Most of them belonged to the Broederbond, were proponents of Hitler's racial policies, and were opposed to South Africa joining the Allies in undertaking to defeat him. Today they would be described as Neo-Nazis. It is a testimony to Smuts's stature that he was able to bring South Africa into the war at all on the side of Great Britain.

[36] Margaret's father, Major Matthew Hosking Eddy, MBE, was stationed with our forces in Italy.

and shape wood, and how to smooth, sand, and finally apply finish (usually French polish) to the end product.

Chilli taught me to speak Italian (haltingly) and told me stories of the great Italian operas, singing many of the arias in his sweet tenor voice. When I eventually went to a live Verdi or Puccini opera it was with some sense of familiarity. Chilli taught me everything I know about woodworking, which became one of my lifelong passions. He made exquisite furniture, filling our home with handcrafted pieces he designed himself. One of these pieces, a display cabinet, still occupies an honored place in our present home. It was the one article of furniture I received after my parents' divorce—and the one piece of furniture we brought with us when we left South Africa at the end of 1973 to begin a new life in California.

There were other days when I went to see and talk to one or another of my two revered local heroes. Mr. Wishart lived further down on Sugarbush Road with his daughter. He was an old Scottish stonemason. He now had a tiny workshop, in which he polished gemstones and made beautiful clock cases out of granite and marble. My parents bought one of them, and it was prominently displayed on the mantelpiece above our fireplace. Mr. Wishart would reminisce about his native Scotland, tell me something of what he knew about gemstones, and show me how to cut and polish stone.

The second older friend was Percy—I never knew his surname. He rented a room from the Sussens[37] family, who lived on the opposite side of our farm from Mr. Wishart. Percy was a ham radio enthusiast. He had a little radio shack in which he built components for his radio system and operated it, making contact with people around the world. Each contact

---

[37] Incidentally, their son Aubrey Sussens was the oldest child in the family, and though a noted newspaper journalist, he was still living at home. He went on to have a distinguished career in South African journalism. He drove a little three-wheeler Morgan sports car, which I greatly admired. The Morgan is still a highly desirable marque.

was confirmed with a postcard sent from whomever he had been able to talk to, and there were literally thousands of postcards pinned to the walls of his radio shack. Percy could fix anything electrical or metallic. Whenever I had something that needed that sort of attention, I would go over to endlessly obliging Percy, and watch him patiently and methodically work on whatever it was I had asked him to help me with until he had restored it to proper functioning. From Mr. Wishart and from Percy, I learned something of the art of improvisation—making do with whatever was available to come up with creative solutions to seemingly intractable problems.

When World War II ended and the prisoners of war were all repatriated, Chilli elected to stay on in South Africa. He had come to love the country. My parents helped his wife, Elena, and Gabriella, the daughter Chilli had fathered before being sent on the Ethiopian campaign but had never set eyes on until she was six years old, to emigrate from Italy to make their home in South Africa. The Bertucelli family lived with us on our farm for a couple of years before Chilli had saved enough money to buy a piece of property and build his own home, also in Bedfordview.[38] My father helped set Chilli up in a furniture-making business. Chilli was joined by another Italian immigrant, Sandrelli, a designer. Sandrelli and Bertucelli eventually became South Africa's premier cabinet-making and furniture-manufacturing company. They won the gold medal, year after year, at the Rand Easter Show—in recognition of the excellence of their craftsmanship.

It was in my final year at Jeppe that I had another of several close brushes with death that I have survived in the course of my life. Neither Sugarbush Road nor River Road (which crossed the creek in which Stanley and I would try to float our homemade canoes) was paved. When the creek flooded, as it did nearly every year when debris from further upstream built

---

[38] Both Chilli and Elena are now deceased.

up against the columns of the bridge, the flooding on either side of the bridge extended for perhaps a quarter of a mile. When it was impossible to cross the bridge, my father stayed home from work—and we boys stayed home from school. When the waters eventually receded, River Road had typically turned to mud, and trucks left deep troughs in the mud that eventually hardened into formidable ruts.

One morning, I set off on my bicycle for school, crossing the creek and continuing up River Road until it came to the main paved road. When I got to that junction, I suddenly remembered that I had left my rugby boots at home. I had rugby practice after school that afternoon so I turned around, pedaling furiously because by the time I went home, got my boots, and started off again, I knew I would be late for school.

As I was going back down River Road toward the bridge, I could see Mr. Sussens's three-ton truck coming toward me in the opposite direction. Just before we passed each other, my bicycle got stuck in one of the deep ruts I have described and I was thrown off the bicycle, landing underneath the truck. I remember this event as if it happened in slow motion. I thought, "This is what it must be like to die." How Mr. Sussens stopped his truck I shall never know. But stop it he did, literally with the double-rear wheels touching my head. Had his reaction time been a split-second slower, my skull would have been crushed. Both of us were badly shaken. Mr. Sussens insisted on taking me home, putting my bicycle on the back of the truck and me in the passenger seat. When we got home, Mom decided that I needed something to calm me down. She gave me a cup of hot milk with brandy in it—the first time I had tasted brandy in my life. It must have done the trick because I was then pronounced ready to go to school. Mom drove me there in the car.

I matriculated from high school in 1948, with a university pass, about two months before my sixteenth birthday. There was no thought of my going on to university. I had no idea what I wanted to do with my life, and even if I had dreamed of entering a chosen profession, there was no money for a university education. Explaining why requires a digression.

From the time our family went to Gran and Pop's house on York Road to play tennis every weekend, my father had coached me.[39] Once Gran and Pop sold their Kensington home with its tennis court, moving to their farm Trekdrift,[40] Dad had taken me to either the Jeppe Quondam Club or to Mr. Louw's home to play tennis. Mr. Louw was in the business of building tennis courts, and he had both a grass court and a clay court at his magnificent home in Bedfordview. One of Mr. Louw's neighbors and a fellow tennis player was Tommy Smith, a stockbroker.[41] Tommy Smith mentioned to my father that the Merriespruit mine in the Orange Free State, one of the first really deep gold mines, going down some three miles into the earth, was a tremendous investment opportunity. Trusting his advice, my father used every penny he had saved and could scrape together to buy Merriespruit shares. Had he stopped there, the setback that followed would not have become a disaster. But he did not stop there. He borrowed money to buy more shares. At the time, the shares were selling at something like the equivalent of one dollar, and my father had bought thousands (I don't know how many, but I would guess fifty thousand). And then tragedy struck in the form of the twin nemeses of deep-level mining— heat and water: the deeper the mine, the greater the heat that has to be dissipated and the greater the risk of flooding.

At Merriespruit, while they were still trying to pump cool

---

[39] Later I was coached by Mr. Damacius, and then by Jaraslov Drobney, who had played Davis Cup tennis for what was then Yugoslavia.

[40] After Pop's death, Gran sold Trekdrift and bought a house in Malvern, #9 Naaid Street. Later she moved in to our home in Bedforview and lived with us for many years, as did Uncle Dick after his divorce from Aunt Bessie. Following my parents' divorce, when Mom sold Bella Vista and bought a house in Parkhurst, Gran and Uncle Dick moved with her and lived there until they died.

[41] Both Mr. Louw and Tommy Smith are now deceased.

air down into the mine shafts, massive flooding occurred. Those drilling must have hit an underground aquifer. The entire network of mine shafts, vertical and horizontal, became unworkable and the mine had to be abandoned. It became difficult to sell shares that had cost one dollar for a single cent. Dad had an enormous debt to repay. This overshadowed our family for the next twenty years. My father, embittered, never spoke to Tommy Smith again. Our days of tennis at Mr. Louw's home ended abruptly. And paying for a university education for any of his children was out of the question.

It was then that I joined the Kensington Tennis Club, which had an active social component for us younger people. Mr. and Mrs. Holloway, who had been professional ballroom dancers, were also members of the tennis club. They had no children of their own. To attract young people to the club, they offered free lessons in ballroom dancing in the tennis clubhouse each Wednesday evening. Neville Webber, another member of the club, was an excellent pianist, and he played for the Holloways, providing whatever music they wanted—the waltz, the foxtrot, the slow foxtrot, the tango, the samba, the rhumba, and, best of all, swing.

On the last Saturday of every month, the Holloways rented the Kensington Hall adjacent to the tennis club, hired a band, and provided a whole evening of dancing for a nominal fee to cover their expenses. None of us needed partners. We simply showed up. What a marvelous opportunity for me, who had been to a school for boys only, to meet girls and become comfortable in their company. And the Holloways always had intervals during which we exchanged partners while the music played. This was the one feature I missed most when, a few years later as my tennis improved and I began to play matches in the third and then the second league, that I joined the more prestigious Turffontein Tennis club.

I now return to my major concern at the time: the choice of a career. Since going on to university was out of the question, not only because we could not afford it but also because I had no idea what I wanted to do with my life, I turned to Uncle Tom for advice about what direction I might go in now that I had finished high school. Uncle Tom had his own advertising agency, and he extolled the beauty of the printed page, or typography, as it is known. He spoke of Johannes Gutenberg in Germany (1436), William Caxton in England (1476), and Christophe Plantin in Belgium (1555), and of how these pioneers in printing with moveable type transformed the world and were instrumental in ushering in the Renaissance and then the Reformation. He told me how honorable a trade printing was; in England, for example, printers were the only tradespeople recognized as "gentlemen" and were accorded by the Crown the privilege of being able to carry swords.

Eventually, after talking with him about this for several weeks, I made up my mind. I would seek an apprenticeship as a printer, more specifically, as a typographer—a compositor or linotype operator. Unfortunately, at that time there weren't any apprenticeships available in Johannesburg. Men returning from World War II had availed themselves of every opportunity to learn a trade. The South African Typographical Union insisted that there be a strict ratio of three journeymen to every one apprentice. This imposed a strict limit on the number of openings. So my name was placed on a waiting list. During the almost twelve months I had to wait, Uncle Tom gave me my first job, as a darkroom assistant to his photographer at Young's Advertising Agency. I loved this work, and it taught me everything I have ever known about developing and printing black-and-white photographs (something Margaret and I were to do together to do later in our own bathroom cum darkroom after we were married). Eventually, in December of 1949, an apprenticeship became available, not in Johannesburg, but in Roodepoort, thirty miles to the west, and almost forty miles from our home in Bedfordview. It was in Roodepoort that the next chapter in my life was to begin.

PART 2

Printer, Theological Student

3

The Model Stationers and Printing Company, Roodepoort, Transvaal

The Model Stationers and Printing Company (Pty) Ltd. was owned by two partners: Mr. Dunstan, who was responsible for the stationery store, and Mr. O'Toole,[42] who ran the adjacent printing shop. This arrangement worked well, considering the unfortunate fact that they could barely get along at a personal level. Yet both were fine men of the utmost integrity, for each of whom I came to have the highest possible respect. Dunstan, O'Toole, and their foreman Len Lloyd, my primary instructor, a kind and gentle thirty-five-year- old family man, were the three journeymen at Model necessary for them to have an apprentice—in compliance with the unbending requirements of the South African Typographical Union. I was their first.

Theirs was a small shop, with a linotype machine, scores of trays of moveable type,[43] a guillotine for cutting reams of paper

---

[42] Both are now deceased.

[43] The alloy used for casting type in linotype and monotype machines and in fonts of metal moveable type was composed of lead, antimony, and tin. Lead has a relatively low melting point. Tin adds hardness to the lead. Antimony expands when it cools, offsetting the shrinkage of the lead and the tin as they cool, thus keeping the height of the letters constant. Larger fonts, such as those used in posters, were made of wood.

to size, five presses (one small, for business cards, checks, and the like, one slightly larger, two medium-sized machines, and a huge flatbed press capable of printing books and large posters), as well as a bookbinding department. The printing was done by an alcoholic letterpress operator named Sydney Green. I mention his disease only because alcoholism killed him while I was working there. Mr. O'Toole operated the guillotine.

According to ancient custom and the union's regulations those composing type (whether by hand or on the linotype or monotype machines), operating the letterpress or lithograph machines, cutting paper, and bookbinding were designated as members of different guilds. Apprentices could only be trained and qualified in one of these guilds. An apprenticeship typically lasted six years. However, the Model Stationers and Printing Company was a small firm, and I was soon moving across these traditional lines of demarcation and on my way to becoming a master printer, proficient in each of these areas. I later came to realize that I had been incredibly fortunate in comparison with most of my apprentice friends who worked for larger printing establishments. They were only permitted to learn the trade of the particular guild in which they were apprenticed.

My father, whose ambitions for me included most things he had not succeeded in doing—having a good education, being a world-class tennis player, and becoming a wealthy businessman—was openly disappointed when I resolved to become a printer. Centuries earlier, the British Crown might have dignified printers as gentlemen, but for my father to have three sons who were tradesmen[44] was consistent neither with the ambitions he harbored for his children nor his ego.

Since I was below the age of twenty-one and becoming an indentured apprentice required the signing by my parents of a

---

[44] Leaving school at the end of the eighth grade, my twin brothers followed me into the printing trade, not as compositors/linotype operators but as letterpress and lithograph machine minders.

legally binding contract, I had to have my parents' permission. My father agreed that I could become an apprentice, but only on one condition: if I was going to become a printer, he decreed, it had to be as an eventual manager of a printing company, or better still, the owner of my own printing works. To that end, he insisted that I study to become an associate of the Chartered Institute of Secretaries (ACIS) in order to acquire managerial competence. The CIS in the British Commonwealth is a qualification similar to that of certified public accountant (CPA) in the United States. The only way I could prepare myself for the CIS examinations would be by attending night school twice a week in addition to the two nights a week of schooling at the Johannesburg Technical College—mandatory for all apprentices. Undeterred, I agreed, thus committing myself to four nights of evening classes a week for the next six years.

Roodepoort was a medium-sized town to the west of Johannesburg, about thirty-five miles from Bedfordview, an eastern peri-urban suburb of Johannesburg. The major difficulty in serving an apprenticeship so far from my home was getting there by eight o'clock in the morning, and getting home after night school ended at nine. The railway station nearest to Bedfordview was Tooronga, about five miles away. There were early morning and late afternoon commuter trains from Springs, the eastern terminus, to Krugersdorp, at the western end of the line, and *vice versa*.

Tooronga was a small station, and not every train stopped there. Roodepoort was larger, but often the express trains from Krugersdorp into Johannesburg passed it by. If I missed one train in the evening, I had a long wait for the next train going east. Likewise, if I was late for a morning train, I had to wait for the next train that did stop at Tooronga (and be late for work) or quickly go on by car to Jeppe station to catch the first train that pulled in there. Since I did not have a car, it was usually Mom who had to drive me and pick me up again late at night. My alternative in the summer months was to ride my bicycle to

Tooronga and lock it to a fence or pole while I was away all day, hoping that it would still be there when I came back that night. Once I came back, and my bike had been stolen. My options were not entirely satisfactory.

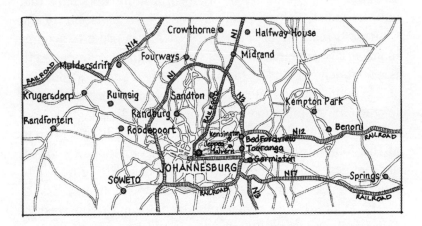

One of the tremendous advantages of commuting to work and back by train was the time it afforded me to read. I always had a book with me, often a paperback edition of one of Aristotle or Plato's works since I was fascinated by—but had had no formal exposure to—philosophy. On the train, I also started reading the New Testament for an interesting reason. My Dad had always stressed the importance of character. But, I wondered, what *was* character—and *how* did one acquire character? In part, my reading of Greek philosophy was to try to answer these questions. But it also occurred to me that Jesus was an exemplar of good character, so it seemed that I needed to read what he said or was said to have said to find any answers, and read the New Testament as well.

John McMillan was one of my friends at the Kensington Tennis Club. We played singles against each other and were doubles partners. In 1950, John, who was working as a bank clerk, bought himself a new motorcycle, a 250 cc Panther, a lesser-known British brand.[45] This seemed to me to be the perfect solution to my own transportation problem. But first, I had to persuade my parents of this. Like most parents, Mom and Dad thought motorcycles highly dangerous.[46] However, eventually recognizing the burden my long commute was imposing on me and on Mom who acted as my chauffeur, they relented and gave me permission to purchase a Panther identical to John's. The brand-new Panther cost 120 pounds sterling (about $250). This was a considerable sum for an apprentice earning three pounds and ten shillings (about $7) a week. But, unbeknown to me, Mom had been saving the wages I handed over to her every payday, and there was enough in the savings account by then to buy the motorcycle outright.

Incidentally, both Panthers, John's and mine, provided an insight as to why British motorcycles, once the best in the world, took fourth place to German, Italian, and Japanese machines in the years following World War II. With the exception of a few exclusive brands like Norton and Velocette, they were erratic, unreliable, poorly engineered, and shoddily made. Once, on the road between Florida and Roodepoort, the engine of my motorcycle dropped to the road when the frame snapped. Without warning, the machine came to a dead stop, which propelled me off the saddle, into the air, and then onto the tarmac—fortunately without injury. The next challenge was getting to work and having the Panther taken to a repair shop. Fortunately some large-hearted passerby pulled over and invited me to load my motorcycle onto the back of his truck. He was kind enough to help me do this and then take me to work, broken motorcycle and all. It remained there until I could retrieve it, have it repaired, and sell it at a considerable loss.

---

[45] When the British refer to the make of vehicles, particularly those of higher quality, the word *marque* is used rather than *brand*. As far as I know, John is no longer alive.

[46] I felt the same way when I eventually became a parent myself.

This experience, as well as one or two minor accidents on the bike, made me realize that I had to get a car of my own as soon as I could find one at an affordable price.

I loved learning to be a compositor and linotype operator. Because of Uncle Tom's influence, my principal interest was in typographical design. I subscribed to and became an avid reader of the two leading journals in the field: *The British Printer,* as the name implies, published in the United Kingdom, and the *Typographical Journal*, an American publication. Both stirred my imagination, and I tried creatively to translate the ideals that these journals and my night classes were holding up before me into the work I was doing day by day.

Recognizing and understanding the reasons for the subtle differences between typefaces—Caxton, Plantin, Garamond, Bodoni, and Perpetua, for example, and *sans serif* fonts such as Eric Gill's Sans Script; coming to know which complemented one another and which clashed; learning when to use bold or italic; and most of all, matching the mood evoked by the typeface to the message to be conveyed, became intoxicating. Likewise, balancing blocks of type on a page and getting the correct margins were satisfying experiences. I tried to use all this new knowledge when I was given the opportunity to design a customer's order *de novo* and to improve the designs of orders that would come in on a recurring basis. Both Mr. O'Toole and Len, my foreman, encouraged this kind of creativity; they were also forthright in telling me when I had gone over the top and then did not hesitate to order me redo something I had worked on for hours.

In different ways, Mr. Dunstan and Mr. O'Toole each tried to mentor me. For example, Mr. Dunstan came into the print shop one morning and announced that he was taking me to lunch that day to his Rotary Club meeting as his guest. I protested that I wasn't properly dressed; in summer, I always went to work in shorts and long socks. He brushed aside my scruples and proudly introduced me to his club as his apprentice, with unexpectedly fulsome praise for the work I was doing.

Mr. O'Toole stood by me in a different context. There was a sexy young woman in the stationery shop who came through our side of the building each morning and stopped to chat with me in a manner I took to be flirtatious. One morning, I decided to try my luck and tried to kiss her. Immediately she told me she was going to tell her fiancé—and did. Next thing I knew, her fiancé, a huge firefighter from the fire station up the street, came in and challenged me to come outside to the sidewalk where he was going to give me the thrashing of my life. I told him I couldn't leave work until my lunch hour, but that I would then meet him at the vacant lot next to the fire station. Mr. O'Toole witnessed all this, and then he told me quietly that he was coming with me to act as my second and referee the fight to ensure there was no foul play. I think he saw how scared I was. Mr. O'Toole had been a well-known amateur boxer in his youth, and he was familiar with all the ways in which an unscrupulous opponent could break the rules, giving himself an unfair advantage.

Promptly at one o'clock,[47] the two of us walked up to the firehouse where the fireman was waiting. Mr. O'Toole made us face one another and explained the rules: there was to be no hitting below the belt and no hitting a man when he was down— any infringement and he would stop the fight. The fireman was much taller and bulkier than I, but it didn't take me long after we started our bare-knuckled bout to realize that he knew little about boxing. Every time he swung at me, I ducked or weaved and then hit his nose with a straight left. Fairly soon, his nose was bleeding profusely, and I could tell he was becoming more and more frustrated. The angrier he got, the more wildly he swung at me. I could easily avoid his lunges and got in

---

[47] Lunchtime in South Africa was always from 1:00–2:00 p.m., rather than from noon–1:00 p.m.

several more straight jabs to his nose and one or two right-hand punches to his belly. Then, much to my enormous surprise and relief, he burst into tears! At this point, Mr. O'Toole stopped the fight and made us shake hands. Needless to say, I never tried to kiss his girlfriend again. And I silently gave thanks to the Paulist Fathers. At least something of what they had tried to teach me had sunk in.

During the years of my apprenticeship, there were several developments in my personal life. I'll begin with the most mundane before going on to describe the spiritual. At the most mundane level, I learned a little dentistry and a new woodworking skill: chip carving.

My unexpected and involuntary foray into dentistry happened in the following way. We had two Africans working at the Model Stationers and Printing Company, a refined man whom we knew only as "Coffee" who cleaned the shop and made the morning and afternoon tea and "Alfred," who made our deliveries. Alfred had served in the South African armed forces during World War II, and came back shell-shocked. To put it mildly, he was a little crazy, in the most endearing way. Today he would be diagnosed with post-traumatic stress disorder. One afternoon Alfred came to me, presented me with a pair of pliers, squatted down in front of me, pointed to one of his front teeth, and insisted that I pull it out. I think he had pyorrhea because the tooth was loose. Alfred's faith in me disarmed me completely, and I couldn't let him down. After making sure this is was what he really wanted me to do, I tightly gripped the loose tooth with the pair of pliers he had handed me, held his forehead with my left hand, and gave a good, hard pull with my right. The tooth came out cleanly, with a minimum of bleeding. From that day on Alfred trusted me implicitly and he would come to me at regular intervals to have yet another loose tooth extracted. I must have taken out four or five of his incisors and molars during my apprenticeship.

The circumstances leading up to my learning chip carving

were unfortunate. One Monday morning, Sydney Green, our letterpress machine minder, failed to show up for work. Around midmorning, Mr. O'Toole walked over to the Craig Hotel a couple of blocks down the street where Sydney lived alone and found him dead in his bed. He had drunk more than usual over the weekend and had finally succumbed to cirrhosis of the liver. After the funeral, the first I went to of someone I knew personally, a series of letterpress machine minders came and went. By the time I had qualified as a master printer and left Roodepoort I don't think they had found anyone permanent to replace Sydney Green.

One of those who worked with us for a few months was an enthusiastic chip carver who offered to teach me what he knew. So my lunch hours were spent carving wood with an extra sharp pocketknife under his watchful eye. Thanks to Chilli, I already knew a lot about woodworking, but this was something Chilli had not taught me, and I took to it as the proverbial duck to water. Later, when I started dating girls, I would fall in love, make for the latest object of my affections a chip-carved jewelry box, give it to her, and then move on to the next girlfriend and box. This became a standing joke in our family. When I later decided to make a jewelry box for Margaret, my brothers warned me that this was the kiss of death. But Margaret still has the box I made and carved with my pocketknife, and gave to her on April 29, 1958, her birthday, the day we chose to become engaged.

At a spiritual level, two ministers of religion sequentially came to have a profound influence on my life. One was a simple pastor of the Church of the Nazarene named Thomas W. Thomas.[48] Thomas Thomas had been stricken with polio and had braces on both his legs. He would limp into our printing shop to have various evangelical tracts printed. Whenever he came in, he would ask me point blank what I was doing about

---

[48] Thomas W. Thomas is now deceased.

God. The man terrified me because I was doing absolutely nothing about God. Tennis was my religion, and I worshipped faithfully every Saturday and every Sunday. Gradually, he won my respect because he not only asked *me* what I was doing about God—he put the same question to Mr. O'Toole and Mr. Dunstan. That, I thought, took courage.

Eventually, to save his church some money, I would set up the type for his tracts during my lunch hour so that all he had to pay for was the paper and the time on the letterpress machines. And then Pastor Thomas invited me to a "big tent" meeting one Saturday afternoon when a prominent American evangelist would be preaching. I agreed to attend, but I sat as far from the front as I could. Before the evangelist spoke, a man and his wife got up and sang a duet. I was shaken to the core by the beauty of the song they were singing and even more by the love for each other and for God that shone in their faces. I burst into tears. In contrast to them, my life seemed to revolve only around myself. My selfishness shamed me. I did not hear a word the American evangelist said, but when he invited those who wanted to give themselves to Christ to go up kneel at the front of the tent, I went forward.

Not fully understanding what had happened to me any more than I did myself, Thomas Thomas believed he had made a new convert. Almost every day he fed me literature that I read diligently. Most of this emphasized the things good Christians did *not* do, like drinking alcohol (which I did not do anyway), going to the cinema, dancing, playing sport on Sundays, or in the case of women, wearing makeup or jewelry. His denomination, as Pastor Thomas represented it, had about twenty-three prohibitions of this nature. Not knowing any better, and thinking this is what God wanted of me, I gave up one by one many of the activities that I loved, especially dancing and playing tennis on Sundays. What was worse, I became extremely judgmental of anyone who did these things, including my friends and members of my family.

Then, unbeknown to me, my mother, wise woman that she was, stepped in. She went to see Thomas W. Thomas (only telling me about this several years later). She said something like this to him: "Ernlé is not thinking for himself; he is parroting your thoughts. If you have sown good seed, it will bear fruit. But I want you to leave him alone for six months, so that he can begin to find his own way." I'm sure no one had spoken to Pastor Thomas like this before. But to his credit, he did as my Mom had asked of him and ceased coming to the print shop to pressure me one way or another. It was then that I began to regret and turn away from the narrow, judgmental approach to Christianity Thomas W. Thomas had been inculcating and returned to my former love of tennis, dancing, and the cinema as well as to a more inclusive and less judgmental form of spirituality.

And this is where the second minister, Joseph Benjamin (J. B.) Webb came into my life. Ever since childhood, I had loved to sing. The most memorable evenings I can recall have Mom or Uncle Tom at the piano and either Gran singing solo or all of us singing together. This was simply the way it was. I knew I had a good but untrained voice. And at the age of nineteen, at some deep inner level, I knew I wanted to have voice lessons. But who was to teach me? The recommendations of friends steered me to the studio of Rupert Stoutt, an Irishman from County Cork, reputedly the best voice teacher in the city of Johannesburg. Tentatively, I approached him, and he graciously agreed to take me on as one of his students. Somehow, I fitted voice lessons into my already hectic schedule of work, night school, tennis, and the rudiments of a social life. After a few months of coaching, Mr. Stoutt invited me to sing in his choir. I did not know it when I first went to him for voice lessons but soon discovered that he was the organist and choirmaster of the

Methodist Central Hall in Johannesburg, where Joe Webb—as he was popularly known—had been the minister for twenty-three years.[49]

Singing in the Methodist Central Hall choir, where the attendance at the main Sunday evening service was close to two thousand, brought several unforeseen benefits. My parents soon followed me and joined the choir; through J. B. Webb's preaching, I was exposed to a type of Christianity that truly made sense to me. It caused me inwardly to exclaim, *If this is what being a Christian is all about, count me in!* I met a woman there who would later become my beloved wife, Margaret Mavis Eddy. I will dwell on each of these points in turn.

My mother, an accomplished musician with a fine alto voice, soon decided to join Mr. Stoutt's choir; shortly after that, my father, an off-key baritone, followed suit. Mom soon became friends with Mavis Eddy, sitting next to her in the alto section of the choir. And because Mavis's husband, Matt, had church meetings on Thursday evenings she brought her daughter, Margaret, then twelve or thirteen years of age to choir practice with her. Margaret would sit at the back of the church far below the choir loft and do her homework. I shall say more about this presently. Dad and I both sang in the baritone section of the choir. It felt good to have this bond between the three of us.

But one Thursday evening, my Mom, for some reason, was unable to go to choir practice. Dad and I set off by ourselves, with me driving our little Morris Minor from Bedfordview into the center of the city. As we were going through Bezuidenhout Valley my father threw one of his inexplicable tantrums and began furiously shouting and swearing at me. This was one occasion when I knew with absolute certainty that I had done nothing to deserve this tirade—and something snapped inside me. I stopped the car, turned off the engine, and said, "Dad, get out of the car, and repeat what you have just said."

---

[49] J. B. Webb and Rupert Stout are no longer alive.

We both got out and stood on the sidewalk. My father continued to berate me in the foulest of language. And then I hit him. He fell down, and I helped him up. He stood there, shaken and silent, and I handed him the car keys, turned on my heels, and started walking the six miles back to Bedfordview. Neither of us got to choir practice that night. Mortified, I sobbed all the way home. I was trying to be a Christian, and I had hit my own father!

When I got home, Dad was already in bed. I went in to apologize for what I had done and ask his forgiveness. He told me to get out of his room and did not speak to me for the next three weeks. This was his pattern after any of our many domestic disputes. With one exception (on the day Heather was born), he never again abused me verbally. Nor did he lift a finger to hit me, something he had done unpredictably and regularly before.

Joe Webb, educated at Oxford University, combined his rigorous intellect with a passionate faith, uniting faith and reason, science and religion, in a way I found utterly compelling. After all, in Luke's Gospel, the first great commandment is summed up in these words: "You shall love the Lord your God with all your heart, and with all your soul, and with all your strength, and *with all your mind*" (Luke 10:27).[50] J. B. Webb was truly a man of God; with the passion of a Hebrew prophet he was equally concerned about social justice. For the first time in my life, I heard someone fearlessly denouncing apartheid and the terrible injustices it inflicted on the nonwhite majority in our country. He spoke of such things as the inequity of the thirteen percent of the population who were white owning and occupying more than 80 percent of the land as well as claiming

---

[50] All Scripture quotations are from the New Revised Standard Version of the Bible, copyright 1989, the Division of Christian Education of the National Council of the Churches of Christ in the United States of America. Used by permission. All rights reserved.

all the country's mineral resources and rights. He decried the oppressive pass system whereby Africans had to have a pass, an identity document, with them at all times. Without it, they could be arrested and thrown in jail. He dramatized the plight of the men who worked the gold mines of South Africa who had to leave their wives and children behind in the rural areas from which they had come for years at a stretch, living in same-sex dormitories where homosexual rape was commonplace.

Besides, Methodist worship services were so different from the Catholic services to which I had been exposed as a child. Instead of Latin, the liturgy was in English. Instead of having to kneel to pray, one could sit. And there was a sense of joy and liveliness in the whole worship experience. Not many months after joining the choir, I decided that if this is what Christianity was all about, I really wanted to be part of it. Little did I know at the time that Dr. Webb would later perform our marriage ceremony and that in the last year of his ministry, before he retired and not long afterward died of cancer, I would become his assistant minister and work closely with him almost every day.

Having decided to become a Methodist, I went all the way. I joined the Wesley Guild, a social and service club for young people. Matt Eddy was its leading light, and I came to know and admire him before I had even spoken to his daughter. And then I decided to become a Sunday school teacher. Without realizing it at the time, this seemingly small decision would lead me to one of the pivotal turning points of my life.

I had left the Kensington Tennis Club and joined the Turffontein Tennis Club, where the standard of tennis was far higher. Turffontein was one of the strongest clubs in the whole of South Africa. Four of us younger players were particularly close. Peter Murray, with whom I later went to London, was my doubles partner, and Alf Menges, Brian Pike (I was Brian's best man at his wedding years later), and I played singles and doubles together constantly and were on the team playing in Johannesburg's second league. These matches were on Saturday afternoons. Then the four of us were selected for Turffontein's first-league team. This was a tremendous honor because the first team played not only against other first-league teams in Johannesburg but in different cities around the country as well. I couldn't have wished for a better way of improving my tennis. But the matches were all played on Sundays, and I now had to choose between playing first-league tennis and becoming a Sunday school teacher.

After agonizing over the decision I felt I must make—and with tremendous regret—I went to the team captain and told him I could not play in the first team. He looked at me as if I had become unhinged. How could a young player turn down the opportunity I had been given? But there was no doubt in my mind. Something deep within me was impelling me to become a Sunday school teacher. I know now that, had I not made that decision, the story I am telling would not have been written. It would have been a different story—not necessarily better or worse, but not this story, not the story of this life I love and I am trying to recount.

Meeting Margaret changed my life. Up until that time, and even afterward, I had many girlfriends. I met girls at the Kensington Tennis Club and at the dancing classes run by Mr. and Mrs. Holloway in Kensington Hall. I would go out with several of them to movies or to dances. I would even fall in love with some of them, briefly, and then move on to the next. It was as if I was searching for the "right" one but had not yet found her. These girls were nothing more than good friends, and we had enjoyable relationships with one another.

At choir practice one Thursday night, Mavis saw a "hobo" (a homeless "wino" of whom there were many in the central part of Johannesburg) enter the church where Margaret was sitting demurely at the back of the sanctuary doing her homework. Mavis nudged Peggy. Peggy turned round and beckoned to me. They wanted me to go down to check on Margaret. I left the choir loft and quickly began walking down the stairs to the sanctuary. Simultaneously Margaret, having become uneasy in the presence of the hobo, had started walking up the stairs to the choir loft. We met on the mezzanine landing. I looked into her eyes and instantaneously—without a word having been spoken—knew this was the woman I would marry. At the time, she was thirteen. I was nineteen—a huge age difference at that juncture of our lives. This was not so much love at first sight on my part as instant recognition. It was as if I recognized my soul mate. Seven years would go by before we became man and wife. But that was the night I unquestioningly knew my destiny. I have no idea of what became of the hobo.

My twenty-first birthday (a major milestone in British and South African culture) was on December 14, 1953, and my parents hosted a splendid party to celebrate my emancipation from minor to major in the hall of the Turffontein Tennis Club. Scores of family members and friends came to enjoy the evening. Among my friends was Margaret, then just sixteen years old. Doug and Jean Cole,[51] mutual Central Hall acquaintances, brought her to the party with them. Although I had asked Margaret to dance with me, Doug and Jean had to leave early and took Margaret away with them. So she and I did not dance; nor did we have our first date until a year later.

The years of my apprenticeship ended more quickly than I had anticipated. Because of the shortage of skilled labor in South Africa, the government and trade unions jointly made it possible for apprentices to be certified as journeymen after five years instead of six—if they passed a stiff nationally certified trade test. I jumped at the opportunity to take the examination, feeling that the Model Stationers and Printing Company had taught me everything it had to offer. When the results came out, only six apprentices in the entire country had passed. I was the

---

[51] Both are now deceased.

only compositor/linotype operator in the group, and of the six came in with the highest marks. On Christmas Eve, 1953, at the age of twenty-one, I left Mr. O'Toole, Mr. Dunstan, Len Lloyd, Coffee, Alfred, the Model Printing Company, and Roodepoort as a fully qualified master printer.

My printing qualification played an indispensable role in my life. It enabled me to stand on my own two feet financially and move as a man among other men, to see and experience something of the wider world, and eventually to pay my own way through university. But looking back I regret to say it was a dying craft. Within two decades typography had migrated from the world of moveable type and letterpress machines to the personal computer—thanks to technologies introduced by International Business Machines (IBM) and Apple, and the genius of people like Bill Gates and Steve Jobs.

The end began in my day and accelerated rapidly. It started on newspapers. For example, at the *Rand Daily Mail,* a morning paper where I worked the night shift while at Rhodes University, we had thirty or so linotype operators. Early in the shift, the editor would give each of us complete stories to set in type for the newspaper's inner pages. This was the most interesting part of the work because much of what we were setting in type was well researched and written. We usually did this for the first four or five hours. Then toward the end of the shift later-breaking stories destined for the front pages of subsequent editions would be divided, paragraph by paragraph, between the thirty operators so that an entire article could be set in type in a matter of minutes and the front page of later editions could be repeatedly re-composed.

Not long after my time, the newspaper's linotype machines were automated, and the operators were replaced with less highly skilled and less highly paid typists who transformed copy onto continuous tape rather than moveable type. The tape was then fed into the now-automated linotype machines. One operator could oversee five or more machines; the automated machines broke the tape into lines, justified the lines (ensuring equal space between each of the words in a line), and then fed the lines on matrices into the machine to be cast in metal.

From this seemingly innocuous beginning, everything we did as typographers rapidly became redundant. Selecting the type font, the size of the font, the symbols, the special characters, the face (italic, bold, or underlining), writing the article, story, or book (as I am doing at this moment)—to printing, with words or characters in different colors, can now be done sitting at a desk in front of a computer.

Today the craft of printing from metal endures only in small towns and in rural areas, but even there, it is an endangered species. But the computer, however versatile, is a sterile companion. It provides no smell of printer's ink, none of the roar of the great rotary presses, no more "printer's fingers" seemingly impervious to the burns inflicted on skin by the constant handling of hot metal. To be sure, much has been gained. From the perspective of one who was proud to become master of an ancient craft, much has also been lost.

4

Temple Press, London, England

After leaving the Model Stationers and Printing Company, I enjoyed working in different well-known printing establishments in Johannesburg. To my delight, I discovered that compositors and linotype operators were constantly in high demand and that there was no shortage of job opportunities. The first position I applied for was at a medium-sized company with the reputation within the trade for typographical excellence—reputedly it was one of the best in the country. My application was accepted, and I started work there almost immediately after leaving Model.

At first, it seemed exactly the right move. The company was indeed doing some outstanding work, and the people employed there were congenial colleagues. I liked and respected the two brothers who were the co-owners. I was allowed a good deal of creative latitude. I was learning a lot, and I was contributing considerably, particularly in terms of making minor improvements to standing orders that I thought not quite up to the high standard the company set for itself.

Several months later, my typographical ideals got me into trouble. One customer came in regularly to have books of checks printed, and the foreman asked me to complete the latest order. As I looked at the checks the firm had been printing for this customer over a period of many years I was appalled. According to everything I had been taught and had come to believe in, the layout, the mixture of typefaces, the spacing, and the font sizes were all wrong. I designed a completely new check and—pleased with my efforts—handed proofs to the foreman, who in turn showed my work to his boss, the co-owner and shop manager. This man then came to me and ordered me to redo the checks. He wanted them to remain as they had been. I tried to explain my reasons for the redesign and what I thought was wrong with the old layout, and asked him at least to show the proofs to the customer, who could then decide which he preferred: the old or the new. He refused to listen, adamantly insisting that I do as he said. So, getting on my high horse, I told him I was not going to violate the typographical principles I had been taught and that if he wanted the checks changed, he could do this himself. I knew that this would not sit well with the co-owner of the company, so before he could fire me, I gave him my notice, announcing that I would find another job elsewhere.[52]

There is a somewhat ironic sequel to this story. Years later, when I was an ordained minister, I discovered that this same co-owner of the company was a lay leader in the congregation I had been appointed to serve, and that we would be working closely together over the course of the next several years. Either he had forgotten that I had once been his employee, or he had graciously decided to forgive my youthful idealism and impetuosity. Now that our relationship was on a completely different footing, we got on famously. I want to think that perhaps the incident that prompted me to leave his printing company, if he remembered it, had left him with a grudging respect for me.

For the next year, I was employed at one or two other printing shops, moving on when I thought I had learned all they could teach me. The one exception was the Electric Printing Works

---

[52] The person whose identity I have concealed in this paragraph is now deceased.

to which I returned in future years.[53] At the same time, a larger plan was formulating in the back of my mind. Although I was a member of the Wesley Guild, was a Sunday school teacher, and was singing in the choir, I felt there was more that I could do to express my faith. I began to wonder about becoming a minister. Two doubts had always driven the thought away. One was the realization that I had led a relatively sheltered life. Many of the men I had worked with in the printing trade had fought in World War II. Some of them had been prisoners of war, some had even escaped from prison camps, and all had had challenging experiences completely beyond my ken. I wondered what a youngster like myself could possibly have to say to those who had seen and, in many cases, suffered so much. The other reason for questioning my notion of becoming a minister was that I naively thought that a *call* to this vocation required a celestial voice or vision, and I had heard or seen neither.

I began to consider going overseas to work—to travel, experience as much of life as I could, and test my ability to stand on my own feet. I discussed this idea with my parents, who were supportive, and with Peter Murray, my doubles partner,[54] asking him whether he would like to join me. He jumped at the opportunity, and we agreed that we would save all the money we could and leave for England later in 1954.

Before going on to describe what turned out to be a life-enriching year-long adventure, I have to say something about my relationship with Margaret. We would see each other from afar and sometimes chat briefly, but we had never gone out on a date. Early in 1954, I asked her out for the first time. Her Mom and Dad were in Uppsala, Helsinki, attending a meeting of the World Council of Churches, and Margaret was staying with her aunt in Parkhurst.

---

[53] I will say more about the Electric Printing Company and the job security it afforded me in the following chapter.

[54] As will be related later, Peter drowned in 1955.

Aunty Gwen gave her permission to go out with me one Saturday afternoon. We decided to visit the famous Sterkfontein caves. Modern excavation of the caves began in the late 1890s by limestone miners who found fossils and brought them to the attention of scientists. It was not until 1936 that students of Professor Raymond Dart and Dr. Robert Broom of the University of the Witwatersrand began methodically to excavate the site. In 1936, the Sterkfontein caves yielded the first adult *Australopithecine*, substantially strengthening Raymond Dart's claim that the skull known as the Taung child was a human ancestor. There was a pause in excavation during World War II, but after the war, Dr. Broom continued digging. In 1947, he discovered an almost complete skull of an adult female. The skull *Plesianthropus transvaalensis* (near-human from the Transvaal) became better known by its nickname, Mrs. Ples, now defined as a member of *A. africanus*.

I can't remember if that afternoon my secondhand car was temporarily out of commission, a frequent occurrence, but I vividly recall borrowing my Brother Winston's Ariel 350 cc motorcycle to take Margaret on our first date. We set off after lunch. Because the sky looked ominous, Margaret had her raincoat with her. She folded it up and arranged it on the pillion to sit on. We had a wonderful time at Sterkfontein caves. Neither of us had been there before, and we both found it fascinating. Margaret was taken aback, although she was too polite to say so at the time, when on our return trip I bought us each a pint of milk instead of a soda. I was on a health-foods kick and simply assumed that she and the rest of the human race were as well!

As we left Sterkfontein, without her being aware of it, her raincoat began to slide off the pillion. Eventually it became entangled in the chain of the motorcycle. We ground to a jarring halt. Fortunately, neither of us fell off the bike, and we were able with difficulty to extricate the raincoat, now in shreds, from the chain and resume our journey back to Aunty Gwen's house.

The first present I ever gave Margaret was a replacement blue raincoat.

Later that year, Matt Eddy was appointed general secretary of the Methodist Youth Department, the first layperson to hold that important position. His office would be in Durban, so the whole family moved from 33 Galway Road in Parkview to 55 Bartle Road in Durban four hundred miles away, and Margaret transferred from Parktown Girls High to Durban Girls High to complete her schooling.

Mom went overseas shortly after the Eddy family moved, sailing from Durban. Mavis had told her she would come to the dock to see her off. I wrote Margaret a letter, the first of many hundreds of letters, asking my Mom to give it to Mavis to give to Margaret. Margaret received my letter on April 29, 1954, her sixteenth birthday. We began corresponding regularly.

When Peter and I eventually set off for England, we arranged to meet in Cape Town, hoping to be able to work our passage to the United Kingdom on one of the Union Castle liners that plied their way between Southampton and Cape Town and other South African ports. Peter, whose parents were the wealthy owners of a brickyard, traveled to Cape Town on the Blue Train. I hitchhiked. I decided to go first to Durban, to see Margaret for a few days, and then on to Cape Town, passing through Umtata in the Transkei to visit Uncle Dyer and Aunt Laura.

My time with the Eddy family in Durban, though brief, is indelibly etched in my memory. Her Mom made Cornish pasties, a family tradition that Margaret has faithfully continued. She says I made having Cornish pasties a condition of our marriage. I probably did, only partly in jest. And when Margaret and I had a few minutes to ourselves she played a 33 rpm vinyl recording of one of her favorite songs from the musical *Carousel*. Looking into her beautiful eyes, nothing else needed saying. Without a word being spoken, I knew she loved me as I loved her. I went on my way to Cape Town, knowing that our time would surely come.

Uncle Dyer, a magistrate in the Department of Native Affairs, was stationed in a small town not far from Umtata, the capital of the Transkei. I dropped in on him and Aunty Laura for a few days. While I was there, Uncle Dyer was judging a murder case that illustrated the difference between tribal law and Roman-Dutch law. A man from one tribe had been killed by someone from a second tribe. Then one Saturday night, after drinking considerable quantities of *magau* ("kaffir" home-brewed beer laced with methylated spirits), fifteen men from this second tribe had avenged the murder by brutally slaying the murderer. According to Roman-Dutch law, the evidence against them was overwhelming. They would likely have been found guilty and hanged. According to tribal law, however, they had merely upheld the tribe's honor, a traditional tribal duty. I can't remember how Uncle Dyer eventually ruled in this case, but I have clear memories of his anguish as he tried responsibly to balance these two competing legal systems.

Peter and I rendezvoused in Cape Town and rented a small, inexpensive flat in Milnerton for a month, figuring that it would take us at least that long to get hired on an ocean liner going to England. Each day, we went down to the docks and made the rounds, with disappointing results. We eventually discovered that the taking on of crew typically took place in Southampton, the Union Castle liners' home port, rather than in Cape Town, and then was only of certified seamen. So shortly before the month was up, he and I bit the bullet, dipped into our savings, and bought the cheapest tickets we could (fifty-six pounds sterling each) for berths on the *Athlone Castle*. Our cabin must have been immediately above the engine room because the noise at night was deafening. Since we spent so little time in the cabin, and being young, it made little difference.

Our adventure had begun. I was only slightly seasick toward the end of our passage, when our liner encountered the swells of the Bay of Biscay. There was a dockers' strike at Southampton, so the *Athlone Castle* was diverted to Antwerp, Belgium. We passengers bound for Britain were driven by coach to Hoek van Holland and then transported by ferry across the English Channel to Dover. We hitchhiked from Dover to London, and the very first car to stop to give us a lift was a Rolls-Royce! The gentleman farmer who was driving must have seen the South African flags we had sewn onto the outside pockets of our backpacks and taken pity on two lads from the Commonwealth. He introduced himself as Sir Arthur Penn and told us he was the queen's surgeon! We never did have such a luxurious drive again. Later, in Italy, we were lucky enough to be picked up by the driver of a brand-new bus he was delivering from the factory in Milan to Naples and had the bus all to ourselves. Still, it was not a Rolls-Royce.

In London, we found rooms in a Toc H hostel[55] on Denmark Hill Road in Camberwell, near the Elephant and Castle underground railway station. There were about forty young men in the hostel. For our rent, we were given bed, breakfast, and dinner every evening except Saturdays when the cook had the night off and would put out raw ingredients for us to make

---

[55] Toc H is an international Christian movement. The name is an abbreviation for Talbot House, "Toc" signifying the letter T in the signals spelling alphabet used by the British Army in World War I. A soldier's rest and recreation center named Talbot House was founded in December 1915 at Poperinghe, Belgium. It aimed to promote Christianity and was named in memory of Gilbert Talbot, son of Edward Talbot, then Bishop of Winchester, who had been killed at Hooge in July 1915. The founders were Gilbert's elder brother Neville, then a senior army chaplain, and the Reverend "Tubby" Clayton. Talbot House was styled as an "Every Man's Club," where all soldiers were welcome, regardless of rank. It was "an alternative for the 'debauched' recreational life of the town." In 1920, Clayton founded a Christian youth center in London, also called Toc H, which developed into an international, interdenominational association for Christian social service. I fulfilled the social service requirement by working with troubled adolescents one night every week at a boys' club in Camberwell.

our own suppers. I remember the bedroom being unbelievably cold. But nothing could have been more convenient.

Almost opposite the hostel on Denmark Hill Road, there was a small printing shop with a sign in the window advertising a vacancy for a compositor. I went in to apply for the job. The owner of the firm seemed delighted to have an applicant. After we had chatted for half an hour and he had looked at my qualifications and letters of recommendation, he offered me the job at an unexpectedly generous weekly wage. But first I had to transfer my membership in the South African Typographical Union to the London Typographical Association (LTA); the two had a reciprocal relationship. I had no difficulty joining the LTA but discovered, to my chagrin that since I would be placed on probation for the first year, I would be required to work wherever the union chose to assign me.

Despite my pleading the LTA was adamant about not allowing me to accept the job I had been offered at the printing works opposite my hostel on Denmark Hill Road, about which I had told them. Instead, I was instructed to report to Temple Press, a major publishing house near Fleet Street on the other side of London. This was an extremely large establishment, the largest printing company I had ever seen, let alone worked in. There were hundreds of printers belonging to every guild, as well as scores more administrative and clerical staff. In addition to three or four foremen, there were several shop stewards representing the trade union.

The wages I would receive were much lower than those I had been offered by the shop on Denmark Hill Road. And getting to work each day would prove as difficult and would take as long as it had to get from Bedfordview to Roodepoort. I had either to go on the tube and then a bus, or two buses. To get to work at eight, I had to leave at six fifteen. Peter, who did not have a trade or other qualification, found work as a typewriter repairman. After a few weeks of initial training, his company would send him to offices all over London to clean and service typewriters. This suited Peter's temperament. He did not have the same work ethic as I, but he was extroverted and gregarious. He enjoyed moving at a leisurely pace from one office to another, meeting new people, and getting into conversations with strangers he would probably never meet again.

Despite its size, Temple Press was surprisingly behind the times. According to the union's rules, one could not be both a compositor and a linotype operator; it had to be one or the other. I was qualified to do either, but the LTA decreed I would work as a compositor. Being the new boy in the shop, the work I was given at first was hand-setting the "smalls," the classified advertisements in five-point type (the smallest type) that appeared in the various magazines published by the company. In South Africa this would have been done on the linotype or monotype machines. But here at Temple Press it was done as it always had been, manually, letter by letter. It was boring, repetitious work requiring no talent for design and layout, which was very much in contrast to what I had been doing for the last six years. Since I had no alternative but to leave the LTA and find work in a nonunion shop,[56] I made the most of it. The men with whom I worked quickly accepted me, and we became congenial colleagues and companions. Many of these men had lived through the "Blitz," the bombing of London by the Nazis, and then through Hitler's V1 and V2 rocket attacks. Once again, I felt naïve and sheltered by comparison.

Dr. Webb had written a letter of introduction for me to present to Dr. William Sangster, the superintendent minister at the Westminster Central Hall. William Sangster was a nationally acclaimed preacher, the most stirring I had ever heard—bar none—and rapidly became a role model. His

---

[56] I was reluctant to leave the LTA and the SATU because in South Africa there were virtually no opportunities to work in nonunion shops, and in the back of my mind, I knew that my trade and ability readily to find work would be invaluable if I ever needed to pay my own way through university.

sermons were the epitome of clarity, with a definite, easy-to-remember structure, replete with vivid illustrations drawn from his extensive personal experiences. I wasted no time before enrolling in the Wesley Guild (the youth group) and the choir.

I also wanted to begin studying and taking the requisite exams to become a lay preacher. But again, one door closed on me even as another was opening. Before I could become a lay preacher, I was informed that I had to be a member of the Methodist Church. In Johannesburg, I had simply assumed I was already a member because of my involvement in so many church activities. But in London, things were more formal and considerably stricter. Church membership required going to classes and passing an examination. So the door to lay[57] preaching was closed for the time being.

The membership class I entered was led by a retired seventy-seven year old minister named J. Clark Gibson and opened the door to a friendship that would last for the next twenty years, until he died. He clarified my understanding of what it meant to be called to the ministry and proved to be another inspiring mentor. The class was held in the early evening each Tuesday. I would go to classes directly from work by tube to Westminster, get something to eat at the Lyons Corner Tea House, then walk past the Houses of Parliament, Saint Margaret's Church, and Westminster Cathedral on to Westminster Central Hall.

J. Clark Gibson was an engaging teacher. He brought Methodist history, polity, doctrine, as well as Bible study to life, and he had a tremendous sense of humor. Ours was a small group, and he and I took to each other immediately. He had retired to Worthing, so after class, I would walk (and sometimes run) with him to Victoria Station where he would catch a train home and I would take the tube to the Elephant and Castle. Very soon, he asked me to call him Padre (he had

---

[57] Lay preachers are also called local preachers in the Methodist Church.

been a chaplain in World War I, and chaplains were given this affectionate title by the troops they served).

Padre was one of two people I met in London who continually opened my eyes to the full horror and scandal of South Africa's apartheid system. He was incredibly well informed and was a voracious reader. He kept me abreast of what was happening in my home country, not only in the mostly white circles in which I had moved, but in the population as a whole. The other was a man from Jamaica. Wilfred Saunders was a fellow resident in our Toc H hostel. On Saturday evenings, when we had to fix our own meals, Wilfred offered to take the ingredients set out by the Toc H cook for as many of us as were interested in his own style of gourmet cooking and then prepare some typically exotic Caribbean dish that we finished off with Jamaican coffee, of which he seemed always to have an abundant supply. A concert pianist, Wilfred was in London to further his professional musical career. I was in awe of him. He was the first person of color I had met in my life who in every imaginable way was my superior—intellectually, educationally, musically, and culturally. He was never judgmental of Peter and me, representatives of a country that was becoming odious in the larger world. By simply being who he was and allowing us to come to know him as a human being, he showed us the utter irrelevance of the color of one's skin.

My colleagues at work were largely secular, at best indifferent and in some cases hostile to religion. A few weeks before our first Christmas in London, I asked permission from my foreman to organize a carol service on the roof garden above the sixth floor of the building. Incredulous, the foreman told me I would have to get the approval of the general manager (the CEO). I asked him who he was and where his office was located. Such was the rigidity of the British class system that the foreman did not know the answer to either question and seemed taken aback by my temerity. So during a tea break that day, I somehow found my way to the administrative section of the enormous building and asked to speak to the manager. I was ushered almost immediately into the largest office I had ever seen. He did not invite me to sit down. So standing before him, I quickly introduced myself, told him of the Christmas Eve carol service that I wanted to arrange on the roof-top of the building, and asked for his permission. After what I had been led to expect, he surprised me by being spontaneously supportive of my idea. With his agreement, I next asked Padre to help me organize what I believed could be a significant event. Padre immediately decided to invite a ministerial friend who had been a Spitfire fighter pilot during the Battle of Britain, a man's man if ever there was one, to preach. I was able to recruit an ensemble from the Central Hall choir in which I sang to lead the singing.

On Christmas Eve, the manager allowed us to finish work early so that we could go up to the roof garden for the event while it was still light (in wintertime it typically grew dark in London from 4:00 p.m. until 8:00 a.m.). Not in my wildest dreams did I imagine what a success the carol service would be. Hundreds of employees—printers, bookbinders, clerical staff, and administrators—as well as company executives, attended. We printed out the words of the carols so that everyone had a sheet to sing from, and the singing was lusty. Padre offered a brief prayer and did a reading. The ex-fighter pilot gave an outstanding, pithy homily. The whole experience made the celebration of Christmas richly meaningful for those who worked at the company—and certainly for me.

Uncle Tom and my Mom had been to see their cousin, Dick Young, and his wife Maggie, in Alnmouth[58], Northumberland. Since arriving in England, I had corresponded with Uncle

---

[58] Alnmouth is downstream from Alnwick on the river Aln. It is close to the river's mouth and the North Sea.

Dick and Aunt Maggie[59], promising to visit them as soon as possible. They had invited us to come to them for Christmas. After the carol service on Christmas Eve, 1954, Peter and I left London with the optimism of youth, venturing to hitchhike to Northumberland—four hundred miles to the north—mainly on little country roads, since Britain had not yet introduced its motorway system.

We arrived somewhere in Yorkshire around midnight when it started snowing. It was the first time in my life I had seen snow! I remember it being a brilliantly moonlit night, and as we walked (as we always did while hitchhiking) on that country road, passing fields with sheep huddled in the snow, all the Christmas card images I had ever seen materialized. I could almost hear the angels singing "Silent Night."

Somehow, thanks to the generosity of British motorists and truckers, we arrived in Alnmouth at about seven o'clock on Christmas morning, a quite remarkable run of luck considering that we had left London the previous afternoon only fourteen hours earlier. Aunt Maggie and Uncle Dick, childless, were awaiting us as if we were long-lost or long-hoped-for children. Uncle Dick was the foreman in charge of maintaining an extensive section of the railway line between London and Edinburgh along which the old *Flying Scotsman*, then still a steam-powered locomotive, would roar with a deafening noise. The front of their cottage was literally six feet from the railway line, and whenever the *Flying Scotsman* surged by at close to a hundred miles an hour, the whole cottage would shudder as if an earthquake had struck. Their hospitality on Christmas day was absolutely unbelievable, especially for two young people starved for home cooking and with insatiable appetites. The

---

[59] Although, strictly speaking, Dick was my second-cousin, he and Maggie were almost three times as old as Peter and me. In deference to their seniority we always addressed them as Uncle Dick and Aunt Maggie.

table was repeatedly and abundantly laden with home-baked food. We had breakfast; then morning tea was set out; then we had lunch; then we sat down to afternoon tea, then supper, then evening tea. Finally we came to Christmas dinner, replete with plum pudding. It went on and on until we were utterly gorged. And still Aunt Maggie wanted reassurance that we would not go to bed "hongry."

The next day, Boxing Day as it is still called in Britain, reprised all of this. Finally, around lunchtime, I could eat no more and announced that I was going to swim in the North Sea. Incredulous, Uncle Dick and Aunt Maggie told me how crazy I was. There was snow on the ground. The temperature of the water was barely above freezing. No one in their right mind would go near the North Sea: I could not have been, and I did. I ran to it and plunged in before I could change my mind—and had the shortest swim of my life. It was so cold that I must have been in and out in about fifteen seconds flat. But even in that short time, I was in danger of freezing and getting hypothermia!

With the memory both of their hospitality and their accent (the Geordies pronounce "hungry" as "hongry" and "shirt" as "short") still vivid after all these years, I still marvel at their simplicity, authenticity, and largeness of spirit. Uncle Dick's little garden provided them with vegetables. Aunt Maggie's skill in the kitchen turned these simple ingredients into the most delectable meals. And both treated us as if they had known and loved us all our lives. Leaving them to hitchhike back to London, I felt bereft. I had found and then lost part of my family.

Before finally leaving England to return to South Africa, Peter and I visited them again, spending four or five memorable days with them. In later years, I went back to Alnmouth to visit them a third time. Alas, by then Uncle Dick had died. Aunt Maggie was still living in Alnmouth, but in a pensioner's flat. We had a splendid afternoon together, and then we said goodbye. Both of us knew it would be for the last time.

It was early in the New Year, back in London, that Padre asked me whether I had ever considered going into the ministry. I told him how diffident I was about preaching to people who had so much more life experience than I and also about my assumption that a *call* to the ministry required some kind of celestial summons—a voice or a vision. He chuckled and pointed me to the call of Isaiah, emphasizing that *the need is itself the call*: "Whom shall I send, and who will go for us? And I said, Here am I, send me!" (Isaiah 6:8).

He went on to talk about the need in South Africa for leaders who would stand up and speak out for social justice, for love of and compassion for all people, irrespective of their color, their ethnicity, or their culture, and challenge the power structure that was ruthlessly extending the ideology of apartheid into every facet of daily life. That conversation was another of my life's turning points. I knew finally that I had to offer myself for the ministry. The only question was whether I would stay in the United Kingdom to be trained or return to South Africa. Margaret and my family were back in South Africa, so the decision was obvious: I would return in order to be able to enter university at the beginning of 1956.

But first, Peter and I had planned to hitchhike our way around Europe, starting in the spring of 1955. So in April, after leaving our places of employment and with what money we had saved, with bedrolls, a pup tent,[60] our leather jackets, army-surplus khaki woolen pants, and one suit crumpled into our small backpacks, we set off. We crossed by ferry from Dover

---

[60] We also planned to stay in youth hostels when the weather was really bad and when we thought we could afford it. Later, in various youth hostels around Europe, we met young people of different nationalities, speaking a plethora of languages. Somehow, we all communicated and in the evenings had tremendous fun together, cooking and sharing what meager food we had, talking about our home countries, singing various folk songs, and learning something about one another's countries and cultures.

to Hoek van Holland and then hitchhiked through Holland, Belgium, and on to Paris, Lyon, the French Riviera (where it was so warm sitting on the beach that I decided to cut off the legs of my woolen khaki pants with my pocketknife and make them into shorts), Genoa, and then into Italy.

In Italy, we looked up all the former prisoners of war who had worked on our farm. Attillio Bertucelli's parents were small farmers in a village west of Venice, and when we got to them, they were busy harvesting their potato crop. We worked with them in the fields for several days, digging up potatoes, glad to repay their lavish hospitality. In Viareggio, we discovered that Giovani Fornaciari had won a football pool, had used the money to start a construction company, and was now a millionaire— and also the mayor of the city. So glad was he to see me and to meet Peter, that on the spur of the moment he arranged a mayoral banquet, complete with brass band, that evening. In the afternoon, he took us barhopping around Viareggio— quite an experience for a teetotaler like myself. At Giovanni's insistence, every cup of espresso I drank had to be well laced with *grappa*. Little wonder that I remember almost nothing of the evening except that it was magical and that, despite my rumpled suit, I felt we had been treated like royalty.

In Milan, Phillipe, who now had his own barbershop, gave us free haircuts and trimmed my abundant red beard (Italians called me "Barbarossa"). Leaving Milan, the driver of the brand-new bus being delivered to Naples gave us a ride. When we got to Rome, he dropped us on the corner of a street in the middle of the city and told us that if we waited there for him, he would be back in two hours to take us on to Naples. We decided to accept his offer and get to Naples while we could and come back to explore Rome later in our trip. Not knowing the city, we decided to stay where he had left us.

While we were waiting on the corner, we noticed a new Vespa motor scooter parked on the sidewalk. This being something of a novelty at the time, we examined it closely.

Suddenly we heard someone yelling at us from the open window of the sixth floor above. The man was shaving and had nothing on but a pair of undershorts. His face full of shaving cream, and brandishing his cutthroat razor, he shouted, "You leave-a ma Vespa! You leave-a ma Vespa!" I shouted back, "Buon Pasquale" (Happy Easter). This infuriated him even more, and the next thing we knew, he was down the stairs and out on the sidewalk, his face still lathered with shaving cream and still wielding his razor. This was becoming serious. But then, as can only happen in Italy, we were surrounded by about a dozen women, all swinging their handbags at the man as if they were weapons and telling him to leave us alone. Peter and I were unharmed, and no damage was done to the Vespa.

In Naples, before touring Pompeii, Peter and I decided to climb Mount Vesuvius and sleep the night on the summit so that we could look down on the city at sunrise. It was a difficult ascent because of the volcanic ash that covers the slopes. One slips and crawls up the mountain rather than climbs. To make matters worse, there was a bitterly cold wind. Just below the summit, we found a windbreak of sorts beneath the cable car station, a flattish spot on which to pitch our tent, and tried to get a little fire started to cook our evening meal of spaghetti and ground beef. Again, there was a voice from a window above us, but this time the shout was friendly. The operator of the cable station wanted to know what we were doing. When I told him in my halting Italian, he invited us up to sleep in the cable car station and told us he would teach us how to cook spaghetti. We needed no second invitation, packed up our tent, and moved into the shelter of his warm abode. True to his word, he took what little meat and dry spaghetti we had and then began adding all sorts of gourmet ingredients from his own larder, coming up with the most fantastic meal either of us could ever have wished for. We talked long into the night, learning all sorts of interesting details about Naples, Capri, Pompeii, and the surrounding region. The descent early the next morning was like skiing. Each step forward in the volcanic ash equaled a slide of several yards. It took us about a tenth of the time to get down as it had to climb up the previous evening.

And so, our exploration of Europe continued. After spending a couple of days in Naples and Pompeii we turned northward again, sightseeing in Rome for a few days, before going on through the Dolomites into Bavaria. I particularly wanted to see Neuschwanstein—something I had dreamed of ever since first seeing a picture of this, the most beautiful of mad King Ludwig's five castles, on a Pan American Airways calendar—and Garmisch-Pattenkirchen, even though it was not the year for the Passion Play at Oberamagau. Three unforgettable experiences are worth mentioning.

We had to walk the entire hundred miles from Innsbruck to Salzburg, in constant rain. Not a single vehicle stopped to offer us a lift, so we had no option but to slog it out. To make matters worse my shoes now had holes in the soles, and since we were trying to live on five shillings a day (about fifty cents) I could not afford to have them repaired. Instead, I lined the insides of my shoes with birch bark. Nevertheless, it was one of the most glorious hikes I have had in my entire life. The road ran next to the River Inn, in full spate because of the incessant rain. The trees were clad in fresh green leaves, and there were spring flowers everywhere.

Then, weeks afterward, leaving Berne late one afternoon, we hoped to find a forest or at least a wood where we could pitch our tent for the night. As we were walking up a slope out of Berne, a man got off his bicycle and pushed it alongside us, striking up a conversation. He told us he was an architect and was going home. His house was just outside the city limits. When we told him our plan for the evening, he advised us that camping (except in designated campgrounds) was not permitted in Switzerland. He offered us the front lawn of his home to pitch our tent. Delighted, we accepted his gracious invitation.

When we got to where he lived, his wife wouldn't hear of us sleeping on their front lawn. She insisted that we occupy their guest bedroom and invited us to have a bath. After weeks on the road, this was an incredible luxury! They provided us with a delicious meal, and we chatted well into the evening. Finally, they showed us to our room. Only after looking around did we discover that this was not a guest room but the couples' own bedroom, which they had vacated for two complete strangers! On the nightstand next to my bed, next to the alarm clock, there was a small, well-worn copy of a German New Testament. This young couple obviously lived their faith without needing to talk about it, and this was a lesson I never forgot.

The third indelible experience was in Holland, where we went to Keukenhof Botanical Gardens. Never in my life had I seen such a profusion of color or so many tulips. There were millions of them in every imaginable hue (including one pitch-black tulip named *Johannesburg*), all tastefully arrayed in the spacious garden beds with which the park abounds. The flowers of Keukenhof were as spectacular in their own way as Rembrandt's *Natchtwag* in the Rijks Museum.

From Duisburg in Germany we cruised on the Rhine as far as Cologne on a coal barge. We had been taken on as deck hands and were given food and bunks to sleep on in exchange for the laborious work of chiseling and scraping old paint off the rusted railings of the vessel all day long. Then, after more than four months, our savings were exhausted. We decided to head back to London before leaving for South Africa. The two cities we had very much wanted to spend time in were Vienna and Prague. But we were unable to see either, because both Austria and Czechoslovakia were in the Russian zone of occupation and it was almost impossible for Western visitors to enter them. Wherever we had been, we had experienced immense kindness. There was no way to repay directly those who had given us rides, befriended us, or offered us meals and hospitality. All we could resolve to do was pay our debt forward and indirectly by showing kindness to any in need who we might meet in years to come. This is a resolution I have tried to keep ever since.

Leaving London after being away from home for more than a year, I felt more mature and eager to get back to work in Johannesburg in order to earn enough money to pay my way through my first year at Rhodes University. Margaret and I had been writing two or three times a week throughout the months Peter and I had been away, and I was eager to see her again. My last gesture, before leaving for home, was to take the train down to Worthing to say goodbye to Padre. By then, he had retired altogether. It was a cold and rainy day and his little house was poorly heated. I gave him the leather jacket that had served me so well throughout our travels, still as good as new, and he was truly moved. We promised to keep in touch, and we did for the next twenty years until his death. I was to see him again only once, in 1972, on my way back to South Africa after attending a meeting of the World Council of Churches in Geneva.

On board the ship to Cape Town, toward the end of our voyage, there was a fancy dress dinner one evening. Simple prizes were awarded for the most original costumes, male and female. I asked Peter to shave a tonsure in the back of my head. One of the sailors with whom I had become friendly located a piece of brown sackcloth, and with his needle and thread we fashioned it into a facsimile monk's habit. Dressed as a Franciscan friar, I won the men's competition. Ironically, not many weeks later, I was in the pulpit for the first time as a lay preacher on probation—tonsure and all. The Methodists must have been bemused, if not confused, by having to listen to a tonsured preacher!

The other memorable shipboard experience was more harrowing. A dozen or so young people were sitting on the deck late one pitch-dark night, looking up at the stars and listening to one of our fellow passengers playing his clarinet. He was an Oxford graduate who had been in Colombia and was now traveling to Africa. Someone offered a dare: to climb up to the crow's nest at the top of the ship's sixty-foot radio mast. Since no one else responded to the dare, I foolishly did.

Although it meant climbing vertically up a narrow metal ladder, getting to just below the crow's nest was fairly straightforward despite the fact that the only shoes I possessed were fairly new and still had shiny leather soles. But to get into the crow's nest itself, one had to lean back and climb another short ladder about thirty degrees out from the mast and then pull oneself up over a railing. The closest analogy I can think of is that of a rock climber slowly clawing up the face of a cliff and then coming to a huge overhanging rock and having to get above it. Once that was accomplished, the truly terrifying phase of this madcap escapade began.

Every time the ship rolled or pitched, one was slung forward, backward, or sideways, the height of the mast accentuating the roll or the pitch dramatically. To get back on to the ladder on the mast, one had to climb over the railing around the crow's nest and work one's way down using one's arms only until finally one's feet hit the ladder on the mast. I don't think I've ever been as frightened in my life. I had to take time to fight my fear, battling to get my emotions under control in order to get down safely. I can remember doing this by wrapping both my arms around the mast and clinging there without moving until I felt more composed. To have panicked and let go would have meant plunging sixty feet either onto the deck or into the ocean.

When we arrived in Cape Town, Mom had driven the thousand miles from Johannesburg in fifteen hours to meet us in my dad's new Fiat 2200. Once in Johannesburg, Peter and I went our separate ways. Two or three months later, I was devastated to open the evening paper, the *Star*, to read of his death. He and another friend from the Turffontein Tennis Club, Eric Suttie, had been in Eric's ski boat on their way to Inhaca Island, some fourteen miles off the Natal coast, for a weekend's fishing. Apparently, about halfway there, toward evening, the boat had capsized in a sudden squall. Neither of them was wearing a life jacket.

They began swimming back to land. Eric succeeded in reaching the beach the following morning, despite being attacked by sharks a few hundred yards off shore. He had been bitten repeatedly in the stomach and had taken off his blood-soaked shorts and thrown them to the sharks. This diverted them long enough for him to crawl onto the sandy beach. Sewing up his abdomen required hundreds of stitches. He stated that he had left Peter, utterly exhausted, on a sandbar about three miles from the beach, at about seven o' clock that morning. Search-and-rescue boats and planes looked for Peter for several days. Sadly, my buddy's body was never found.

In the course of the next several years, I went to see his parents as often as I could. They found it impossible to get over Peter's death. He was their only son. And since his body had never been recovered, they always clung to the desperate hope that he had been washed up safely on shore somewhere suffering from amnesia. They could not let go of the illusion that one day he would come home, walking breezily through the front door. Tragically, it was not to be.

5

Rhodes University

Grahamstown, Eastern Cape, South Africa

For the remainder of 1955, I had two principal objectives. First, I had to study, pass the required exams, and then preach a trial sermon in order to be accredited as a lay preacher—a prerequisite for offering myself as a probationer Methodist minister. Second, I had to earn all the money I could to pay my way through my first year at Rhodes University in Grahamstown—a lovely old 1820 settler city in the Eastern Cape. At Rhodes, the Methodist, Presbyterian, and Congregationalist churches had endowed a department of divinity. The Anglican[61] church had its own seminary in Grahamstown, Saint Paul's; but Saint Paul's seminarians would come to Rhodes to take various academic courses, so there was a truly ecumenical group of theology students (we were called "theologs") in Grahamstown.

The sorry truth, looking at this retrospectively, is that we were all white. African Methodists, Presbyterians, Congregationalists, and Anglicans studied and were trained at the University of Fort Hare in Alice, near to King Williams

---

[61] In the United States, the Anglican Church is known as the Episcopal Church. Similarly, Anglicans are known as Episcopalians.

Town.[62] The only contact between the two groups of theological students was the annual cricket match, played alternately at Rhodes and at Fort Hare. This was simply a reflection of the fact that all education in South Africa at the time, at every level—from elementary school through university—was segregated. To make matters worse, elementary and high school education for whites was free of charge. For those who were black or colored, elementary schooling was free, but if students wanted to continue through high school, they had to pay for it themselves—a considerable burden for people whose income was extremely meager. And to compound the injustice of the apartheid system, the medium of instruction for black students was Afrikaans, the language of the hated oppressor.[63] If after graduating from high school, black students wanted to go overseas to further their education, Afrikaans was of little or no use when studying at any of the institutions of higher learning in the Western world.

I must further interrupt this narrative to point out yet another major injustice. By the late 1970s, the medical school of the University of the Witwatersrand had been given permission by the government to admit a handful of black students, between six and nine out of a class of more than two hundred. All medical students rotated through the Baragwanath Hospital in SOWETO.[64] Baragwanath was the largest hospital in the

---

[62] Nelson Mandela had obtained his undergraduate education at the University of Fort Hare and then began studying for his law degree there as well. He completed his studies in law at the University of the Witwatersrand in Johannesburg where he then worked as a lawyer.

[63] This was a major factor (in addition to the draconian pass laws) leading to the Sharpeville riots in which South African police shot to death sixty-nine black students and wounded two hundred more.

[64] SOWETO is the acronym for South Western Townships, containing row upon row of concrete boxes with a kitchen, two small bedrooms, and a bathroom. SOWETO had been established after an historic township, Sophiatown, was razed to the ground to make way for a

southern hemisphere, with two thousand beds and at least that number of patients sleeping on the floor on mattresses under the beds. Yet it was one of the finest hospitals in Africa, and for medical students in training, because they encountered at firsthand diseases associated with poverty, unsanitary and unhygienic living conditions, and rare infectious diseases—none of which were prevalent in the more affluent white population. White medical students were the immense beneficiaries of this. But when it came to rotating through the Johannesburg General Hospital (for whites only), the black students were not allowed to attend white patients. This prohibition extended to postmortem dissections. Black medical students were not permitted to be present when autopsies were being performed on whites.

Back now to my own story. I passed the necessary local preacher's examinations. Then I had to preach a trial sermon. William Sangster's preaching had electrified me in London. His sermons always had a discernible structure, and one could seldom forget the three or four points that he had hammered home with the most vivid illustrations. Though J. B. Webb was one of the finest orators I had ever heard, his preaching, in contrast to Sangster's, was more like a spoken essay than a sermon: inspiring to listen to but difficult to remember.

I had decided to model my own preaching on that of Sangster. I wanted to have a clear outline of what I was going to say in my own mind in the hope that if I could remember it, so might those who listened to me. Although I recollect still having the tonsure from our shipboard fancy dress competition, I forget where I preached my trial sermon, what the subject was, or precisely where or when I preached it. But it satisfied the three ministers designated to decide my fate, and I was formally appointed a local preacher.

---

new white suburb and its inhabitants forcibly removed to this sterile new environment.

The reason I had to earn all the money I could in the remainder of that year was that when I told my parents of my intention to offer myself for the ministry, my father's response was to inform me that if that was what I wanted to do, I would have to do it without his help. He still harbored the hope that I would become a businessman (or else resentment that I was "doing it my way" and not his).

I found a well-paying job, with plenty of overtime, at the Electric Printing Company in Doornfontein, which I mentioned in the previous chapter. The foreman, who was Jewish, was so impressed with what I was planning to do that he offered me a job whenever I wanted to come back to work during my university vacations. I took him up on his offer and went back to Electric each time I was up in Johannesburg on vacation. I also worked the night shift at the *Rand Daily Mail*, Johannesburg's morning newspaper where I had received the same generous offer. With these two jobs, I was able to earn enough each year to pay my way through Rhodes, without any help from my Dad and without any loans.

At the beginning of 1956, when I entered Rhodes, Margaret, having graduated from Durban Girls' High, began her nursing training at Entabeni Hospital in Durban. Entabeni was a beautiful, old Victorian building, reputedly haunted by "the gray lady." The young nurses in training were always given the night shift, having to make rounds every couple of hours, checking on their patients with only a flashlight. The senior nurses took a perverse pleasure in frightening the novices with stories about "the gray leady." I learned from her letters how terrified Margaret had been. By this time, we were writing to each other almost every day.

My own undergraduate experiences at Rhodes were idyllic in comparison. I began running regularly to stay fit, played tennis and cricket, and also took up squash, which I would play late at night after studying until about ten o'clock. I found a faculty member in the Music Department with whom I continued my singing lessons, and joined the Rhodes Chamber Choir under the direction of George Grüber as well as the choir of the Methodist Memorial Church in the center of Grahamstown. And my studies were pure pleasure: English, philosophy, Greek, New Testament, Hebrew, Old Testament, ecclesiastical history, apologetics, theology, comparative religion, sociology, and psychology, among other subjects. The work ethic I had acquired during my years as an apprentice and then as a journeyman printer stood me in good stead. I worked diligently in all the courses I signed up for, especially in my two major subjects, biblical studies and systematic theology. As far as I was concerned, a sign placed below the clock in one of our lecture halls asking the question "Time Will Pass; Will You?" was unnecessary.

My closest friend at Rhodes was Paul Welch. He, like me, was a cricketer. The university's first team (for which we had both been selected) always played matches on Sundays. Since we theologs had various preaching assignments on Sundays, often at the local mental hospital (challenging, to say the least), Paul and I both decided to play for the Rhodes second team that played its matches on Saturdays (I was elected team captain). At Jeppe, I had been younger than my classmates, not yet fully developed physically, and did not excel in rugby or cricket. At Rhodes, I was older than many of my contemporaries, and physically mature, which made me a far better player. The Eastern Cape is a fertile agricultural area, and the teams we played against in various towns like King Williams Town, Alice, and Bathurst were composed mostly of farmers. The matches were played in bucolic surroundings. Often, we had to clean cow patties off the pitch before games could begin. And the highlight for us students was the morning and afternoon teas and the lunches provided by the farmers' wives: mouth-wateringly delicious, especially for students who were reconciled to dining-hall fare.

Paul and I loved hiking together in the hills around

Grahamstown. We helped each other prepare for exams by quizzing one another on Greek vocabulary, theories of the atonement, or the findings of critical biblical scholarship— whatever we were to be examined on next. We took Sunday assignments together where alternatively one of us would do the children's sermon and the other would preach the main sermon, in cities like Port Elizabeth and East London, each two hundred miles away from Grahamstown. To get there, we had to hitchhike, leaving early enough to get to our destinations by 10:45 a.m. Somehow, we invariably made it, although I often remember showing up at the designated church with a full bladder and only minutes to spare.

I will say more about my experience at Rhodes later, but now I should mention the tremendous sadness I subsequently felt about my friendship with Paul. He and Valmai Storey were married three weeks before Margaret and me. They were stationed in Stilfontein, near Kroonstad. We were in Northmead, Benoni. I assumed that the four of us would have the same close relationship that Paul and I had had at Rhodes since Margaret and Valmai had known each other from childhood. But then Heather was born, followed by Andrew, and Jenny (Timothy is ten years younger than Heather).

Paul and Valmai seemed unable to have children, and it must have been painful for them to be around married couples with young families. And so we drifted apart—geographically as well as in our friendship. Years later, when we had lost touch with them on any regular basis, they adopted a child. As so often happens following an adoption, they then had three children of their own in fairly rapid succession. We never met their children. However, fifty years or so later, we bumped into Paul and Valmai in Fish Hoek when we were visiting Jean Smythe, Margaret's oldest and dearest friend from their first grade, and arranged to have lunch together. It was as though the hiatus in our relationship had never happened. We picked up where we had left off. Shortly after that, we heard that Paul had died, unexpectedly, of kidney cancer. Valmai died not long after him. I cherish his memory. He was the dearest of friends and one of the gentlest of men.

At the beginning of 1958, a young theology student by the name of Robert G. Hamerton Kelly transferred to Rhodes University from the University of Cape Town. He had a brilliant mind and was a fine athlete. I can remember entering the cross-country race that year. I thought I was doing fairly well until he streaked by me going up a long hill. He went on to win the race. I finished thirty-fourth. However, I did redeem myself somewhat when I came fourth in the mile in a time of four minutes and thirty-two seconds, running barefoot because I didn't have any spikes. It was the first mile race I had ever entered, and considering that I had not trained specifically for it, it was an impressive performance at the time. Bob later represented Cambridge University and was on the British Universities cross-country team. He dazzled us all with his intellect. He and I did not become particularly close at Rhodes, yet he was destined to play an absolutely crucial role in my later life, which I will come to in due course. For what he did for me then I will be indebted to him forever.

While the Eddy family was living at 55 Bartle Road, and when I visited them in 1954 on my way to London, Margaret's brother Kenneth Michael had been a boarder at Kearsney College.[65] From there, he went on to study engineering at the University of Natal, in Pietermaritzburg. As a student at the University of Natal, Ken drove a Coca-Cola delivery truck to earn extra money (his parents paid for his university education). His passion was sports cars. He was turning a Singer sedan into a sports car by designing and building a completely new body for it—and for that, he needed an income of sorts. After

---

[65] My brother-in-law and sister-in law, Ken and Deanne Eddy, have provided their written, notarized permission to include their names in various places in my narrative.

graduating as an engineer, Ken decided to enter the Methodist ministry. He arrived at Rhodes the year after me. He knew how extremely close Margaret and I were, so he and I had a natural affinity for one another and bonded in the ensuing years.

By the end of 1957, the Eddy family had moved back to Johannesburg.[66] Now that our families were in the same city once again, both Ken and I would go home to Johannesburg at the beginning of the short Easter and spring breaks, and for several weeks during the long summer vacation. The year before Ken came to Rhodes, and before I had a car, I would hitchhike the seven hundred miles from Grahamstown to Johannesburg, always wearing my university blazer in the hope that this would assure anyone willing to give me a ride of my bona fides.

Mostly, I had no difficulty getting rides. Motorists were extremely generous in those days. However, on one occasion in the middle of winter, my luck ran out. I had reached Aliwal North in the Karoo[67] at about sundown. The Karoo is semidesert, bleak, sparsely populated, and at that time of year cruelly

---

[66] Matt had left the Methodist Youth Department, and was working at Harris and Jones (before World War II, he had been an executive at Hunt's, the Chevrolet dealership in Johannesburg). Margaret had transferred from Entabeni Hospital to the Johannesburg General, where she would complete her training as a nurse. Matt and Mavis rented an apartment close to the General, first #40 and then #10, Brooklyn Heights in Hillbrow so that Margaret could walk home on her days off. While she was working, she had to stay in the probationer nurses' residence under strict supervision. After she and I were engaged and when I was back in Johannesburg from Grahamstown in between terms, she would often come with me to Bedfordview on her days off.

[67] The Karoo formed an almost impenetrable barrier to the interior from Cape Town, and the early adventurers, explorers, hunters, and travelers on the way to the Highveld unanimously denounced it as a frightening place of great heat, great frosts, great floods, and great droughts.

inhospitable after dark. Instead of finding a room in town for the night, I unwisely decided to press on to Jamestown, another hundred miles north. Someone stopped as I was walking out of town and invited me to jump in, which I gladly did. That is the good news. The bad news is that the person who picked me up told me he was only going about twenty miles out of Aliwal North and would have to drop me on the main road when he turned off—leaving me with about eighty miles still to go to the nearest town. Trusting my good fortune, I agreed to go with him as far as he could take me.

By the time he left me on the main road, it was pitch dark and freezing cold. A biting wind cut through my clothing, so I opened the suitcase I was carrying and put on my raincoat. That made little difference, and I kept walking just to keep myself warm. At one point, I stopped and tried to light a fire in a culvert, thinking that was where I would be sleeping that night. The wind blew out my matches before the kindling caught alight, so I kept on walking. At about nine o'clock, I saw lights approaching in the distance behind me. As the car drew closer, I opened my raincoat so as to show my university blazer and stood almost in the middle of the road, hoping that the driver would have pity on me and take me on to Jamestown.

My luck didn't hold. The driver slowed down, but then accelerated again and kept going. I had no choice but to continue walking, which I did for what must have been another forty-five minutes. By then, it was so cold that I knew I would be in serious trouble if no other car came by and took me in. Then, coming toward me from the direction of Jamestown, I saw the headlights of what proved to be an old truck. When the driver saw me, he stopped, opened the door, and indicated that I was to toss my case onto the bed of the truck and climb in next to him—which I was only too delighted do! He was an old Afrikaner farmer. He said that his daughter, a nurse, who worked in Aliwal North, had arrived home not long before. The family had waited to have dinner until she returned, and at the dinner table, she casually mentioned that she had seen a young student walking and hitchhiking on the main road to Aliwal North, but had been too afraid to stop and pick him up. Her father, the old farmer, was indignant. That his daughter would have left someone out on a bitterly cold night was a violation of everything he believed to be right. So he got up from the dinner table, jumped into his truck, and came out to take me in from the cold!

The family insisted that I join them for dinner when we got back to the farmhouse. Since I was ravenous, I needed no second invitation. They were curious about me, and I told them my story in brief—speaking in Afrikaans. Then they gave me a bed for the night, breakfast the next morning, and after breakfast, the old farmer took me back to the main road. I made it back to Johannesburg later that same day. That Afrikaner farmer's kindness and the family's generosity of spirit have remained among my most cherished memories.

By 1957, I had the first of two old cars, both Austins, which I kept at Rhodes and used to travel back and forth to Johannesburg. The first was a 1936 Austin 7, in very poor condition. That Christmas long vacation, midsummer in the Southern Hemisphere, Ken and I drove it in turn, nonstop, from Grahamstown to Johannesburg in thirty-six hours, at an average speed of about thirty miles per hour! The weather was extremely hot. The car's radiator was leaking badly, and the engine boiled.[68] Every few miles, we had to stop to refill the radiator with water. But before being able to do this we had to find water on that desolate road, which by then I knew like the back of my hand. The solution to the problem was to stop whenever we saw a windmill, fill what bottles we had with water

---

[68] In those days, radiators were filled with water, and the water frequently boiled, causing engines to seize up, especially going uphill and in warm weather. Only later did coolant take the place of water in cars' radiators.

from the cattle drinking trough the windmill supplied, hoping to get as far as the next windmill without the engine blowing up. Somehow we managed the long journey, but the Austin 7 clearly was ready for the scrap dealer.

My brother Winston, who had married Jean Chapman, an Englishwoman, was leaving for England with his bride.[69] Before they left, Winnie gave me his 1938 Austin 10, a car he had restored to much better condition. The Austin 10 was a wonderful vehicle, utterly reliable, and served me well for the next several years. Ken and I made many trips between Grahamstown and Johannesburg in this car. Finally, my days of hitchhiking were at an end.

During one long vacation, the Rhodes Chamber Choir, with about eighteen sopranos and altos and the same number of baritones and basses, went on a month-long tour of what were then Southern and Northern Rhodesia—now Zimbabwe and Zambia. We traveled from Grahamstown on the South African Railways and on the Rhodesian Railways after crossing the border, as well as by bus. We performed some afternoons and almost every night in large cities like Salisbury (now Harare) and Bulawayo, in small towns like Livingstone, in hotels such as the magnificent Victoria Falls Hotel overlooking the Zambezi River and the falls, in churches, and in halls—wherever there was an audience to hear us. It was the trip of a lifetime, rich in memories. Six, in particular, stand out.

First, I was overwhelmed by the natural beauty of the Rhodesias with their verdant savannah plains, teeming with wild-life, seemingly untouched by human hands—a fertile land waiting to be developed. It is utterly tragic that Zimbabwe has been despoiled by a tyrant like Robert Mugabe. Second, the

---

[69] Winston and Jean's first son, Gavin, was born in England. Their second son, Barry, was born in New Zealand, and their third son, Robin, was born in Australia. Both Winston and Jean are now deceased.

simple grave of Cecil Rhodes after whom the Rhodesias were named in a large, flat rock at the top of one of the mountains in the Mtopos range, looking out over the most majestic scenery imaginable, was deeply moving. Third, while we were touring a game park near Gwelo, a large elephant charged our bus. Its tusks cut right through the side panel of the bus into the luggage compartment (fortunately empty at the time). I imagine that somehow our driver had come between a mother elephant and her baby—and she was rightly enraged. The power of these magnificent animals, when seen and experienced at close range, is both frightening and awe-inspiring. It was as if our bus had landed in the epicenter of an earthquake 7.5 on the Richter scale. Fourth was a tour of the Zimbabwe Ruins, shrouded in mystery. It is thought that they date from about 1,500 CE; no one has yet identified the people who constructed this maze of stupendous stone walls twenty-five feet thick at the base—or the reason for doing this. Fifth was my first sight of the Victoria Falls, surely one of the seven wonders of the world, over which Margaret and I were to fly, several decades later, each with our own MicroLight aircraft pilot and then together in a helicopter. The sixth memory warrants space unto itself.

The Kariba Dam was under construction at the time we were on tour. An Italian civil engineering company had been awarded the contract. The Chamber Choir had been invited to perform for those working on the site. After being taken on an inspection tour, seeing the coffer dams then being constructed in the Kafue River (a major tributary of the Zambezi), and realizing that the dam wall would rise between the two sides of a gorge twenty miles wide and that the dam would then extend some four hundred miles upstream, we were duly humbled by the sheer scale of the project. That evening, we sang in the camp for the Italian workers on the construction site. They had not seen a woman for at least a year. The Italian men gave the music marginal attention; their primary focus was on the sopranos and altos in the choir. The applause was deafening, again, not for the music, but for the beautiful young females who had appeared in their midst. After the performance we all went to our designated sleeping quarters: little caravans, males on one side of the construction site, females on the other, with each trailer sufficiently large to accommodate two people. No sooner had we men gone to bed than there was a frantic call for help from the women. The Italian workers were trying to break into their trailers. The women wanted the men in the choir to guard them. So we did this in two-hour shifts, throughout the night, forgoing even the prospect of uninterrupted sleep. We left early the next morning, bleary-eyed but fortunately with our sopranos' and altos' honor unsullied!

Although separated for most of the year by a distance of seven hundred miles, Margaret and I wrote to each other almost every day, and we saw each other constantly during my vacations. When she was on duty, she lived in the nurses' residence, where there was a rigorously enforced curfew. She was only allowed out for two nights a week and she had to be back strictly by ten. On her days off, she could go home to Brooklyn Heights or sometimes come with me to Bedfordview when I was back in town. Despite these constraints, or maybe because of them, Margaret came down with mononucleosis—supposedly contracted through kissing. This laid her up for several weeks, long after I had returned to Rhodes.

Our relationship flourished, and I eventually asked Margaret to marry me. Once she had agreed, the next hurdle was for me to seek her parents' permission. I shall never forget the night I did this. I had been invited to the Brooklyn Heights flat for dinner. Margaret must have tipped her Mom off that I was about to ask her Dad for his daughter's hand in marriage because the two of them kept away, busying themselves in the kitchen. Matt Eddy was sitting in his favorite armchair, reading the evening paper, the *Star*. I don't know how I interrupted him, but I do remember how scared I was to broach the subject. I think he was taken so much by surprise that he almost dropped his newspaper. But broach it I did, and he called Mavis into the living room, told her what was afoot, and almost as embarrassed as I was, they gave us their consent. The evening meal was truly a celebration.

With Matt and Mavis's blessing, we decided to get engaged on Margaret's birthday, April 29, 1958, during the Easter break from Rhodes. Before the end of the vacation, I remember my friend John Rees taking me to a diamond merchant where he knew I could buy a good stone at a reasonable price. Before I left to go back to Rhodes, Margaret and I chose a setting for the diamond. I returned to university, and in the evenings with my well-worn chip-carving but razor-sharp pocketknife, made the last of the many jewelry boxes I had presented to various girlfriends before I met Margaret—my brothers had jokingly called this the kiss of death, for no sooner were they given than the relationship ended. Margaret's and mine did not end in the same way, and now, fifty-nine years later, we are still together. Margaret still has her jewelry box, and it looks as good as it was when I gave it to her.

Back in Johannesburg for the Easter break I met Margaret at 7:00 a.m. on April 29, 1958, as she was coming off from the night-shift at the E. P. Bauman Hospital. She was then taking care of children with congenital, genetic, or developmental disabilities—including hydrocephalus, in the days before shunts were placed to drain the fluid from their watermelon-sized skulls to the kidneys. We drove back into the center of Johannesburg, parked, made our way to the Methodist Central Hall, and went up to the mezzanine landing where we had first met and where I knew that this was the woman I would marry. After formally proposing, I placed the ring on her finger and gave her the jewelry box. Then I took her back to Brooklyn Heights to sleep. That night, our two families went out to celebrate. After dinner, J. B. Webb joined the Eddys and the Youngs at His Majesty's Theater, where much to the embarrassment of

Margaret's parents, we saw Marilyn Monroe in *Some Like It Hot!* Dr. Webb, however, seemed to enjoy the film

Our engagement was a long one—eighteen months. In those days, Methodist probationer ministers were not allowed to marry until they had completed their six-year probation. Fortunately for us, at some point after we became engaged Methodist policy was changed to allow probationers to marry after five years instead of six. But for that we would have had to wait two and a half years. Nevertheless, it felt like an eternity.

Toward the end of 1958, two important events occurred. First, the Methodist Conference in October appointed me to serve my first church, beginning in January of the following year. I was to go to Northmead Methodist Church, in a suburb of Benoni on the East Rand, with a small and struggling congregation. And second, I took my final examinations at Rhodes. I really studied hard, determined to do the best I possibly could. So intense was my preparation that I developed a boil in my nostril, the one and only boil I have had in my entire life. It was excruciatingly painful, but fortunately, it burst before I sat for my exams. Bob Kelly, Andrew Milne (a Rhodesian Presbyterian), and I were the only three students to be awarded double firsts.

PART 3

Pastor, Preacher, Graduate Student, Political Activist

6

Early Ministry in South Africa

Northmead, Benoni, Transvaal

As legend has it, it was on a Sunday in March 1886 that an Australian gold miner, George Harrison, stumbled across the rocky outcrop of a gold-bearing reef on what would come to be known as the Witwatersrand (White Waters Ridge) and where the city of Johannesburg would soon rise on the Transvaal Highveld. He registered his claim with the then-government of the Zuid Afrikaanse Republiek (ZAR), and the area was pronounced open to prospectors. His discovery is commemorated with a monument at Langlaagte, a "dorp"[70] where the original gold outcrop is thought to have been located, and a park is named in his honor, as is one of the main streets of Johannesburg. Ironically, Harrison is believed to have sold his claim worth billions for less than ten pounds sterling before leaving the area, and he was never heard from again.

The Witwatersrand extends about a hundred miles from Krugersdorp, in the west, to Springs, in the east, with a score of mining towns in between. Roodepoort lies between Krugersdorp and Johannesburg, and Benoni (a Hebrew word meaning "Son of my Sorrow") is similarly about midway

---

[70] The Afrikaans word *dorp* means a settlement or very small village.

between Johannesburg and Springs. From north to south, the gold-bearing reef is approximately five hundred miles in extent, from Johannesburg in the Transvaal to Welkom in the Orange Free State, like a giant saucer dipping ever deeper into the ground, so that at Welkom the miners have to toil three miles or more below the surface.

In October 1958, all of us at Rhodes who were to graduate that December anxiously awaited news of where the Methodist Conference would station us. I learned that my posting was to Northmead, a place of which I had never heard, one of several new suburbs springing up north of Benoni. Later that year, before graduating and before taking up my new post, I made an appointment to spend an afternoon with the probationer minister who had been at Northmead for the previous two years. He was dispirited. Only four or five people came to the Sunday evening worship service (the main service in South African Methodist churches was then in the evening, not the morning). There were no young people involved in the life of the church, and there was not much of a Sunday school either. And he indicated that, in his opinion, this satellite of the main Benoni Methodist church, about five miles away, should be closed down. However, after driving around Northmead and the adjoining suburbs of Airfield (where there had been a World War II air base), Rynfield, and Rynfield North for a couple of hours, I had a different impression. It seemed to me that all the present and future population growth would be in these suburbs where young married couples could afford to buy homes and raise families. I was struck by the tremendous potential and the strategic location of what was to be by my first church.

In January, I took up my assignment. Cyril Wilkins was the superintendent minister stationed at Benoni, David Jones was the minister at Boksburg and Boksburg North (David was married to and later divorced from Rita, the only child of J. B. and Cora Webb), and Vivian Harris was in Springs. Vivian was one of the few who, after graduating from Rhodes with a bachelor's degree had gone on to take the BD degree. I had turned to him for tutoring in Hebrew before taking my first formal Hebrew courses at Rhodes, and knew him well. I was the new kid on the block. David, Viv, and I soon became good friends as well as colleagues. Mr. Wilkins remained somewhat aloof, conscious perhaps of his standing as our superintendent.[71]

Since the Northmead Church had no manse,[72] arrangements had been made by the church leaders to rent two rooms for me (one a bedroom, the other a study) from Mrs. Small, a widow living in Northmead who was also a registered nurse. For two weeks of the month my evening meals were to be with "Ma" and "Pa" Gush (who had recently lost their only son, George, in a motor accident), and with Jim and "Tinkie" Darroch[73] for the other two weeks. Mrs. Small allowed me the use of her small kitchen so I could prepare my own breakfast and lunch.

I do not recall what topic I preached on when I occupied the pulpit at Northmead for the first time, but I do remember that only a handful of people showed up. I felt something of

---

[71] In South African Methodism, several churches were grouped together in what was called a "circuit." The ministers were responsible for the pastoral care of those in their own congregations, but they moved around the circuit to preach in one another's pulpits. Usually, one was in one's own church either for the morning or evening service, and elsewhere for the other. Occasionally, one had to preach at both services in the same church and prepare two sermons for that Sunday.

[72] Manses are known as a parsonage here in the US.

[73] Jim and Tinkie had two daughters; the older girl was named June. Years later, when I was at SMU and we were living in an apartment in Kessler Park, a suburb of Dallas, June showed up on our doorstep asking if she could live with us for a while. We took her in, moving Heather and Jenny from their separate bedrooms into one, so that June could have the other. She lived with us for about a year, and we took her with us on one of our summer vacations in which we explored parts of the United States we believed we would never see again. After she moved out and was living elsewhere in the United States, we heard from her that she had married an American.

my predecessor's gloom engulfing me. But I had inherited from him a little black book in which were typed the names and addresses of all the families in the various Northern suburbs of Benoni who had indicated some sort of interest in or allegiance to Methodism. At Rhodes, Professor William Maxwell had given those of us who were to graduate some parting advice. He told us to establish early on in our ministry a pattern of studying in the morning, visiting in the afternoon, and attending meetings in the evenings, and if there were no meetings, reading (preferably history and biography).

I took his counsel to heart. Having earned my BA, I immediately enrolled for the BD degree at Rhodes, and spent my mornings studying and preparing sermons and other talks. Each afternoon, using as my guide the little black book left me by my predecessor, I visited families in their homes after I had been to the hospitals—the Boksburg-Benoni Hospital in Boksburg and the Glenwood Nursing Home in Benoni. In the evenings, I attended various circuit meetings, and when there were no meetings, I read. For transport, the church provided me with an old, beaten-up Ford Anglia. This was later replaced with a spanking new Ford Anglia from "Pa" Gush's Ford dealership after a fire had started in the engine of the old one on my way to a funeral.

The mention of funerals reminds me of the first funeral I had to conduct. Mr. Wilkins was away on vacation, and I received a call alerting me to a double tragedy involving two families belonging to the main Benoni Church. The two families were traveling to a Durban vacation in convoy. A husband and wife were in the lead car, a Studebaker, with one of their own children and two children belonging to the other couple, who were in the second car in which two of the children of the couple in the lead car were riding. Just outside Pietermaritzburg (about sixty miles from Durban), as they began the long five-mile descent into the city, the brakes of the Studebaker failed and simultaneously the gearshift stuck in overdrive—meaning that there was no engine compression to slow the car down. The vehicle rapidly gathered momentum. The driver tried desperately to reduce the car's dangerously increasing downhill trajectory (afterward it was apparent that he had literally pulled the handle of the emergency brake out of the dashboard of the car). Eventually, on a corner too sharp to be taken at speed, the car went off the road, colliding head-on with a tree. All five in the car were killed instantly. The parents and children in the second car saw the accident happen. Helplessly the parents witnessed the deaths of their children and the children of their parents.

After visiting both stricken families, they asked me to conduct the funeral, my first! Lined up at the front of the church were five coffins, two large and three small. The church was packed to capacity. These were well-known and well-loved families. The sobbing was almost hysterical. The grief was indescribable. This was no time for pious platitudes—not that I was ever given to the platitudinous. Whatever was said had to be from the heart, acknowledging the enormity of the tragedy, the utter waste of life, and the indescribable anguish of those left behind—at the same time offering solace and hope to the mourners. Somehow, I was able to make it a meaningful service.

While on the subject of funerals, the second funeral I conducted is equally memorable—for a different reason. A young Roman Catholic couple had gone to their priest to make arrangements for their baby's baptism. The week before the baptism, the baby was found dead in her crib, a victim of sudden infant death syndrome (SIDS). The priest refused to bury the baby. He could not conduct a Roman Catholic burial for an unbaptized child! I was asked to perform this sad little service, which I did without hesitation. The callous way church polity got in the way of ministering to those in such profound need was an instructive lesson—a lesson I took to heart in my own approach to ministry.

By the end of my first year, the Northmead Methodist Church was becoming a thriving community. Both morning and evening services were increasingly well attended. There was an active and enthusiastic youth group. The Sunday school was flourishing. And, since the conference had given me permission to marry before I was ordained and Margaret and I were to be wed later in 1959, the church had to begin to think of providing us with a manse.

A house under construction by a developer in Rynfield came on the market. Margaret and I were invited to look at it, and once we had approved it, the church decided to buy it for occupancy later that year or early in 1960, whenever it was finished. Since the congregation was now to have a physical presence not only in Northmead but also in Rynfield, I proposed to the church leaders that we should rename the Northmead Methodist Church the Northfield Methodist Church—descriptive of our intent to minister to people not only in Northmead, but also in Airfield, Rynfield, and Rynfield North. The leaders agreed, and the change was made.

On November 20, 1959, Margaret and I were married by Dr. J. B. Webb in the Methodist Central Hall in Johannesburg. Her bridesmaids were her cousins, Sheila and Gillian (daughters of Aunty Gwen, Margaret's Mom's sister, and Uncle Harry), and her flower girl was my nine-year-old cousin Gillian (Uncle Tom and Aunty Ivy's daughter). Ken, Margaret's brother, was my best man, and Matt, their cousin, and Justin, my brother, were my groomsmen.

The wedding ceremony was joyful and dignified, as only J. B. could make it. I remember him making self-deprecating references to the "Greek scholars" standing before him—as if he were not one himself. After the service, we had our reception in the hall of the Civic Center YMCA. Following the speeches, music for the dancing was provided by Bill Prideaux (a member of the Northfield Church) and his band.

In 2009 Ken was with us when we celebrated our fiftieth wedding anniversary, giving one of the tributes at the gala event our children put on for us. The week he was with us, we discovered an old tape recording of our wedding ceremony and the speeches at the reception following, that David Jones had made for us and we listened to it for the first time.

My Dad lent us his new Peugeot 204 for our honeymoon, and after the reception, we set off, spending our first night at a hotel in Vereeniging, going on the next morning to Cathedral Peak, in the Drakensburg, where we spent a week hiking,[74] horseback riding, swimming, and delighting in one another's company. From the Drakensberg we drove to Durban for Ken's wedding the week after ours. After Ken's wedding, we drove south to Cape Town along the garden route that includes South Africa's wild coast. We spent the second half of our honeymoon at a beautiful old hotel in Kalk Bay. Unfortunately, the hotel is no longer there, having been pulled down to make way for more modern structures. It was the first time either of us had really explored the environs of Cape Town including the magnificent Table Mountain overlooking the city and the harbor beyond it. All in all, we had the most marvelous time—the best holiday of our lives.

After returning to Northfield, early in 1960 we moved into the new manse, 11 Impala Street, Rynfield, bringing with us the wedding present Viv Harris and his wife Dorothy had given us—a purebred boxer puppy bitch we named Bess. Margaret, now a registered nurse, worked the day-shift at the Joubert Park Nursing Home in Johannesburg. Aunt Elizabeth ("Aunty Bis," Margaret's Dad's sister) had given Margaret her old car (another Anglia). Margaret would drive to the station, leave her car there, catch the train into Johannesburg, walk from the station to the Joubert Park Nursing Home, and then reverse the process in the evening. One day, she fainted on the train coming

---

[74] One of the Drakensberg Mountains we hiked around had the Zulu name "N'tunja." N'tunja means "eye of the needle." At the mountain's summit there was a massive rock with a hole right through it the size of an automobile. The hole had probably been eroded by rain and wind.

home. That was our first indication that she was pregnant. We made arrangements for her to be taken care of by Dr. Melzer, a female obstetrician-gynecologist, who told us that the baby was due sometime toward the end of August—a mere nine months after our wedding.

One of the unplanned events in the Northfield Church that yielded huge dividends in years to come started with an impulse. The church's sanctuary was a beautiful little structure, but it had been badly neglected. Most noticeably, the paint was peeling from the steep, corrugated iron roof, detracting from the appearance of the whole building. I went to the trust committee (which handled the church's finances) and asked the trustees whether they would have the church painted. They demurred. There weren't sufficient funds put aside to meet this kind of expense. I then offered to enlist some of the men in the congregation to help me paint the roof ourselves—if they would pay for the paint. They agreed, and I rounded up three or four of the men who never came to worship services but whose wives were involved in the life of the church. Soon, the three or four of us increased to a regular half dozen.

We worked every Saturday,[75] scraping off the old paint before sanding the roof and repainting it. When the roof was done, the gutters and downpipes looked shabby, so we painted them. Then the outside walls of the church looked drab in comparison with the gleaming roof and gutters, so we repainted the outside of the church. Finally, having done the outside, we couldn't ignore the inside of the church, and redid the entire interior of the building. I suppose this project took us about six months.

Each Saturday, one or more of the wives would bring us

---

[75] As a probationer minister, I was not yet allowed to perform marriages (or celebrate Holy Communion) so I had most Saturdays free. (I was, however, allowed to perform baptisms and conduct funeral and memorial services.)

lunch. Margaret made Cornish pasties several times. Cornish pasties, as already mentioned, were a "condition of our marriage." My first taste of one had been in Parkhurst at Aunty Gwen's home. I hopefully and half-jokingly urged Margaret learn the art of pasty making, which she did in earnest. By now, she must have made at least twenty-five thousand pasties for us, our family, and our friends.

I alluded to the dividend painting the church paid out. The men who worked with me, who previously had never set foot inside the building, were now among its most stalwart members. It was *their* church. They had a stake in it. And they were proud of what they had accomplished. Decades after I left Northfield, these men were still the church's leaders. One of them, a rough diamond named Willy Green,[76] told me when we were sitting on top of the roof about a brief extramarital affair that was threatening his marriage. I talked to him about forgiveness and the possibility of new beginnings that is at the heart of the Gospel, arranged to meet with him and his wife, and was able to bring about their reconciliation. Later, he mentioned that he practiced and sometimes taught yoga. I asked if he would like to offer a yoga class in the church hall. He jumped at the opportunity, and every Tuesday night, we had thirty to forty people taking instruction from this plumber who also proved to be a gifted teacher. Margaret and I joined his class as well. Willy taught me to stand on my head in the yoga manner. This is something I did, every day of my life, until I shattered my pelvis more than fifty-three years later (not standing on my head, by the way; the full story is to be told in chapter 11).

If Saturday, November 21, 1959, the day of our wedding, was the most unforgettable day of our lives, Sunday, August 20, 1960, was the next most memorable. On Friday morning (my day off, two days earlier), Margaret and I had played a round of golf, pushing our own homemade double golf cart on

---

[76] I have used a pseudonym to protect Willy's privacy.

the Crown Mines golf course where ministers were given the courtesy of the course during the week. Margaret was very pregnant, and she could hardly swing her club around her protruding belly. Yet she walked and played the entire eighteen holes. The Saturday night following, after we were in bed, she woke me to announce that the membrane surrounding the baby had ruptured and that we had better get to the hospital. After alerting Dr. Melzer, we left for the Boksburg-Benoni Hospital where Margaret was admitted to the maternity ward. I wasn't allowed to stay very long with her after she had been settled in bed, and I returned home. Those were the days when fathers were thought to get in the way of the birthing process and were only permitted to see their wives and babies after the delivery. At about two o'clock on Sunday morning, I got a phone call to say that our baby had arrived safely. I rushed out in the pouring rain to greet my first child and hug my wife.

Margaret remembers me squelching my way into the maternity ward in my soggy shoes and euphorically waking and greeting the other ladies as I made my way to her bed. She was radiant, and she was holding the most beautiful little seven-pound, eight-ounce girl—whom we named Heather Margaret. In those days before routine ultrasound scans during the pregnancy gave parents the option of learning their baby's gender while it was still in utero, whether it was a girl or a boy was invariably a complete surprise. Both of us were ecstatic that our firstborn was a girl, and I couldn't wait to hold her and her mother.

I was only allowed to stay with them for what seemed like an incredibly short time before being told politely that I had to leave. I don't know how I was able to get back to sleep or preach the next morning. I was so excited. Somehow I did both and then went back to Bedfordview to share my excitement with Mom and Dad at lunchtime before going back to the hospital for the three o'clock visiting hour—eleven hours after Heather was born! How different it all is these days.

At this point, another painful memory of my father comes to mind. Mom was elated to hear the news of Heather's birth, and when I arrived at Bella Vista after the morning service she asked for graphic descriptions of the whole process so far as I knew it and of her first grand-daughter. My Dad was playing golf and had not yet come home. While we were waiting for him, I sat outside the kitchen in the sun glancing at the *Sunday Times*. Eventually he drove his car up onto the back lawn outside the kitchen, and I got up to tell him all that had so enthralled my Mom. He gave me no time to do this. For some obscure reason, perhaps because the one girl he and Mom had had was stillborn and he was jealous of my good fortune, he started shouting at me as he had done that night we were driving to choir practice. I stood there in disbelief, unable to comprehend what or why this was happening. Finally, I turned, went back into the kitchen, told Mom I couldn't stay for lunch after this totally inappropriate outburst, picked up my coat, and left. He never once visited Margaret in the hospital, nor did he refer to this incident again. He saw his granddaughter for the first time when we returned to Bedfordview for lunch a couple of Sundays later.

Margaret came home early the following week, and we began our new life as parents with a brand-new baby. Our friends Ella (also a nurse) and Billy Clements,[77] immigrants from Ireland, had their first baby at about the same time. Billy had been a carpenter in Ireland, but he was now employed in the men's department of the Benoni branch of John Orr's, an exclusive retailer. Billy and I worked together on our days off making various items for our respective babies. We started by designing and then jointly building two cabinets (one for each

---

[77] Billy and Ella and their children returned to Northern Ireland after we left Northfield. Billy became a police officer. Later, he was assassinated with other officers in his police station by members of the IRA. Ella died not long afterward.

family) the top of which opened out to form a changing table, exposing a little bathtub that could be filled with warm water, with drawers below for shampoos, powder, baby oil, diapers, and baby clothes.

I continued my baby furniture-making by building a little wardrobe with drawers and hanging space for Heather's clothes and a tiny chair, the seat of which slid out to allow a child to sit on the potty beneath it. These were later used by all our children and eventually by their cousins. Another project was a cage for Fluffy, a white rabbit Heather was given when she was older, which had an enclosed nest on one side and an open play area on the other, with a door through which Fluffy could be fed and her cage cleaned.

Later woodworking items included a model of Mostert's Mill, the only working Dutch windmill in South Africa (which still stands in Cape Town), a homemade children's slide for the backyard, a model of a three-stage Delta rocket, a Wendy house for the children to play in, which could be disassembled in sections for transportation (as happened when it was donated to various nieces and nephews after we left for the United States), and steam-bent Masonite "surfboards" for sliding down the large sand dunes when we went to the coast for our annual vacations.

Andrew Ernlé was born twenty months after Heather, also at Boksburg-Benoni Hospital, and with Dr. Melzer as our obstetrician. His birth was special—not only because we now had a boy as well as a girl but because he arrived on Margaret's birthday, April 29, 1962. He, too, was hefty (eight pounds, two ounces) and healthy. When she first saw him, Heather, barely twenty months old, exclaimed, "See, he's sucking his fin-gars!"

Our boxer, Bess, had six puppies at about the time Andrew was born and turned out to be the prototypical mother. She would take all Heather's toys that she could find into her kennel with her puppies, and when Andrew was in the back yard in his baby carriage getting some fresh air, and woke up, Bess would try to get him into her kennel as well.

Andrew had a voracious appetite. Frequently we would wake up in the morning to find the little fellow squatting on the kitchen table next to the sugar bowl, shoveling spoonsful of sugar into his mouth as fast as he could. He would open his mouth, trustingly, to eat whatever we offered him. Occasionally, I would take cruel delight in putting Marmite or mustard on the spoon and watching his grimace as the tart taste surprised him, giving way to a broad grin as he shared in our laughter at the joke we had played on him.

Our little family grew even further during our time in Rynfield. On September 12, 1963, Jenny Anne was born. With Margaret having had two uneventful confinements, we were determined that this time I would witness the birth of one of our children this time. The only way to do this was to have the baby at home. Dr. Melzer did not approve, so we decided to have the district midwife attend Margaret.

This was truly one of the most transcendent experiences of my life. I boiled gallons of water, with a large pot on every ring on our electric stove (why I thought so much water would be needed escapes me now), and squeezed Margaret's hand as she went into labor and eventually gave birth to another healthy little girl, this one weighing seven pounds and three ounces. I can remember vividly how blue Jenny was at first and then how pink she became after taking her first few breaths, how perfect she was in every way, and how much joy there was in our living room (where a bed had been prepared for Margaret) when her Mom and Dad, Heather and Andrew, came in to see her for the first time. This was the first birth I had ever witnessed, and it forever gave Jenny a special place in my heart. Incidentally, her birth was the least expensive of the three. The bill for the services of the district midwife was R3.50, probably the equivalent of $1.75.

Each November for four years (1959–1962), we would go

back to Rhodes so that I could sit my final examinations. We would borrow my father's folding caravan,[78] tow it down to Port Alfred (about forty miles from Grahamstown), and camp out. Each day that I had an examination to write I would drive to Rhodes and then return to the campsite in the evening. By this time, Heather was walking, and one of our many photographs of her at about fifteen months shows her carrying a quart bottle of milk almost as big as she was, with a baby doll strapped, African-style, to her back.

My BD thesis, entitled "The Meaning and Significance of Intercessory Prayer for the Christian," was inspired by the death of a lovely young woman in the congregation by the name of Colleen Claasens. At the age of nineteen, Colleen was diagnosed with inoperable, metastatic brain cancer (a glioblastoma). Her parents and her many friends in the church started praying for her—as Margaret and I did—and continued to do so for the many months before she died. This tragedy raised countless questions in my own mind. Did our prayers do Colleen any good? If they did, how could we know this and, more importantly how could this be demonstrated objectively? If they didn't, was there any point in praying at all? And if so, what was the point? What did we, as Christians, expect when we prayed for others? When people came to me requesting that I to pray for them how was I to balance my experience of seemingly unanswered prayer with the clear New Testament mandate to make intercession for others—both as a private obligation and a public congregational duty?

There were scores more questions raised by Colleen's illness and death, But to find answers to at least some of them

---

[78] The folding fiberglass caravan was an ingenious piece of equipment. When closed, it was only about three feet high so that one could easily see everything behind the car in the rear-view mirror. In the open position, the canvas walls with mesh windows allowed one to stand upright, with the beds in the lower half and the upper half providing the waterproof roof.

I decided to do research into intercessory prayer from several perspectives: philosophical, historical, theological, liturgical, psychological, and practical. The resulting thesis could have been expanded into a doctoral dissertation. It clarified my thinking enormously and was helpful to me throughout my ministry.

Two findings, in particular, stand out. One was that, more frequently than not, prayers are answered through human agency. The word "intercession" is derived from the Latin *inter cedere,* meaning "to yield between", or surrender oneself to serve as the "go-between" the one prayed for and the Divine. This means that truly to pray for another person requires that one be willing to be the agent through whom the divine purpose can be worked out—whether this means supporting medical research, providing medical or nursing care, preparing meals for those who are ill, or driving them to the hospital. And secondly, doing this can be costly—in time, energy, and resources. Praying for others is demanding work, not to be undertaken lightly. A readiness to sacrifice, to yield to the need of the other, is always entailed.

At the end of 1963, I was awarded my bachelor of divinity degree, majoring in systematic theology with first-class honors.[79]

---

[79] My thesis was entitled, "The Meaning and Significance of Intercessory Prayer for the Christian." At the time, I had no idea how important this piece of work, which took about eighteen months to complete, would be for our lives. Years later, my acceptance into the PhD program at Southern Methodist University in October 1967 (about which more will be said later) was contingent on my passing the Graduate Record Examinations (GREs). However, the American Consulate in Johannesburg was not holding the GREs for another year. In lieu of passing my GREs, Professor Herndon Wagers, the dean of the graduate program in the sciences and humanities at SMU, asked me to send him a copy of my thesis, which I did. The thesis was read by Professors Wagers and two of my future advisors, Professors John Deschner and Albert Outler. Evidently, it satisfied

We served the Northfield congregation for five years, from 1959–1963. Because of its strategic location almost in the middle of Benoni's northern suburbs, my confidence in the viability of the church and its future was justified. The church and hall that had served us so well during most of our tenure became too small for the rapidly expanding congregation. My successor would preside over the selling of that building, the purchase of an empty lot in Airfield, and the construction of a new church with seating for 2,500 people, several halls, and classrooms. Today, it is one of the biggest Methodist churches in the country.

In October 1963, the Annual Conference of the Methodist Church appointed me, no doubt at his own request, as assistant minister to Dr. J. B. Webb. In January of 1964, we would be going back to the Methodist Central Hall in Johannesburg, at that time the largest Methodist church in South Africa, where we had first met and where we had been married, this time as members of the ministerial staff. We left Benoni saddened to bid farewell to the dear friends we had made there, but excited at the opportunity we had been given and keenly anticipating what lay ahead.

Methodist Central Hall, Johannesburg

It was said of Joseph Benjamin ("Joe") Webb, who had been at the Methodist Central Hall for twenty-three years when I joined him as his assistant, that it was he who put the "Jo" into Johannesburg. Certainly, he was the best known and the most widely beloved minister not only in Johannesburg but indeed in the whole of South Africa—as Harry Emerson Fosdick had been at roughly the same time in the United States. As an example of his national stature, in 1950 he had been asked by

them of my readiness to do doctoral-level work, and I was accepted into the program.

the family to deliver the eulogy at the funeral of the former two-time South African Prime Minister, Field Marshall Jan Christian Smuts.[80] I counted it an immense privilege to have been chosen to work with the man I had revered since I had first heard him preach at Central Hall. Unfortunately, we would work together for that one year only. J. B. Webb announced in January that he and his wife Cora would retire at the end of 1964, principally because of Cora's poor health.

But that was still in the future. In addition to the excitement of being at Central Hall, we would now be closer to Margaret's Mom and Dad, who still had their Brooklyn Heights flat, to my parents (regrettably, they would divorce later that year), and to Jean McFarlane (neé Lobban),[81] who had been Margaret's best friend since they were in the first grade together, and her husband, Robert. They were now next-door neighbors; they lived at 48 Lurgan Road in Parkview, and our manse was 46 Lurgan Road.

Typical of his largesse, Dr. Webb made it clear from the beginning of our time together that if people asked me, rather than him, to perform weddings, funerals, or baptisms for them, that was perfectly acceptable and something he encouraged me to do. Looking back, this may also have been because he knew

---

[80] The cremation service for Prime Minister J. C. Smuts was held in the Chapel of the Braamfontein Crematorium, Johannesburg, where my Mom was the organist. When I was eighteen, she was able to smuggle me into the chapel for the funeral. I sat on the organ bench beside her and had the proverbial bird's-eye view of the whole impressive service. Thousands of mourners were in attendance, the majority standing outside the chapel, seeing nothing but hearing everything over loudspeakers that had been specially installed for the occasion.

[81] Years later, after Robert MacFarlane's death, Jean married Michael Smythe, who unfortunately died of brain cancer soon afterward. Jean Smythe's name recurs throughout my narrative. She has graciously provided written, notarized permission for me to include her in my memoir.

even then that he would be retiring at the end of the year. In any case, he was in constant demand as a speaker at all sorts of civic and religious events and had burdensome administrative duties as well—he was superintendent minister of the Johannesburg Central Circuit, chairman of the Southern Transvaal District, and had been president of the Methodist Church of South Africa numerous times. As his junior colleague, he asked me to do the bulk of the pastoral visitation—in the Johannesburg hospitals and in the homes of congregants spread out over the entire city. Also, since he was often away, sometimes overseas, I would do a considerable amount of preaching at Central Hall— an amazing opportunity for a young minister. In my almost four years at Central Hall, I would be in four or five hospitals every day of the week, and in the course of each year, I would visit every one of our more than 1,500 members in their homes spread out across the metropolitan Johannesburg area—about five hundred square miles.

My parents' divorce, though not unexpected, came as a tremendous shock to us all. I have mentioned my father's temper before. Once the three of us children were married and out of the home, Mom must have found Dad's tantrums increasingly intolerable. Finally, for some reason, the breaking point came—and she told him to leave the house. He moved out, but not very far away. By this time, they owned not only Bella Vista, #10 Sugarbush Road, but #12 as well. Previously, my father had built chicken houses and chicken runs on #12, on the other side of the wall enclosing our backyard. He now turned the chicken houses (minus the chickens) into an apartment and took up residence there. He pleaded with Mom to take him back, but she refused.

He came to see Margaret and me at 46 Lurgan Road, asking us to intervene and persuade Mom to let him return home. I tried to reconcile them, but Mom had made up her mind and she made it clear there was no going back. She proceeded with the divorce. In the settlement, she was awarded #10 and Dad kept #12; they divided the furniture Chilli had built and the paintings some of which had been done by Giovani Fornaciari as well as other household items. Shortly after the divorce went though, Mom sold 10 Sugarbush Road and bought a small house on Thirteenth Avenue in Parkhurst, where she, Gran, and Uncle Dick lived. Both Gran and Uncle Dick died there while we were in Dallas, and Mom continued to stay on in that home until she sold it in 1974 shortly before coming to live with us in California.

Because we had failed to prevail on Mom to take him back, and from this had drawn the conclusion that we had taken her side in their dispute, my father effectively cut us off in 1964. From then on he would have nothing whatever to do with us. Even when we left for Dallas in 1967 and I asked him whether he would allow us to bring his three grandchildren to see him to say their goodbyes, he refused. Our reconciliation in 1980, about which I will say more in a later chapter, was heartwarming (from my perspective) but short-lived.

Otherwise, life in Parkview was truly happy. Margaret had grown up in this northern suburb, and she felt as if she had come home to her old familiar places. She was working again as a nurse at a private hospital in Johannesburg; she loved nursing and was excellent at what she did. Jean and Robert were next door, and in what free time we had, we would see a lot of them. The children loved going next door to Jean's backyard swimming pool in which they had learned to swim. We saw Margaret's Mom and Dad and my Mom every week, often more than once. They were enthusiastic babysitters when we both had to be out in the evening. And Heather, then Andrew, started at kindergarten and primary school there.

The kindergarten, which used classrooms at the Saint Francis Anglican Church, was a quarter of a mile from our house at the bottom of Lurgan Road. With pride and joy, I would walk Heather, carrying her little lunch case in one hand and holding mine in the other, down the road to her first school each morning. By the time Heather was ready to start grade one at Parkview Junior (where Margaret and Jean had at one time been pupils), Andrew was enrolled at Saint Francis. Heather and I would walk with him down the road to Saint Francis, and then she and I would continue on to Parkview Junior where I would take leave of her. We would conjugate Latin verbs and do declensions of Latin nouns as we walked: *Amo, Amas, Amat...* *Mensa, Mensas, Mensam* ... Heather went further with her Latin than ever I did, and I'm sure it is because we had so much fun on our walks to school.

I was determined to continue my own education, especially after J. B. Webb retired. His successor, Stanley Pitts, and his wife Daphne[82] were insecure. They had been at a remote mission station for decades and now found themselves at the largest metropolitan Methodist church in South Africa. Whereas J. B. Webb had a national reputation and was beloved throughout the country, they were relatively unknown. J. B. was a gifted preacher and a brilliant orator—and Pitts was not. Pitts jealously guarded his prerogatives as senior superintendent minister whereas J. B. had welcomed the opportunity to share these with me. It soon became apparent that Mrs. Pitts, especially, was envious of the affection people had for Margaret and me. As noted earlier, Margaret had grown up at Central Hall and I had been a Sunday school teacher and member of the choir and Wesley Guild years before coming back as the assistant minister.

Particularly galling to Mrs. Pitts was the fact that Pitts had a BA after his name (J. B. had an Oxford MA and a several honorary DDs), and I, his junior, had a bachelor's and an honors degree. In all sorts of little ways, we began to realize that she was trying to undermine me at every opportunity. I'll mention one example. The University of the Witwatersrand had recently created a new department of religion, chaired by Dr. Albert

---

[82] Both Mr. and Mrs. Pitts are now deceased.

Geyser, a former Dutch Reformed Church minister who had been drummed out of his church on trumped-up charges of heresy, but in fact because of his opposition to apartheid. He was also the department's sole professor. Wits, as the university was known, had taken the opportunity to create this new department partly because Professor Geyser was available and needed an academic position (he was a brilliant scholar with doctorates in New Testament studies from the University of Leiden and Saint Andrew's University) and partly because there was an enormous pent-up demand for courses in religion for schoolteachers in training at the normal college.

I went to Professor Geyser to inquire about being enrolled as a PhD student at Wits in his new department. After reviewing my transcripts and interviewing me at length, he arranged for me to be admitted as his first graduate student. Our understanding was that I would be a part-time student and would meet with him for one hour each month. Since he was the only faculty member, there was no course work. He would assign me readings and exegesis of various texts in the Greek, which I would do, and then when next we met, we would go over the work I had done and discuss its implications for the research I was doing for a dissertation. At that early stage, he thought my dissertation should be on the intercessor in the Scriptures generally and particularly in the letter to the Hebrews. This was an area of his expertise and interest, and logically it seemed also to continue the research I had done for my BD thesis.

Mrs. Pitts started circulating the story, which came back to me from three different sources in three different suburbs in the course of my pastoral visits, that I was doing no work whatever in the church and was spending all my time at Wits. Nothing could have been further from the truth. When I finally confronted her about this, she denied having ever said such a thing about me. My response further soured our relationship: "If you did not say this, then three different people in the congregation, living in completely different parts of the city, each having volunteered the same story to me, must be lying." Partly because of the fact that working with Mr. and Mrs. Pitts was becoming unpleasant and partly because I was seeing Albert Geyser so sporadically and was by now doing research on a topic in which he was more interested than I was myself, Margaret and I made the decision toward the end of 1966 that I would enroll at a university overseas as a full-time PhD student. I wrote first to the University of Saint Andrews, with an accompanying letter of recommendation from Professor Geyser. Since we had three children, I inquired about scholarships and part-time employment to support the family. Their response was discouraging: there were no scholarships available, and PhD students at Saint Andrew's were not allowed to take part-time employment.

Our next application was to the University of Chicago. After reviewing my transcripts and letters of reference, I was accepted into the PhD program at the divinity school, pending successful completion of the Graduate Record Examinations (GREs). I was also offered a scholarship to cover the cost of my tuition. However, there was still the problem of how we were going to pay for our accommodation and support our family. We knew Margaret could eventually find work as a nurse, but since the children were so young, we were both reluctant for her to have to work full-time.

How could I find part-time employment without a green card, conferring permanent residence status (and the Catch-22: unless I had a job offer, how could I obtain a green card?)? One possible way around this problem was to develop a slide show about South Africa, complete with commentary and musical soundtrack, and go on the lecture circuit in my spare time. With Ken's help,[83] we did this. We still have it, but we never needed

---

[83] After his divorce and consequent enforced resignation from the Methodist ministry, Ken had become a professional filmmaker,

to use it to raise a single dollar because luck or providence[84] intervened to take us in a different direction. This will be explained as I return to the main narrative.

Shortly after J. B. Webb retired from Central Hall, the trustees made a business decision to sell the land on which the church and the large fellowship hall next door to it were built and buy a smaller property not far from the old site right in the heart of Johannesburg This would net enough profit from the sale for the congregation to be able to build everything it had in the way of space, and more—by expanding vertically. Eddie Gill (I had been best man at his and Avril's wedding) was appointed the architect, and he drew up the plans that were eventually approved. The large hall and classrooms were in the basement, the sanctuary occupied the next two floors. Offices for the staff and flats for the superintendent minister (Mr. Pitts) and the organist and choir director (Rupert Stoutt) were on the top floor. The basement hall was built first, and after the sale, we moved out of the old building so that it could be demolished by the new owners and began to use the hall as the temporary sanctuary while construction above it continued.

One Sunday evening (always the larger service), I was appointed to lead worship and preach. As usual, after the service, I stood at the door and greeted people on the way out. One man thanked me enthusiastically for the service and mentioned in passing that he was an American Methodist bishop. I did not catch his name. Because our children were so young, Margaret had stayed at home, and when I got back, I mentioned casually that I had met an American bishop after the service.[85] Immediately, she asked, "Did you ask him to help you

---

subsequently specializing in ariel photography.

[84] I will return to my understanding of the notion of providence in the final chapter.

[85] The Methodist Church of South Africa had its roots in British Methodism (as did the American Methodist Church; John Wesley

had spent three years establishing Methodism in Georgia, one of the original ten states colonized by the British). Despite being cousins, they differed in the terms they used for their officials and their functions. A superintendent minister in the British and South African churches was the spiritual leader of a "circuit," a group of churches in a discrete geographical area, and was also the senior minister of the largest church in the circuit. The ministers in a circuit preached not only to their own congregations, but circulated from one pulpit to another throughout the circuit according to a roster drawn up by the superintendent minister and his staff. In the United States, a circuit was called a "district," and the minister in charge was a district superintendent or DS. A DS had no congregational responsibilities of his own, but he circulated throughout his district, preaching in each church from time to time according to a timetable he drew up; nor did the ministers in a district preach in one another's churches except by special arrangement. In British and South African Methodism, all the circuits in a larger geographical area (a province or county) comprised a district, and with oversight over all these churches was a "chairman of the district" who also had responsibility for his or her own congregation. These churches had an annual synod, at which the chairman was elected. In the United States, the district chairman was termed a bishop, who had no primary congregational responsibility but was responsible for all the churches in his or her diocese. In Britain and South Africa, there was an annual conference of which all the ministers in the country were members, as well as lay representatives elected by each of the churches. Chairmen of district rotated annually to become president of the conference, and the conference enunciated church polity and issued considered statements on important issues of the day (in South Africa, these statements included annual affirmations that Methodists were united regardless of color as brothers and sisters in the one church as well as denunciations of the Nationalist government's apartheid ideology). In the United States, all the districts in a state or collection of states meet in an annual conference under a presiding bishop, and all the representatives of the various dioceses meet in a quadrennial general conference, which sets policies at the national level. J. B. Webb had simultaneously been superintendent minister of the Johannesburg Central circuit, Chairman of the Southern Transvaal district, and President of the Methodist Church of South Africa. Since my time in South Africa, the names—but not the functions—of the leadership find a job in Chicago?" I told her that the idea hadn't occurred to me. Besides, there had been so many people in church that night that there hadn't been time at the door for more than a brief exchange. She insisted that we had to find out who he was, where he was staying in Johannesburg, and that I was going to see him.

That very night, we made one telephone call after another to each of the major Johannesburg hotels, asking whether among their guests there was an American Methodist bishop. After about three phone calls we found him. The bishop's name, incongruously, was W. Kenneth Pope. The receptionist put me through to him, and after explaining why I was calling, he gave me an appointment to meet with him the next day at his hotel.

When we met, I told Bishop Pope (who was from Dallas) about having been accepted as a graduate student at the University of Chicago but needed to find a job to help support our family while I was in graduate school, and that I had come to ask for his help in doing this. He gazed at me thoughtfully for some time without saying a word. Finally, looking me in the eye, he said, "I am going to take a chance on you. If you are willing to consider coming to Southern Methodist University (SMU) in Dallas, where I am a on the board of trustees, I will recommend that you be accepted into the doctoral program. I will also appoint you to a part-time position somewhere in Dallas as a minister in the Texas Conference."

My immediate response was to ask how SMU compared with the University of Chicago. He replied was that the Perkins School of Theology at SMU was one of the finest in the country—as good as if not better than the divinity school at the University of Chicago—and that among the distinguished

---

have changed: chairmen are now bishops, and the annual conference is chaired by an annually appointed presiding bishop. This was done to clarify for government officials in South Africa the status of Methodism's leadership. Bishop Kenneth Pope is now deceased.

faculty were Albert Outler, John Deschner (both of whom became my advisers and are now deceased, about whom I will say more later), Herndon Wagers (the dean of the graduate school in the sciences and humanities), and Schubert Ogden, perhaps the preeminent exponent of the theology of Rudolf Bultmann. SMU, said Bishop Pope, was endowed with ninety-six producing oil wells. This made possible the recruiting of the best faculty in the world and enabled it to have one of the finest university libraries, the Bidwell Library, comparable to those of any of the great institutions of higher learning. Needless to say, I was enthusiastic and asked him whether I could discuss this with Margaret and get back to him the following day.

Margaret was unhesitating in her urging that this was an offer we had to accept. J. B. Webb, whom I called on the telephone at his home in Saint Michael's-by-the-Sea, was equally affirmative. And what finally clinched it was my learning that John Deschner had studied with Karl Barth in Basel. Barth was *the* preeminent Reformed theologian of the twentieth century. He had been a professor at the University of Tübingen. But in 1933 he had refused to begin his lectures with the by then mandatory salute, *Heil Hitler!* He was immediately dismissed from his professorship at Tübingen and expelled from Germany. The University of Basel welcomed him with open arms. From this strategic base in a neutral country he continued his resistance to Nazism and drafted the Barmen Declaration—the manifesto of the church's opposition to all that Hitler was doing and would do in the years ahead. What better opportunity could I possibly have to learn more about the Reformed tradition[86]; to understand the reasons why Barth, the supreme current exemplar of the Reformed tradition, opposed the Third Reich as demonic; and the implications of this for

---

[86] I knew next to nothing about the theology of the Dutch Reformed Churches in South Africa which were all justifying apartheid biblically and theologically.

relations between church and our increasingly totalitarian state in South Africa?

I contacted W. Kenneth Pope the next afternoon, as promised, and eagerly informed him that we would accept his offer. On returning to Texas, he was as good as his word. Wasting no time, he appointed me as an assistant minister in the Kessler Park Methodist Church in Dallas and had the pastor, Gordon Casad, write me a letter formally offering me the position with primary responsibility for the young people (eleventh and twelfth graders) in the congregation, with secondary pastoral and preaching duties. This airmail letter was crucially important for meeting the American Consulate's requirements before issuing us with green cards designating us permanent residents and thus enabling us to work legally in the US. Further, Bishop Pope asked Dean Herndon Wagers to contact me with information about what I would have to do to be accepted into the graduate program in the humanities and sciences at SMU.

Immediately, we began working on two fronts. Armed with a job offer, we went to the United States embassy in Johannesburg and applied for permanent resident status under the quota system the State Department then being applied in various countries around the world. At the same time the consul told me that it was too late to take the GREs in South Africa that year. When I wrote informing Dr. Wagers of this, he asked me to send him my BD thesis instead, which I did. After he and other faculty members had read the thesis, Dr. Wagers formally notified me that I had been accepted into SMU's inaugural class of nineteen PhD students in the newly formed graduate school of humanities and sciences, and that Professors Outler and Deschner would be my advisers.

Simultaneously, in order to get a head start on the two foreign languages required of all doctoral students, I enrolled with Frau Schmidt, a Swiss lady in Johannesburg who taught German and French. (Later, after arriving at SMU, Professor

Outler encouraged me to drop French and take Patristic Greek
as my second foreign language since I had already mastered
classical and New Testament Greek.)

Looking back, I don't know how we managed to do all this,
but accomplish it we did. By August, we had our green cards,
I had informed the Conference of the Methodist Church in
South Africa (which makes all ministerial appointments) that
we would be leaving at the end of August, and our children
were ready to transfer out of their schools before the end of the
school year (December in South Africa) in order to start their
new schools in a higher grade in September (the beginning of
the US school year). I was well along in my studies of German
and French, and Margaret's Mom and Dad and my Mom were
already making plans to visit us in Dallas.

With a scholarship from the Institute of Race Relations, in
which I had been active, we were able to purchase air tickets
to Dallas. Our family had been truly beloved by the Central
Hall congregation, and we bad them a sad farewell; our parting
from Mr. and Mrs. Pitts was considerably less sorrowful. With
four suitcases, we left on an Icelandic Airways propeller-driven
Boeing Super Constellation first for Luxemburg where we hired
a small car and spent a week, then for Reykjavik where we
rented a VW Beetle and spent another unforgettable week—our
only vacation that year—and then on to New York. In Riverside,
New York, we spent a day or two calling on dignitaries at the
World Council of Churches (WCC).[87]

After that, we went on to Dallas. I remember having
dressed in my best suit, heavy serge, since it was winter when
we left South Africa—and we had not the slightest idea of
what summer in Texas would feel like. When we got off the

---

[87] I had been a delegate of the South African of Churches to a WCC
conference on race and justice. The Institute of Race Relations in
South Africa was funded in part by the WCC, so that our air fares
were in fact paid by the WCC. We wanted to meet with and thank our
benefactors.

plane at Love Field, it felt as if I had stepped straight into a hot oven—the temperature was well above a hundred degrees. To make matters worse, the Reverend Gordon Casad (the senior minister of the Kessler Park Methodist Church) and his wife Dee-Dee, who met us at the airport, took us straight to a Mexican restaurant to welcome and get acquainted with us. This was our initial experience of Mexican cuisine. We had no idea how highly-spiced Mexican food could be. Andrew burst out crying at his first taste of salsa (and for Andrew, that is saying something), and I was sweltering in my serge suit.

The Casads's welcome was wonderfully warm (literally and figuratively), but we all were incredibly relieved to be able to change into cooler clothes in our new home—an apartment provided by the church in a complex called the Lamplighter, which had a swimming pool! The apartment was across the road from the Rosemont Elementary School that Heather and Andrew would be attending. In addition to providing us with the apartment, Kessler Park UMC would pay us a stipend of $400 a month. We thought we had arrived in heaven.

7

Southern Methodist University

Dallas, Texas

Kessler Park, when we arrived in 1967, was an affluent, predominantly white suburb of Dallas. In the four years we were there, the demographics were beginning to change as more Hispanics moved into the area, resulting, I'm ashamed to say, in whites moving out. The transition would accelerate in the decade after we left. As we saw ten or fifteen years later when we returned to visit friends we had made in Dallas, the swimming pool was cracked and empty, the Lamplighter furnished apartments where we had lived so comfortably and where our children had been so happy were derelict, and the entire complex was fenced off and scheduled for demolition.

However, at the time we could not believe our good fortune in having a pleasant apartment to live in about five miles from the church, with $400 a month for my part-time job as youth minister with a congregation that took our family into their hearts from the moment we arrived. The senior minister, Gordon Casad, was a good and decent man—even though he was considerably more conservative theologically and politically than Margaret and me. The assistant minister, Montie Stewart, and his wife, Marlee, staunchly Democratic, were more liberal. The four of us soon became firm friends as well as colleagues.

Many in the congregation—Ted Boone, Jack Schull, and Larry Arnspiger among them—were practicing physicians at Methodist Hospital, also in Kessler Park, and we and their wives became good friends from the start. One of the older physicians, Dr. Harrell (no one dared call him by his first name, was an obstetrician-gynecologist who later took care of Margaret without charge when she became pregnant and delivered Timothy; he sternly made it plain at our first consultation that he did not tolerate husbands in the delivery room). Once Margaret started working at Methodist Hospital as a registered nurse, these friendships deepened. As their children and ours came to know each other, we were all accepted into this community despite the fact that most of them were extremely wealthy and lived in luxurious homes, while we were in the same league as the proverbial church mice.

Some sixty of the older children in these and other families were members of either the junior high or the senior high Sunday school class, the youth group, and the youth choir. My job was to minister to these young people: visiting them in their homes, teaching them in formal sessions on Sunday mornings, organizing fun as well as serious and meaningful service programs for the youth group on Friday evenings, singing with them in the youth choir under the direction of Stanley Shepelwich, organist and musical director, and, best of all, taking them away fairly regularly to various conference centers for weekend retreats, with our whole family going along. I also assisted in the Sunday services and preached from time to time, as did Montie.

The church owned an old school bus, and when we went away for our retreats, I was the designated driver. The juniors and seniors were always high-spirited, and our trips were filled with laughter, singing, and horsing around. Preparing the various sessions, usually four or five depending on the theme, took a lot of work. These made up the serious aspect of the retreats. But in the evenings, we would all relax. There would be campfires, sing-songs, skits, and plays. We soon bonded into a wonderfully cohesive group.

Margaret and I were shocked at first by the way these young people wasted food. The meals would all be prepared by the conference center staff and generally were excellent. Nonetheless, these children of wealthy families would literally throw away plates of food barely touched, choosing instead the candy bars and soft drinks from the ubiquitous vending machines. We tried to impress on them the reality of hunger in countries like Africa and India, but they simply had no experience of what it is like to go without, and our pleading with them to recognize how fortunate we all were seemed at the time to fall on deaf ears. In fact, their behavior slowly began to change, perhaps as a result of growing maturity. By the time we left Kessler Park, the improvement in their sense of social responsibility was evident. It is gratifying to note that two members of my youth group, Keith Boone (Ted's and Nell's second son) is now a district superintendent in the Texas Conference of the United Methodist Church, and William Jennings (Bill) Bryant is a professor of theology at Rice University.

Mention of Bill Bryant reminds me that our first major purchase after arriving in Dallas had to be a car. SMU was in Highland Park (where George W. Bush now has his residence), an even more affluent suburb of Dallas than Kessler Park and fifteen miles away on the opposite side of the city. There was no public transportation from the one part of Dallas to the other. So Gordon Casad took us to see a used-car dealer who was a member of the Kessler Park congregation.

After showing us various automobiles, he stopped at one, which he said was exceptionally "clean," the highest form of praise of which a used-car dealer is capable. It was a white 1965 Nash Rambler station wagon, a straight six with pushrod overhead valves and about 75,000 miles on the odometer. Its previous owner was none other than "Red" Bryant, grandfather of Bill and founder of the *Red Bryant Smokehouse* then being run by his son, Bill's father, "Sonny" Bryant. He had owned the car since it was new, three years before. The price was $1,500, which even now, I find hard to believe. That Rambler, which we purchased without hesitation, was a car I could work on, changing the oil regularly, replacing the points and spark plugs, and even taking off the cylinder head and regrinding the valves. We did at least another 100,000 miles in it as it took us throughout the United States on our annual vacations (with one or two mechanical challenges which I will recount presently) before we eventually gave it away when we returned to South Africa. For a fairly large station wagon, it got good mileage— and gasoline was then only 21–23 cents a gallon!

Our next purchases, with a newly opened Sears-Roebuck credit card, were pots and pans, sheets, blankets, pillows, crockery, and cutlery. Sears astounded us because it was open until nine o'clock and was open every day of the week! Every store in South Africa shut its doors at five and closed from Saturday afternoon until Monday morning. What we soon discovered was that credit purchases (provided one pays them off in full every month) are more advantageous than buying for cash. They enable one to establish a favorable credit rating without which no other major purchase (such as an appliance, car, or house) is possible. Ever since, we have used credit cards only for the convenience and benefits they afford, paying them off in full every month. Not once in all the years we have lived in the United States have we owed a cent of interest.

Soon the children were in school: Heather and Andrew at Rosemont Elementary across the road from our apartment, and Jenny in preschool and then kindergarten at Kessler Park. Margaret had gone back to work as a registered nurse at Methodist Hospital. And I began my graduate education at SMU. To that topic I now turn.

Although Perkins School of Theology at Southern Methodist University has a venerable history, the graduate program in science and the humanities, in which I was now enrolled as a candidate for the PhD, had only recently been accredited. I was in the inaugural class of nineteen—the only foreign student.

Soon after our arrival, Dean Wagers and his wife invited all of us and our spouses to a welcoming dinner at his home to enable us to get to know him and one another.[88] Meeting my fellow doctoral students alarmed me. I knew very little about American culture. One of its characteristics, I soon learned, is the tendency to talk about oneself with tremendous self-confidence, unintentionally (or maybe intentionally) parading all one's knowledge and accomplishments. Certainly, my fellow students exemplified this to an extraordinary degree. I felt totally inadequate as I listened to each of them. Our cultural upbringing had been the very opposite. We were taught to be diffident and unassuming, making little or nothing of what we knew and what we had done. It was only at the end of the first year that I began to feel certain of my own worth as a student and was able to assess my fellows with deeper insight.

The PhD program at SMU, like those in most other American universities, is divided into three phases. First, there are the comprehensive exams, taken whenever one felt ready, which are designed to bring everyone in the class up to the same level. In our comprehensives, there were nineteen required subjects plus the two foreign languages. Second, there are the field studies—in my case, five: the history of religion, the philosophy of religion, the psychology of religion, moral theology (ethics), and systematic theology. And thirdly, there is the dissertation.

For the first phase, we could enroll in classes anywhere

---

[88] When I was teaching at Stanford, I followed suit. Margaret and I tried always to invite my students to dinner in our home early in the quarter and again before the course ended.

in the university. I had a rich menu to choose from. Among the courses I took were Albert Outler's on the history of doctrine, John Deschner's on systematic theology and Karl Barth's theology in particular, Schubert Ogden's on Bultmann's theology, Frederick Carney's on moral theology, Van Harvey's on the history of religion, William Farmer's on the New Testament, Herndon Wagers's on the philosophy of religion, and Outler again on the history of doctrine, psychology of religion, and the history of Methodism.

Having already begun work on my two foreign languages, I decided to get them out of the way first. Within three months of our arrival, I had taken and passed the examinations in German and in Patristic Greek, which had been suggested to me by Albert Outler, rather than French. (My French was not nearly as good as my German or my New Testament [*koine*] Greek, and Patristic Greek is similar to *koine* and classical Greek).

For the remainder of the year, I assiduously audited various courses for two reasons. One was that many of the subjects on which I would be examined in the comprehensives were new to me; the other was that, whereas I had been exposed in my previous studies to British scholars, now I was being immersed by my American professors in European, and in particular, German scholarship. By the end of my first year, the only courses I had passed were the two languages. My fellow students had taken and passed nineteen different examinations, leaving themselves only the two foreign languages before moving on to phase two. This was when my sense of inadequacy was at its most acute. However, early in the second year, I successfully completed my comprehensive exams and was able to start at once on my fieldwork. The language requirement held my fellow students back for the rest of that year. It was only then that I began to believe that I was their equal and could successfully complete my PhD.

While I was in the midst of my comprehensive examinations, I received a telegram from my Mom. Gran, eighty-three years of age, had suffered a massive stroke and was in a coma. Mom said that Gran was unresponsive and urged me not to come back to see her since she would not even know I was there.[89] Word of Gran's stroke quickly spread throughout the Kessler Park congregation. A day or two later, I received a telephone call from Pan American Airways informing me that there was an open return-ticket from Dallas to Johannesburg in my name waiting for me and asking whether I would like to pick it up or have it delivered. When I inquired who had purchased the ticket, the agent was evasive, saying only that whoever it was who had done this wished to remain anonymous.

Margaret and I immediately guessed that only one person at Kessler Park would have been so thoughtful and generous: Ted Boone. I went to see Ted and asked him whether he had bought this ticket for me. He admitted that he had. I protested that I couldn't accept it; Gran was comatose and unresponsive, and I was in the middle of my comprehensive exams. I asked him please to take the ticket back. Ted refused, saying that if we didn't use it then, we could do so later. In fact, when it was time to return to South Africa, we exchanged this ticket for one-way tickets home. This is the sort of openhearted man Ted Boone was. I loved him as a brother. Gran died three weeks after I received Mom's telegram while I was writing my comprehensives. We all grieved. She was the most loving, courageous older figure in our lives, and she was the epitome of the joy of music. I will cherish until the day I die the memories of singing in harmony with her while Mom played the piano at Bedfordview.[90]

---

[89] My later work at Stanford with people in a coma or a permanent vegetative state leads me to believe that, at some level, they still are aware that they are surrounded by loved ones, even though they may be completely unresponsive.

[90] Uncle Dick died shortly after Gran; both of them at home in Mom's house in Parkhurst. Uncle Dick had had a deep vein thrombosis in his leg, which led to its amputation. Shortly after that, he had a fatal heart

After we had been in Dallas for two years, Montie Stewart left Kessler Park UMC. He was charged by the conference with building a congregation in a new suburb of Dallas, University Park, which was home to a recently established Roman Catholic university. We missed him and Marlee, although we continued to see them socially from time to time. Montie and I had started running together after I came to the sobering realization that the novel experience of homemade ice-cream socials at the church seemingly every other Sunday evening did nothing for my waistline. We ran every day, either early in the morning or in the evening, and in 1970, I ran my first marathon, organized by the Cross Country Club of Dallas, around White Rock Lake.

Montie was not replaced at Kessler Park UMC, and I had to assume many of his responsibilities, particularly visiting the sick in Methodist Hospital, assisting in worship and preaching more often, and printing the church's Sunday bulletin every Friday afternoon. I had an office on the third floor of the educational building of Kessler Park United Methodist Church (UMC) as it was now renamed.[91] I would go to this office whenever I could to read, study, and do my preparation—sometimes late at night after the children had gone to bed.

---

attack. My memories of him, like those I have of Gran, are cherished. His life was anything but easy, but he lived it without complaint, with deep wisdom, and with a wry sense of humor. Uncle Dick was a man of few words, but when he did have something to say, it was truly worth listening to.

[91] It was in 1968, while we were there, that the quadrennial conference of the Methodist Church met in Dallas. It was then that the name was changed to the United Methodist Church (UMC) when the Evangelical United Brethren (EUB), a German and more conservative cousin to British and American Methodism, united with the Methodist Church. To this day, the origin of the split within the UMC on issues such as the ordination of homosexual or bisexual ministers can be traced back to 1968 when the two branches of Methodism came together. Those opposed typically have their roots in the EUB—those in favor in the larger more liberal Methodist Church.

But it was not all work. Each summer we took three or four weeks to travel somewhere in the United States, intent on seeing all we could of the country's national parks, including the Grand Tetons, Yellowstone, and Yosemite, historical sites such as Jamestown and Vicksburg, and places of breathtaking scenic beauty such as the narrow-gauge railway line in Colorado between Silverton and Durango. We had bought a fourteen-by-fourteen-foot tent at Sears, and when the carpet was being replaced in one of the Lamplighter apartments, we managed to scrounge a fourteen-by-fourteen piece of carpet that had been under a bed and was practically new. We loaded the tent, the carpet, and our luggage onto the roof-rack of the Rambler and set off—to the East Coast one year, to the Midwest the next, to the southern states the following summer, and out to the West Coast in our final year, staying in national park campgrounds whenever we could and in private campgrounds only when there was no other alternative. We learned passionately to hate one chain of privately owned campgrounds in particular; these were always on newly established sites without trees where land was cheapest, and staying in one of them typically meant camping on bare ground without a view or any other redeeming feature.

In 1969, when we toured the southern states, we followed some of the historical milestones of the civil rights movement. In Atlanta, we went to the Ebenezer Baptist Church and met and spoke with the organist and with Martin Luther King, Senior. In Montgomery, we chatted with people who remembered the bus boycott instigated by the courageous Rosa Parks. In Memphis, we went to the Loraine Motel, standing outside the room Dr. Martin Luther King Jr. had occupied, on the very balcony where he had been taking in the evening air when he was assassinated. From the balcony, we could look up to window at the back of the room from which the assassin had shot him. The next morning, we also drove along the street above the motel and saw the same room from the front—it was one of several seedy rooms, mainly used by prostitutes, that could be rented for fifty cents a day.

The three children were crammed into the back of the station wagon. They fought constantly. The days must have been long and tedious for them despite our taking as many breaks and doing as much sightseeing along the way as possible. On one of these vacations, my Mom joined us; on another, Margaret's parents came along; on another, we had June Darroch with us; on yet another, Margaret's brother Ken[92], who had recently divorced his wife Lorraine, and one of Margaret's fellow nurses at Methodist Hospital, a South African by the name of Wendy Hope, accompanied us. How we all squeezed into the station wagon and into the tent at night is something that still amazes me. But by traveling in this fashion, we were able to visit thirty-nine of the fifty states in the union in the four years we were in Dallas. The reason for persistently taking these extended vacation trips was that we didn't think we would ever be back in the US. Our intention was to return to South Africa as soon as I had completed my PhD.

The family will not let me forget one story related to our travels. Before one of our summer road trips, I had seen an advertisement for an instant breakfast. This was a new product.

---

[92] Ken was staying with us when we saw on television the Apollo moon landing on July 16, 1969. We had not seen television prior to coming to the United States in 1967. The South African government did not to allow the South African Broadcasting Corporation (SABC) that controlled all radio broadcasting to include television among its offerings until the SABC had stockpiled enough locally produced program material to counter the liberal influence of what was available for rebroadcasting from the United Kingdom and the United States. In 1971, the SABC was finally permitted to introduce a television service and began experimental broadcasting in the main cities in mid-1975—after we had been forced to leave the country. The service went nationwide at the beginning of 1976, and until Nelson Mandela was elected prime minister in 1994, it was used principally for propaganda purposes by the nationalist government.

I assumed it was made basically of milk with added vitamins and proteins to provide one with a liquid breakfast. The thought occurred to me that if we all drank our breakfast before leaving Dallas, we could get away very early and complete the boring part of our journey, namely, driving out of Texas, before the day became hot and humid[93]. So at about four o'clock in the morning, I rallied the troops and poured us each a glass of this instant breakfast. After quaffing mine, I went out to finish packing the car, assuming everyone else had had theirs as well. This assumption was wrong. After taking sips, all four of my family members had poured theirs into the kitchen sink.

Off we went before it was even light. We had barely been on the road for ten minutes before I had to search for a gas station. I had developed stomach cramps followed by the most dreadful diarrhea. Ten minutes later, I had to stop again—and again ten minutes after that. My constant inquiries elicited the same response: the rest of the family was feeling fine. Only later did I figure out the reason for their uncontrollable laughter and the truth came out.

Three of our more challenging adventures along the road are worth recounting. One year, when my Mom was with us, we came to a national forest in the state of Virginia toward the end of the day. After being allocated a campsite, we pitched the tent. The evening was hot and humid. The children had seen a sign pointing to a "Nature Walk" as we entered the park, so while Margaret and Mom began preparing the evening meal on our Coleman camp stove, Heather, Andrew, Jenny, and I set off on the nature trail. It was exactly what we needed after a long day cramped in the station wagon. We were all in shorts. Neither Heather nor Jenny had shoes on. Andrew had no shirt on. I was wearing a T-shirt and my running shoes. We had not gone very far along the trail when it began to peter out. Obviously not many had hiked this trail that summer! The forest was thick

---

[93] The Rambler did not have air conditioning.

with trees, which made the evening darker than it would have been in the open, soon making it almost impossible to see the sky. Getting a bearing from the stars was out of the question. When it was almost pitch dark, after searching fruitlessly for a way back, I realized and had to admit to the children that we had lost the trail and that I had not the slightest notion which direction to go in order for us to retrace our steps. We had to wait until somebody came to find us, and began to make ourselves comfortable, sitting against a tree, and piling leaves over our legs to keep warm. I warned the children that it would take some time before rescuers found us. But when we did not return for dinner, I reassured them Margaret would realize that something had happened to us and would quickly get help. I took off my T-shirt and put it on Andrew, and the four of us huddled together against the tree under piles of leaves. From time to time, I whistled loudly and we all shouted to give any would-be rescuers a directional clue. And trying to keep the kids from panicking I told them stories and we sang songs for two or three hours.

Eventually, toward midnight, we could hear a ranger shouting through a bullhorn, "Mr. Young! Mr. Young!" Of course, without having a bullhorn as well, our answering reply could not be heard. But we kept on shouting and whistling and finally were found. The ranger put Jenny on his shoulders, I carried Andrew, and Heather walked out on her own. Jenny rewarded the ranger by peeing on his neck. But he led us safely back to the campsite, lectured me sternly about going into the forest inadequately clad and without a flashlight, and then told us that the greatest danger, especially in leafy areas—of which we had been totally unaware—was copperhead snakes, one of the four most venomous snakes in North America!

The two other anecdotes have to do with the car. The first occurred shortly after we arrived in Winston-Salem when the Rambler broke down. Fortunately there was a grassy area at the side of the road where we were able to pitch the tent while

I tried to diagnose the problem. I forget what precisely caused the breakdown, but I soon identified it and hitchhiked back into town to try to buy the necessary part. The Rambler dealer told me that the part was not in stock and would have to be ordered. It would take three days before it arrived. For three days, we camped at the side of the road, walking to the nearest store to buy supplies. The frisbee had recently been invented and Margaret, Heather, Andrew, Jenny, and I spent endless hours learning how to throw it. After three days, we were fairly proficient. Eventually, the part we needed arrived, I was able to install it, and we went back on the road. The fact that we had no fixed itinerary—merely a general idea of where we wanted to go and what we wanted to see—meant that our schedule was not unduly interrupted.

The other anecdote was more stress inducing. We were in Arizona, as I recall, when I noticed that the Rambler's temperature gauge was steadily climbing. This indicated either a problem with the water pump, or with the thermostat, or both. We limped into the nearest campsite at a remote and desolate campground aptly named Fort Courage. After pitching the tent while Margaret began preparing the evening meal, I began to remove the water pump and the thermostat. The bolts holding these onto the cylinder block had rusted, and I was having difficulty loosening them (I had only the most basic tools with me).

After supper, as I continued trying to loosen the bolts by flashlight, a man came over to where I was working, introduced himself to me as a highway patrol officer who lived at Fort Courage, and offered his help. When I explained my problem, he went back to his campsite and returned with an enormous socket-wrench, which he applied to the stubborn bolts with great vigor. Three of the four bolts came out cleanly, but the fourth sheared off. We were able to remove the water pump and thermostat (both of which had failed), but now we had a broken bolt in the cylinder block. We spent the rest of the night drilling out this stubborn piece of metal and re-cutting threads for a new bolt in the cylinder block, finally getting to bed in the wee hours of the morning.

The highway patrol officer had the next day off, and he kindly offered to drive me the seventy miles into the nearest town to buy the parts we needed and back again. I was touched by his generosity, but had to pay a price for it. The officer was a devout follower of Ron Hubbard, founder of Scientology, about whom and whose teachings I knew practically nothing. For the hours he had me captive in his jeep, he preached Ron Hubbard's doctrines to me. Since he had been so good as to take me into town and back, I did not have the heart to tell him I was a Methodist minister and that I was not in the least interested in converting to Scientology, so I bit my tongue and suffered in silence. We got the parts I needed, and I was able to install the new water pump and thermostat without difficulty later that afternoon.

We set off again the following morning. We had not gone very far when again I noticed the temperature gauge climbing precipitously. Once more, we had to stop at the side of the road, this time literally in the middle of nowhere with the sun blazing down on us. Our whole crew looked disconsolate and dispirited. This time, the problem was easy to identify. In drilling the broken bolt out of the cylinder head, iron filings had dropped down onto the fan belt and abraded it, causing it to snap. Fortunately, I always carried a spare. I quickly installed the new belt, and we were on our way in an hour or two—much to the relief of our family.

After living in the Lamplighter apartments for two and a half years, we discovered that however romantic, glamorous, and exciting an apartment complex may initially appear from the outside, actually living in one has major drawbacks—uncongenial neighbors, paper-thin walls, an almost total lack of privacy, and people coming and going at will, often at the most inconvenient hours of day or night. So we began to long for an alternative. There was a woman in the Kessler Park congregation, Mrs. Weaver, who had a lovely little house on Winnetka Street, only a block or two from the church (and my office). Her husband had died recently, and she was going to move nearer to her daughter, putting her furnished house up for rent. At her suggestion, we asked the church leaders whether they would be willing to pay the rent to Mrs. Weaver rather than to the Lamplighter (even though it was somewhat higher). Since I was doing far more than ministering to our young people, the church readily agreed. So early in 1970, we moved into the Winnetka Street house where we lived in greater privacy and comfort until leaving Dallas.

Meanwhile, there were intersecting developments in my graduate studies and at the church. I was well along in preparing for the five field examinations. For each of these fields, I had an adviser. He would outline the area of expertise he expected me to acquire and suggest a substantial bibliography for me to work my way through. I was also free to audit whatever courses might help me with my field studies.

By that time, I had decided on the subject of my dissertation. This proved to be highly advantageous since my fellow students were to spend almost an entire year trying to figure out what topics they were going to research and write about. Alarmed, as many liberal South Africans were, by the increasingly authoritarian nature of the supposedly "Christian" (Reformed Church) Nationalist government in South Africa, with its rigorous laws segregating whites, blacks, Indians, Chinese, and coloreds, with its secret police (the Special Branch), its limitations on freedom of the press, its detentions without trial, and its relentless suppression of dissidents, I was determined to try to understand the process by which the Reformed theologian *par excellence*, Karl Barth, had come to oppose the Nazi regime, and to identify the point beyond which a Christian in any country has to refuse to give allegiance to an increasingly dictatorial and demonic state. Many of Barth's political writings had not been translated into English from the German, and I would read and translate these as I worked away in the general area of social and political ethics. My five fields were tailored accordingly, with each designed to illumine an aspect of this principal theme. It had taken me more than a year to feel that I had mastered the subject matter in each and was ready to write the required eight-hour examinations.

At about the same time, Gordon Casad was moved by the conference from Kessler Park United Methodist Church to the far bigger and more prestigious First United Methodist Church in downtown Dallas.[94] The conference replaced him with a fairly ordinary-looking, skinny little man. Despite his looks, I took to the new minister in the first few months of his brief tenure. He was the very antithesis of Gordon. Whereas Gordon was conservative, he was ultraliberal. Gordon's moral horizons did not extend much beyond the behavior of individuals; he was concerned about matters of social justice. Gordon had been distant and aloof; this pastor was warm and accessible. Gordon was extremely formal; his successor was relaxed and almost casual. The church welcomed the change. There was a more joyful, spontaneous spirit in the worship services, and the new minister's preaching addressing the pressing social issues of the day, including race relations and civil rights, was in stark contrast to Gordon's.

During Lent of 1969, shortly before I was scheduled to take my five eight-hour field exams, I received a sobering telephone call from Irving Gathings, the district superintendent. Without going into details, he informed me that Gordon's successor was being removed immediately from his appointment at Kessler Park and had been asked to resign from the ministry

---

[94] Shortly after returning to South Africa in 1970, we heard that Gordon Casad had had a fatal heart attack while he was the senior minister at First Methodist in Dallas.

for reasons of moral turpitude.[95] Mr. Gathings asked me to take responsibility for the Holy Week services (including the Good Friday service) and the Easter services as well as overall pastoral duties until an interim replacement could be appointed. This was terribly short notice, but I put my academic work aside and got down to thinking about, planning, and preparing three midweek services, a full-blown service on Good Friday, and the Easter Sunday services, morning and evening. Somehow it all came together, and the church survived the loss of a minister who in the short time he had been there had breathed fresh air into the congregation.

Soon after Easter, the district superintendent moved quickly to appoint an interim minister, a retired Perkins professor of homiletics by the name of George T. Baker. I went off by myself for a week to a cabin in the woods that had been kindly offered to me by someone in the congregation, taking with me about seven hundred books[96] to get ready for my field examinations the week after I came back. Without any of my usual church and family responsibilities, I was able to work for about fourteen hours each day and came back ready to confront whatever awaited me.

I had never taken an eight-hour exam in my life, let alone five in the space of ten days with a day between each to shift gears for the following—nor have I since. I arrived at SMU at eight o'clock in the morning with my secondhand IBM Selectric typewriter. I was shown into a room, which I had all to myself, was given an envelope with the examination questions inside, and was told to work until five o'clock, taking an hour for lunch. This process was repeated every other day until I had completed

---

[95] We subsequently learned that he had been having concurrent extramarital affairs with nine women in the congregation.

[96] I had read all these books and summarized the important points on index cards. I wanted to go through the cards and look up the important references, rereading each in context.

all five. I remember feeling pleased with the questions in each exam. They allowed me to demonstrate what I knew rather than probing to expose what I did not know.

Once I had studied the various questions and sketched out an outline of my answer to each, I started typing and kept going until five o'clock, not pausing to eat lunch or even read what I had written before putting my paper into the envelope, sealing it, and handing it in. My preparation paid off. I passed all five with high marks. I still have those five envelopes. They were returned to me with the examiners' comments, but I have never opened them. I knew I had done well, and after the insecurity of those first two years, it was a good feeling. I could start immediately on my dissertation.

But before describing my research, I must interrupt myself to tell of totally unexpected good news on the home front. Margaret was again pregnant, ten years after the birth of Heather. She was working the night shift at the time so that she could be there when Heather, Andrew, and Jenny came home from school. After supper, I would go to my office to work, getting home by ten o'clock to spend half an hour with Margaret before she went off to the hospital for the 11:00 p.m.– 7:00 a.m. shift. She often says, "We are still looking for the star in the East!" We made an appointment to see Dr. Harrell, and he confirmed that she was pregnant and graciously offered to give her regular prenatal care and then deliver the baby in November 1970—without charge. His generosity was such that I could not protest or complain when again he firmly told me that he did not allow fathers into his delivery room, not wanting to be distracted by hysterical men—a generalization I found mildly offensive but chose to ignore.

The congregation, of course, was delighted. They at once arranged a baby shower. One of the gifts was a crib with one-, five-, ten-, and twenty-dollar bills pegged onto cords that were strung back and forth across the top and to the bottom corners of the crib. We traveled west that summer, seeing the Grand

Canyon, the Petrified Forest, the Mesa Verde, and the states of Washington, Oregon, and California, ending up at Disneyland, Universal Studios, and Marine World. Dr. Harrell had insisted on Margaret flying home from Los Angeles. After putting her on the plane to Love Field, the four of us took three days to drive the 1,200 miles home.

Margaret kept working until two or three weeks before our fourth child was born. On November 11, 1970, I took her into the hospital in the afternoon—and Timothy Matthew came into the world before suppertime. After being allowed briefly to hug Margaret and hold my baby, I rushed home to collect our three older children so that they could welcome their new little brother. We were only allowed to see him through the glass window of the newborn nursery. A nurse held him up for us, and we were all enthralled with this beautiful little boy. Heather, in particular, immediately regarded herself as his surrogate mother—and she still does.

At the Annual Conference of the United Methodist Church,[97] Dr. Bruce Weaver was appointed pastor of Kessler Park. I took to him at once. He was not a spectacular preacher, but he was as solid as a rock. He cared about people. He was committed to social justice. And he was a genuine human being, a *mensch*. He and I became firm friends as well as good colleagues.

Bruce did not have an easy time of it at Kessler. There were wounds in the congregation that had to be healed. That said,

---

[97] In 1968, at the Quadrennial General Conference, held every four years, the Methodist Church had united with the Evangelical United Brethren, an ultraconservative German offshoot of Methodism. The newly merged church was to be called the United Methodist Church. To this day, as mentioned previously, over such important issues as homosexuality, the United Methodist Church is anything but united. There are resulting tensions and divisions even at the highest levels of the church's hierarchy. These led to a decision at the 2016 Quadrennial Conference in Portland, Oregon, to defer a final decision on the church's official stance on homosexual ministers until 2020.

one of his first initiatives was to commission a demographic study of the Kessler Park area, which showed, as I mentioned earlier, that the racial composition of the suburb was rapidly changing. Bruce attempted to prepare his congregation for these demographic changes, but racial prejudice against Hispanics and African Americans made it difficult for many in the church to hear what he was saying. The message was repudiated—and so eventually was the messenger. And after the charismatic ex-minister and the melodramatic Dr. Baker—the interim minister—Bruce Weaver's matter-of-fact style did not win the hearts of his people. I became not only his friend but also his confidant, and for the short time we were together, we made an effective team.

Once I started work on my dissertation, my office at the church doubled as a nursery as Margaret and I established a new routine. When Timothy was only three or four weeks old, Margaret went back to working the night shift at Methodist Hospital.[98] She would come home at 7:00 a.m. and breast-feed Timothy. We would see the three older children off to school. Before going to sleep, Margaret would pump breast milk into a bottle and I would go to my office with baby Timothy, his diaper bag and bottle of milk for his morning tea and lunch, my own sandwich for lunch, and whatever other baby toiletries I needed. I would put him down to sleep in his crib in a room adjacent to my office where I could close the blinds, making the room dark. I would work until he woke up two or three hours later. As soon as he woke, I would feed and change him and then put him into his reclining chair on the top of my desk and carry on working for another hour or two. Then he would

---

[98] At about this time, Ted Boone also performed a vasectomy on me. One last surprise in our family planning was enough. I had promised Heather, Andrew, and Jenny that I would take them to "Six Flags Over Texas" when school recessed for the Christmas holiday. I kept my promise the day after my vasectomy and, to put it mildly, that was one of the more painful and uncomfortable days of my entire life!

have another nap. We would go home at about three thirty, by which time Margaret was awake and the three older children were coming back from school. While Margaret prepared our evening meal and the children did their homework, I would go for a run. Heather, Andrew, Jenny, and I would then go over to the church lawn to play baseball or touch football or throw the Frisbee for half an hour or so. After supper, I would walk over to my office and work until ten, come home to spend some time with Margaret before she went off to the hospital, and then go to bed. When Margaret had her days off, I would go over to SMU to meet with my professorial advisers to show them what I had written and to receive their critique and comments.

In this way, I made remarkable progress on the dissertation. By the time I had finished a first draft, I had written more than five hundred pages. These had then to be reviewed by each of my three advisers: Albert Outler, Charles Lloyd, and Leroy Howe (John Deschner, my primary adviser, was away on sabbatical that year). Then there was the arduous task of incorporating my advisers' suggestions into the manuscript and then completely retyping the entire thesis on my Selectric— since those were the days before computers and the facility they afford for pagination, cutting, and pasting. I handed in my finished manuscript on April 19, 1971—"Church and State in the Theology of Karl Barth." By April 29 (Margaret's and Andrew's birthdays), I had successfully defended my thesis in a public oral examination. Graduation was on a Saturday in late May,[99] and after church the following day, we flew from Dallas to Johannesburg via Rio de Janeiro where we would spend a week on vacation.

In anticipation of my graduation in June, we had made a family decision to send Heather, now aged ten, back to South Africa in January to stay with Margaret's Mom and Dad in

---

[99] Of the nineteen who had started studying for the PhD degree four years earlier, I was the first to graduate.

the new home they were building at Halfway House. This was done so that she could begin school at the beginning of the South African school year and was another of the many lateral moves from school to school that Heather, Andrew, and Jenny made in the course of their childhoods. They were all bright enough to complete less than two-thirds of the school year in one country and then enter the following grade in a school in another country without ever falling behind, but it could not have been easy for them. Ours was a happy home, and the long separations from their parents and siblings, however glad their grandparents were to have them, must have been difficult in the extreme.

So early in the New Year, Heather and I flew to New York and spent a night in a Manhattan hotel. The next morning we went by taxi to JFK airport for her to board a direct flight to Johannesburg and where I entrusted her to the care of a flight attendant. Juliet Prouse, the famous South African dancer who had moved to the United States because of the greater career opportunities this afforded, was on the same flight traveling first class. She (and others) took pity on our plucky little ten-year-old and gave her as much attention as any child could have wished for. Grandma, Granny, and Papa were there to meet and make a huge fuss of her when she landed at Jan Smuts International Airport.

This is Heather's own mature recollection[100] written at my request of what for her at the time must have been a truly momentous upheaval:

---

[100] I have not edited these paragraphs in which Heather recently described what she felt as a child in her own words. She has provided written permission for me to include her description in this memoir.

I was quite surprised to learn that I was going back to South Africa ahead of the family, to start the school year in January. I had very mixed feelings about the whole idea. Part of me was excited to go back and be with Granny, Papa, and Grandma, whom I adored. Another part of me was heartbroken to leave my new five-week-old brother who had become the love of my life in his short time on the planet. I was also a bit confused about the plan because I was leaving in the middle of a school year, where I knew my teachers and friends, so it didn't make sense to me as I would be off time either way—this led to a bit of a niggling insecurity about whether this was a plan to get rid of me! But the adventure began—starting with the outfit and luggage. I was so thrilled to wear my navy blue dress with red and white neckline and the coolest slick red boots. I had a new carry-on bag to hold the watch and twenty-four wrapped small gifts some kind person in the church had given me to open, one every hour, throughout my upcoming twenty-four hours of flight.

Dad flew with me to New York to get me on the international flight. This was before flight attendants took charge of small travelers in the way they do now. We stayed in a hotel, and the city was gray and cold with more cars than I had ever seen. Dad told me that night that Uncle Winnie and Aunty Jean had divorced while we were in Dallas, preparing me for this new situation. I was stunned and shocked and couldn't stop thinking about it and about the boys. It was the first divorce I had really heard about, and it scared me and added to my niggling insecurity.

It was so hard to say goodbye to Dad the next day at the departure area, but I was quickly distracted from my tears by the bag-check officers behind the big doors. They opened my bag and asked what was in the wrapped gifts. I excitedly told them I would find out when I unwrapped them on the hour for the next day. To my chagrin, they ordered me to unwrap them right then. In disbelief, I opened each small gift. Then they said, "Fine—repack them." This was easier said than done. Surrounded by paper, I attempted to repack and had a lot of trouble getting them to fit back in the bag. The officials looked on with no offer of help. Just as I struggled to zip it shut, the zip caught in the pompom of my slipper and jammed. Now I was hopelessly stuck. A kind gentleman behind me came to my aid and repacked the bag and said, "Come with me. We will find the plane together." He was in first class but came to visit me and invited me up for a coke with him during our trip to Rio. During our seven hours in Rio, he made sure I had something to eat and got me back on the plane. When we landed, he stayed with me until Granny and Papa found me. I think Papa was surprised to meet my handsome escort, probably fearing a pedophile! He interviewed him about where he worked (a bank) and his name, etc. and we wrote a thank-you letter the next day.

I arrived on Christmas Eve, and it was *so* exciting. Granny had a buffet ready at the Hillbrow flat, and so many family members came. I couldn't believe how happy I felt to see them all. Shortly after I got there Granny handed me a plate to fill, and before I put a thing on the white plate, a huge drop of blood landed on it—the start of a major nosebleed, an embarrassing drama on my first night.

I loved the Hillbrow flat with the old lift, the balcony, and Granny's couch where I slept. We spent Christmas and Boxing Day with Aunty Gwen and all the Rowe family—and that was so much fun—I loved every second of it. Two weeks later, we moved to Halfway House on a very stormy day, to the second of five homes I would occupy in the upcoming seven months. The water was rushing high across the dirt road to our temporary rental home on Pitzer Road, and our car got stuck. Gill and Ron had to get us out of the ditch in the darkness and mud.

The Pitzer house was wonderful—big porch and my own room for the first time in my life. We rented it for three months while construction was getting completed on the new home that Granny, Papa, Ken, and Deanne were building a few fields away.

I loved being there—except for the night I went to the toilet and saw a black mamba coiled in the corner. I climbed up on the tank and yelled. Papa came in and killed it with a spade. I went to Halfway House Primary School, a mixed English/Afrikaans school nearby. Because there were only three English kids in my grade, they were teaching all the classes in Afrikaans. Unfortunately, I did not speak Afrikaans, but I learned enough quickly enough to understand a bit and get by playing with other kids. Weekends were fun, visiting Grandma and the boys, Aunty Gwen, or Gill and Ron.

Construction took longer than the lease, so we moved into Aunty Gwen's kombi, very tight quarters. After a few cramped nights, Papa asked a neighbor if I could sleep at their house, so for a few weeks, he would walk me over there after supper, and I would catch the bus to school from their place in the morning. I hated going there because their house smelled funny and they were mean. But I didn't want to complain about anything because Granny and Papa were so kind to me, and I knew Granny wasn't happy camping either! She singed her hair with the cook stove and dropped her torch down the pit toilet, so I knew it was not her dream!

As soon as we could, we moved into the new house. First on concrete floors with an air mattress, then slowly carpet and furniture came. We were so glad to be in with their radio back on to listen to the BBC world service and the stories. Granny cooked the best food—boerewors and potatoes and gravy, steak and kidney pie, chiffon cake—all my favorites. Then the best excitement of all—the family was coming home. We spent a couple of weeks getting ready, anticipating going to Jan Smuts to pick everyone up. It was strange to have 5 percent of my life unknown to my family, and Tim was so much bigger!

Reflecting back on this experience, I am aware of a lot of the emotions I don't think I let myself feel then. I remember hearing from everyone that I was a brave girl, so I tried to live up to that. I only remember crying once, in the field, after I got a letter from Mom and Dad and felt very homesick. Overall, I thought it was a great adventure, and I loved being back in South Africa with all the family. I think it gave me a sense of self-confidence and courage. I learned to adapt quickly to uncomfortable situations. I am a confident and avid solo traveler to this day. I had a rich inner life, with elaborate fantasies that I could take with me anywhere, even when I didn't have friends. I am still very sensitive to newcomers and make a point of welcoming people whenever that is the situation. I think it helped me be a good nurse, able to focus on what another person needs rather than my own feelings of shock, sadness, anger, and fear—I save those for later, private times. Most of all, I always felt in our family that everything is possible and you just have to do it.

⌒

Five months later, the rest of us left Dallas and SMU—with mixed feelings. The Kessler Park congregation had been amazingly kind and generous to our little family. They had taken us into their hearts and given us a home away from home for four years. We would remain lifelong friends with many of them. But Dallas, as a whole, was and is politically and theologically conservative, something which we did not and do not find congenial. SMU, in contrast, was a liberal oasis in the midst of a largely fundamentalist desert. There were mixed-race couples living at SMU who dared not be seen together off campus, such was the level of racial prejudice in the city of Dallas.

The graduate program in the sciences and humanities had enabled me to have the best possible graduate education I could have hoped for. Bidwell Library at SMU is indeed one of the finest in the nation, and its librarians had been unfailingly helpful to me in my research. In one respect, I was extremely fortunate to have had a foot in the very different worlds of academia and the city.[101] Without my knowing it at the time, this helped prepare me for the struggle that was to come in the ultraconservative city of Bloemfontein, South Africa.

---

[101] Despite what I have said about the conservatism of Dallas, I was pleased to accept the Freedom of the City, which was bestowed on me shortly before our return to South Africa, for the work our youth group had been doing with underprivileged minority youths in the city as part of the service program I had developed at Kessler Park.

8

Concluding Ministry in South Africa

Berea, Johannesburg

During our final year at Southern Methodist University we notified the Methodist Church of South Africa of our expected return and began receiving invitations from various congregations to become their minister at the beginning of 1972. After discussing this between us, Margaret and I decided to accept an invitation to serve in Bloemfontein as the superintendent minister of the Trinity Methodist Church and the Bloemfontein Circuits—white, African, and colored—with oversight of and pastoral responsibility for some forty-two thousand Methodists. As we were serious about working for change in South Africa we felt we should try to do this where change was least likely. And Bloemfontein was notoriously, even frighteningly, *verkrampte*.[102]

But there would be more than six months after our return before the annual conference, meeting in October 1971, would formally appoint me to Bloemfontein—effective the following January. So we decided to accept a second fortuitous invitation from Berea Methodist Church in Johannesburg for that interim

---

[102] *Verkrampte* is an Afrikaans word meaning ultraconservative on socially important issues such as race relations and white supremacy.

period—July until December 1971—to be their superintendent minister *pro tem*. The minister at Berea, Kenneth Wardle, and I had been at Rhodes together for a couple of years; we were well acquainted and on excellent terms. Ken was originally from England and had decided to emigrate from South Africa to Canada because of his pessimism about what was happening in the country under the Nationalist government's apartheid policies. He was leaving at the end of June and wrote to ask if I would fill in for him at Berea for the rest of the year, after which time, a permanent replacement appointed at the October conference would take over. We seized the opportunity with alacrity. Being back in Johannesburg would mean that we would be reunited with Heather without her needing to change schools again, close to our families and friends, and our children to their grandparents. Besides, it was our home town, and in many ways, we would be returning to a familiar and well-loved environment.

Using the open United Airlines ticket that Ted Boone had given us when Gran was so ill, and after selling a piece of property we had bought at Kelso Beach on the Natal South Coast five or six years previously for which we had received a generous offer, we were able to buy the necessary tickets to fly all five of us back to South Africa the day after I graduated from SMU, having earned my PhD.

The flight was via Rio de Janeiro (as Heather's had been when she flew back ahead of us), and we decided to spend a week in that city having a well-earned family vacation. We reserved a large room in a modest hotel near Copacabana Beach. The three children reveled in being able to enjoy most of the day on the flat sands of the beach or in the warm, shallow water of the magnificent bay. We did as much sightseeing as we could; the highlight was the huge statue of Christ that overlooks the city. Timothy, however, got the flu, and we couldn't go out much at night.

Margaret generously stayed in the hotel with the children

one evening while I went on a small guided tour of the city. I had particularly wanted to experience a *Macumba* religious service and was taken to a nondescript, smoke-filled building where such an event was in progress, presided over by an enormous woman priestess smoking an extremely large cigar. The devotees of this cult work themselves into a trancelike state by gyrating, ever faster, to the beating of drums, before falling to the ground, convulsing, and then speaking in tongues. It was a scene unlike any I had ever encountered, and the memory of it has remained unforgettably vivid more than four decades later.

Equally unforgettable was the stark contrast between the opulence of the Copacabana beachfront with its luxurious hotels and apartments and the dire poverty of the teeming multitudes living in *Favelas,* shanties on the slopes of the hills directly above and behind them—without electricity, running water, or sanitation, and with drugs, prostitution, and collateral crime in abundance.[103] It was all so familiar from our experience in South Africa where the contrast between the northern suburbs of Johannesburg, for example, and the surrounding townships of Alexandria, Sophiatown, and SOWETO[104] was as stark, shameful, and tragic.

Our arrival home was indescribably joyful. We were back with Heather. We found my Mom and Margaret's Mom and Dad in good health; we reconnected with our closest friends and

---

[103] One evening as I was strolling outside our hotel after dinner, a girl no more than ten-years-old came up to me and offered to take me to bed with her for a pack of cigarettes. I told her I didn't smoke cigarettes, gave her the few dollars I had with me, and urged her to return home and go to bed by herself.

[104] SOWETO, as noted previously, is an acronym for South Western Townships. After Sophiatown had been razed to the ground to make room for a white suburb, ironically named Triomf (an Afrikaans word meaning triumph), the Africans were moved involuntarily to these newly built townships consisting of row upon endless row of cement boxes with two tiny rooms, a kitchen, and a bathroom in each.

were generally welcomed like prodigals. Until the Berea manse became available, we stayed with Uncle Tom and Aunty Ivy in Forest Town, opposite the Johannesburg Zoo. Jenny joined Heather at Barnato Park School for Girls. Andrew started at the King Edward's Preparatory School for Boys. And as Margaret's Mom and Dad were still building their new home at Halfway House, we worked with them, among other things making and putting in a stairway from the ground floor to the upstairs bedrooms.

At the beginning of July, I took up my interim appointment at Berea. We moved into the manse, an old Victorian house on beautiful grounds adjacent to the church. The children's schools were within walking distance, and Saint John's College was over the road from us. I made good use of its rugby fields for my regular early morning run. Aunt Elaine gave us her fine old upright Steinway piano, and we had it moved into the manse. One of our treasured photographs of baby Timothy at twelve-months-old shows him, barely able to walk, standing at the piano naked, holding himself upright with one arm and reaching up to the keyboard with the other. In retrospect, we can say that he was entranced with the thought of making music from his earliest days.

The congregation at Berea warmed to us immediately. This was an all-white church, but it was fiercely liberal. Under the leadership of Professor Trefor Jenkins, who with his wife Ada lived in Yeoville, several members of the church were involved in regular multiracial dinner meetings at the Jenkins's home and at the homes of some of the colored Methodists in Coronationville. Margaret and I immediately became involved whenever we could find a babysitter. These meetings provided an opportunity for members of different racial groups to meet socially and get to know one another intimately; they also introduced us to the difficulties and dangers being faced daily by those living in the townships. They gave us avenues for collective, constructive action. Today, more than forty years later, Trefor is still a close friend.[105] He is a medical doctor and geneticist who has done extensive genetic studies of the !Kung in Botswana, and was for many years director of the Institute for Medical Research at the University of the Witwatersrand.[106] In 1979 and again in 1980, after we had returned to the United States (and after I had become a US citizen), Trefor invited me to Wits for three weeks each time to work with him in introducing biomedical ethics into the university's medical school curriculum.

Among the clergy already in Johannesburg when I arrived on the scene was a young Scot, a popular Presbyterian pastor.[107] Like many ministers, he had been outspokenly critical of the government's apartheid policies. Johannesburg, at the time, seemed to be fairly tolerant of antigovernment speech. The theater in Johannesburg, for example, welcomed mixed audiences and produced plays by the well-known critic of apartheid, Athol Fugard. I had joined the interfaith, inter-denomination clergy association shortly after my arrival. This enabled me to come to know many of city's spiritual leaders, this young minister included.

A few months later, at one of our meetings, he stood up and said farewell to the group. He had resigned from the church he had served for the previous four years and was leaving South Africa permanently. The reason was simple but sobering. He and his wife had recently been receiving regular anonymous

---

[105] Sadly, his wife Ada died of cancer in 2014.

[106] Trefor had also collected blood samples for genetic analysis from prominent Afrikaner politicians, the architects and enforcers of apartheid. He discovered that all these proponents of racial purity had genetic markers of mixed-race ancestry, much as was true of the progeny of slave owners in the United States.

[107] Details in this and the next paragraph have been altered to protect this family's identity. I do not remember their real names. The circumstances in which I became acquainted with the pastor have been altered, as has his denomination and nationality.

telephone calls threatening the life of their five-year-old daughter. "We know the bus your child takes home from school each day," the callers had stated. "Unless you stop criticizing our government, she will not be on the bus when you go to meet her at the bus stop. You will never see her again." This couple could not deny what their consciences prompted them to say and do. Nor could they risk the life of their only child. Their only option seemed to be to return to Scotland.

A colleague who knew the circumstances of the family's decision better than I mentioned that they had lodged repeated complaints with the police. However, the police were dismissive and uninterested when they asked for protection after these incidents—even when they had gone so far as to make tape recordings of the telephone threats for the police to listen to. This episode opened my eyes. It helped me realize afresh that, beneath the apparently democratic surface of life in Johannesburg, the currents of incipient totalitarianism in South Africa ran powerfully and deep.

A primary reason for concentrating on the Reformed Protestant tradition in general and Karl Barth's theology of church and state in particular during my graduate studies was to be able to enter into an informed conversation with Dutch Reformed ministers about their general accommodation to the ideology of apartheid. With notable exceptions, among them Albert Geyser (with whom I had studied at Wits), Beyers Naudé (subsequently placed under house arrest), Frederick van Wyk (director of the South African Institute for Race Relations), and a young theologian named Pieter Schumann (whom I had met while he was doing his graduate work at Kampen University in Holland where his best friend was a fellow South African colored minister by the name of Allan Boesak[108]), the

---

[108] Allan Boesack subsequently became a professor of theology at the University of the Western Cape. He was elected president of the World Reformed Federation (the WRF). Ironically, the WRF later

majority of the Dutch Reformed Churches' *dominees* (clergy)[109] were solidly supportive of the government's policies. On one occasion I was invited to address a combined meeting of about sixty Johannesburg clergy of the three Dutch Reformed Churches, and in accepting the invitation I announced that "Civil Disobedience in the Reformed Tradition" would be my topic.

Beginning with John Calvin's view of civil disobedience as set forth in the *Institutes,*[110] working my way through the early seventeenth-century Reformed theologian Johannes Althusius,[111] and concluding with my own research on church and state in the theology of Karl Barth, I forcefully made the case that, in the Reformed tradition, the church's highest allegiance and duty is not to the state but to the God of love and justice revealed in the prophets and in the life and ministry of Jesus, and that when these come into conflict civil disobedience is not merely an option but an inescapable moral obligation.

My presentation was greeted with stony silence, broken only by one senior clergyman eventually standing up and saying (in Afrikaans), "If this is what Calvin said, we have no choice but to dissociate ourselves from him." His position

---

expelled the South African Reformed churches (see the following footnote) because of their support for apartheid while Allan remained leader of this worldwide organization.

[109] There were three Dutch Reformed Churches in South Africa at the time: the *Hervormde Kerk*, the *Gereformeerde Kerk*, and the *Hervormde of Gereformeerde Kerk*. The Gereformeerde Kerk was the most liberal (*verligte*), and the Hervormde Kerk the most ultraconservative (*verkrampte*). None of these churches was integrated, as the Methodist Church of South Africa was—at least at the conference level and in its public pronouncements. All had separate *"dogter kerke"* (daughter churches) for Africans and coloreds. In true parental fashion, the white churches were the *"moeder kerke"* (mother churches).

[110] John Calvin, *Institutes of the Christian Religion,* 1536.

[111] *The Politics of Johannes Althusius,* abridged and translated by Frederick S. Carney, Boston, Beacon Press: 1964.

was tantamount to a Muslim declaring that he did not believe Muhammad was Allah's prophet, or a Lutheran denouncing Martin Luther. Needless to say, I received no further invitations from Dutch Reformed clergy to meet with them or discuss their support of the government's apartheid policies.

One of the best things, professionally, about being back in Johannesburg was that I was able to renew my links with the South African Council of Churches, of which my friend John Rees (a fellow Methodist, and also an old boy of Jeppe High School) was the general secretary (the first layperson to hold this distinguished position), and with the South African Institute for Race Relations. These contacts had long-term consequences for my subsequent work in Bloemfontein and were also immediately valuable. The Institute's publications on race relations provided abundant factual material to back up appeals for social justice. The Council of Churches provided ample opportunities for ecumenical work to create a better South Africa. Under the editorship of John de Gruchy—who had written his doctoral dissertation on Dietrich Bonhoeffer (sentenced to death for conspiring to assassinate Adolph Hitler)—I was invited to join the editorial board and became a contributor to the Council's new *Journal of Theology for Southern Africa*. Our six months at Berea were packed and exhilarating.

However, a few weeks before we were due to leave and take up the Bloemfontein appointment, Timothy had a most unfortunate accident. The Berea manse was almost a hundred years old. Since it only had one electrical outlet in the kitchen, we had an electric kettle on a small table at the end of a long passage that led into the kitchen; there was another plug-socket low down in the wall of the hallway, close to the kitchen. One day in December, as we sat down to lunch with the kettle coming to the boil in the passageway immediately behind us, Timothy, who had just started walking, toddled down the passage toward the kitchen, steadying himself with one hand against the wall. When he came to the small table with the boiling kettle, he grabbed the electric cord and pulled the kettle on top of his head and upper body. He was wearing a woolen sweater, and this soaked up the boiling water and held it against his chest. Startled by his agonized screams, we leaped up from the table. Margaret rushed him to the bathroom, stripped off his clothes, and put him into a bath of cold water while I got all the ice that was in the refrigerator to add to the water in the bath and then went to call for an ambulance. Timothy was rushed to the Children's Hospital in Johannesburg where he was admitted to the burn unit. He had severe burns on his chest and face. The physicians attending him told us that it was possible that he would never see again; it looked as though the boiling water had burned his eyes as well as his face. Thankfully, this proved not to be the case, but he remained in the hospital for the next seven weeks.

Meanwhile, I had to leave for Bloemfontein to take up my new appointment. Margaret and the other three children remained behind in Johannesburg and joined me only after Timothy had been discharged five weeks later from Children's Hospital to the care of a Bloemfontein plastic surgeon named Maxine Stillwell.[112] We were delighted to discover that Dr. Stillwell was a Sunday school teacher at Trinity Methodist Church, and she later became one of our few close and trusted friends in that city. The initial concern was whether Timothy's scars would be hypertrophic (raised scars) or, more seriously, keloid (which can be precursors of skin cancer). They turned out to be hypertrophic. We are profoundly grateful that Timothy's face and eyes had no scarring whatsoever and that the scars on his chest and upper arms, while having expanded as he grew from childhood to adulthood, have also become less markedly raised and have faded considerably.

The six months we spent at Berea helped re-awaken us

---

[112] A pseudonym used to protect her identity. The person she represents is now deceased.

to the realities of apartheid South Africa. In the previous decade, without our fully appreciating their significance, signal events had been taking place not only around us but also during our four-year absence in the United States. For example, without warning, on March 21 1960, at Sharpeville, an African township outside Vereeniging, south of Johannesburg in the Transvaal, South African police had shot into a crowd of about five thousand unarmed Africans who were protesting against the government's "pass laws."[113] At least sixty-nine had been murdered in cold blood, and more than two hundred were wounded. Most were shot in the back as they tried to escape the police cordon. As "South Africa History Online," devoted to documenting the struggle for freedom and equality, puts it:

The massacre created a crisis for the apartheid government both inside the country and internationally. The government immediately declared a State of Emergency and banned political meetings. Within less than a month, it banned both the Pan African Congress (PAC), which had organized the action in Sharpeville, and the African National Congress (ANC). After lengthy internal discussions, the ANC and PAC turned to armed struggle and went underground.

Umkhonto we Sizwe, "the Spear of the Nation," was the name in both Zulu and Xhosa for the armed wing of the ANC that had been cofounded by Nelson Mandela, Jo Slovo of the South African Communist Party, Walter Sisulu, and several others. Many of these leaders were now in exile, continuing their resistance from outside the country's borders. Within South Africa, power stations and various other government installations were being sabotaged. On October 30, 1963, ten of the leaders of *Umkhonto*

---

[113] The pass laws required Africans to carry at all times an identity document without which they were not allowed to enter cities like Johannesburg.

we Sizwe, including Mandela, were arrested at an isolated farm near Rivonia, Johannesburg, and subsequently brought to trial for their lives on charges of sabotage.

"In arguably the most profound moment in the trial, Nelson Mandela made a speech in the dock in which he condemned the very court in which he was appearing as 'illegitimate.' He ... argued that the laws in place were equally draconian and that defiance of these laws was justified."[114] The trial ended on June 12, 1964. Nelson Mandela and seven others were sentenced to life imprisonment. Mandela was incarcerated on Robben Island for nineteen years, was then transferred to Pollsmoor Prison in Tokai, Cape Town, for seven years, and finally, for two years to a house on the grounds of Victor Verster Prison in Paarl.

In response to continued unrest, the government was to display less and less tolerance for dissidents. Midnight raids on the homes of suspected "communists"[115] by the Special Branch were a common means of intimidation. Steve Biko had been detained in Port Elizabeth and brutally assaulted during interrogation. The police drove him naked in the back of a police van to Pretoria Central Prison where he died. Minister Jimmy Kruger said that Biko's death left him cold and tried to make out that he had died from a hunger strike; but Helen Zille and her editor at the *Rand Daily Mail*, Allister Sparks, courageously revealed that Biko died from brain damage caused by deliberate police brutality.[116]

Meanwhile, the African, colored, and Asian peoples of South Africa were quietly, steadily, and with inflexible

---

[114] See "South African History Online."

[115] I will go into the insidious nature of the Suppression of Communism Act in the following chapter. Suffice now to note that the term *communist* served as an umbrella description of those who opposed the government's ideology of white supremacy and provided the pretext for harassing, banning, or imprisoning them.

[116] I am indebted to Johann Maree for providing me with details about Nelson Mandela's imprisonment and Steve Biko's death.

determination uniting and mobilizing their energies to overthrow the prevailing political regime. At the same time, the world outside South Africa was beginning to regard the country as a pariah. More and more nations were starting to exert pressure on the South African government through economic sanctions and boycotts to force it to change its inhumane policies. The International Olympic Committee, the Fédération Internationale de Football Association (FIFA), and other international sports organizations terminated South Africa's membership. Such was the prevailing situation in the country to which we had returned to work for change. Without being fully aware of it, our six months in Berea prepared us for the struggle in which we would more overtly and actively be engaged once we began our work in Bloemfontein.

Bloemfontein, the Orange Free State

Bloemfontein (an Afrikaans word meaning "fountain of flowers") is the seat of the South African Supreme Court and is the country's judicial capital.[117] It was also the capital of the Orange Free State—one of the two Boer republics (Transvaal being the other) defeated by Britain in the second Anglo-Boer war of 1898–1903 and then incorporated into the Union of South Africa in 1910. When we arrived in 1972, it was probably *the* most conservative (*verkrampte)* city in the country, comparable to Alabama and Mississippi in the United States circa 1950 (and the emotional temperature of Charlottesville, Virginia in 2017) in terms of its racial intolerance, not to say outright hatred, and its entrenched and outspoken belief in white supremacy.

Trinity Methodist Church, with 1,500 members, "The Church of the Friendly Welcome" as a large sign outside

---

[117] Cape Town is the legislative capital city of South Africa, and Pretoria is the administrative capital. Johannesburg is informally known and recognized as the financial capital.

the building proudly and prominently proclaimed, was the largest church in the Bloemfontein-Kroonstad circuit. As the superintendent minister, I was primarily responsible for the pastoral care of this congregation and visited each of its 1,500 families once a year in their own homes, in addition to visiting every day those who had been admitted to the National Hospital in Bloemfontein or had called for pastoral care.

John Lewis had been assigned by the conference to be my assistant; he and his wife Barbara became our good friends as well as colleagues. Wesley was the other white Methodist Church in the city of Bloemfontein, and Ron Taylor was its minister. Brian Brutus was chaplain to the South African armed forces at the military base in Bloemfontein.[118] I invited him to join our team (my predecessor had excluded him from participating in the life of the circuit despite—or perhaps because of—his being an excellent preacher). We had congregations in the outlying towns of Dewetsdorp, Paardekop, and Westminster. And then there were the numerous African and colored congregations in the townships around Bloemfontein and in Kroonstad.[119] All in all, I had oversight of some forty-two thousand Methodists.

I arrived alone with my books and our few belongings on

---

[118] Brian Brutus is a pseudonym. The person he represents is now deceased.

[119] Despite regular proclamations at the Annual Conferences of the Methodist Church of South Africa that we were a multiracial church, opposed to the government's apartheid policies, the reality was vastly different. Largely because of strictly imposed residential segregation under the government's policies, the Methodist Church in Bloemfontein, as elsewhere in South Africa at the time, was divided into white, African, and colored congregations, with separate circuits and quarterly meetings. One of the accomplishments of which we are most proud is that, by the time we left Bloemfontein, we had united the three separate circuits into one, with a single quarterly meeting attended by all Methodists in the city regardless of the color of their skin. I have no idea whether this unique accomplishment endured after our departure or remains in place today.

the Wednesday before my first services at the beginning of January 1972 and began unpacking and settling into our manse. On Thursday, I received a telephone call from the editor of the *Friend*, Bloemfontein's English morning newspaper,[120] asking whether he could send someone to interview me for the Saturday edition. Having had some previous experience with journalists who had misquoted my remarks or quoted them out of context, I agreed—with the request that the person sent to interview me be a mature, seasoned newspaper reporter. Consequently, I was somewhat taken aback when, on the Friday, a young woman about eighteen years of age, appeared on the doorstep for the interview. She was a journalistic intern home from college for the Christmas vacation—anyone but the mature, seasoned reporter the editor had agreed to send.

Making the best of it, I settled into a wide-ranging conversation for a couple of hours about my background and beliefs. Among other things, the intern asked whether I belonged to a political party. I told her I belonged to the Progressive Party (of which Colin Eglin was the leader and whose sole parliamentary representative was Helen Suzman); it was the one legal political party in South Africa that stood for the integration of all South Africa's ethnic groups.[121] Furthermore, in its platform of racial equality, it was in my view the one political party that most closely mirrored the inclusiveness at the heart of the Christian faith: "There is no longer Jew or Greek, there is no longer slave or free, there is no longer male and female, for all of you are one in Christ Jesus" (Galatians 3:28). The intern pointed out that there was no branch of the

---

[120] Rudyard Kipling was for a short time the editor of the *Friend*. Early in 1900, at the invitation of Lord Roberts, he helped start and then edited the newspaper for the British troops in Bloemfontein, the newly captured capital of the Boer republic, the Orange Free State.

[121] The African National Congress (ANC) was at the time a banned organization, and it remained so until the release of Mandela from Robben Island and then Polsmoor and Victor Verster prisons in 1993.

Progressive Party in Bloemfontein. I told her that I knew this and intended to start one. My words to her were, "If I don't get involved, as is my right and responsibility as a citizen, in working to challenge and change racial discrimination in South Africa, I might as well leave the country."

This young reporter's article, based on our interview, appeared on the front page of the *Friend* the next day under the banner headline: "New Methodist Leader Vows to Launch the Progressive Party in Bloemfontein—Or Leave the Country." Disregarding all else I had tried to say during our extended interview, this distortion of one of my remarks provided the content for the substance of the article. To make matters worse, the Afrikaans language evening newspaper in Bloemfontein, *Die Volksblad*—without contacting me at all—published a leading article on Saturday evening based on what had appeared in the *Friend* that morning. In essence, the leader in *Die Volksblad* pontificated as follows (in translation):

> We have some advice for the new Methodist minister in Bloemfontein. Don't bother even to unpack your bags. Leave the country now. The *Sappe*[122] scarcely dare to breathe in Bloemfontein. The Progressives don't exist in our city, nor will they ever.

---

[122] *Sappe* was a derogatory term for members of the United Party, at the time the official opposition, which had led South Africa from the time of Union in 1910 until 1947 when the Afrikaner Nationalist government came to power. The party had been led by General Jan Christiaan Smuts and after his death Sir de Villiers Graaf succeeded him. Smuts had brought South Africa into World War II on the side of Great Britain when she stood alone against the Nazi menace. In the Nationalist Party there were many, including Hendrik Verwoed, a future prime minister, who belonged to the *Ossewa Brandwag* (the Ox-wagon Fire Brigade), a powerful pro-Hitler Afrikaner faction that endorsed the Nazi ideology of Aryan racial supremacy.

To set the stage for the predictable reaction of the Trinity congregation where I was scheduled to preach at the morning and evening services the next day; I should first describe the composition of its membership (something I only discovered later). There were several large Dutch Reformed congregations in Bloemfontein. All of them held that Freemasonry, being a secret society, was "of the devil." They were curiously tolerant of the fact that the largest secret society in the country was *Die Broederbond,* "the band of brothers." From 1918, this secret organization, initially named *Jong Zuid Africa,* and then from 1920 named the *Broederbond,* worked assiduously and in secret to orchestrate the eventual political triumph of Afrikaner nationalism with the Nationalist government coming to power in 1948. I mention this because, periodically, the Dutch Reformed Churches (DRCs) would conduct a "witch hunt" and purge all Freemasons from their membership rolls.

My predecessors[123] had welcomed these former DRC congregants into the Methodist Church, assuring them that the only difference between the churches to which they had belonged and ours was that in public worship we used English rather than Afrikaans—without ever informing them that the Conference of Methodist Church of South Africa went on record, year after year, denouncing apartheid and proclaiming that we were one, inclusive church implacably opposed to racial segregation. About 80 percent of the members of Trinity were among those driven out of their DRCs either because they were Freemasons or because they had been seen dancing on Saturday evenings (which the DRCs condemned as a violation of the Sabbath).[124]

---

[123] The two superintendent ministers who had preceded me at Trinity are both deceased.

[124] That Saturday was regarded as the Sabbath, *Sha'bat,* rather than Sunday, the day of resurrection, is indicative of how the Jewish Scriptures, rather than the New Testament, provided the foundation for DRC theology.

Knowing nothing of this at the time, I was totally unprepared for the wall of hostility that awaited me in both the morning and the evening services—at which the church was filled to capacity. I use the word *wall* advisedly. The antipathy of the congregation was palpable, coming between me and those sitting in the pews as an impenetrable physical barrier. There was no welcoming warmth. There was not a smiling face to be seen. There was only an angry, sullen, resentment of this new Methodist leader who had dared to come to their city to launch a branch of the Progressive Party and to challenge their unquestioned assumption of racial superiority. At least at the end of that first day in the pulpit, I had some idea of the magnitude of the struggle that awaited me—and the congregation knew exactly what I stood for. That Sunday night, I decided to preach the following week on the subject of *joy,* portrayed in the New Testament as one of the prime virtues or "fruits of the Spirit" in the Christian way of life and so markedly absent from our worship services that first unforgettable Sunday.

Those initial five weeks in Bloemfontein before Margaret and the children arrived were lonely; I was temporarily isolated and without the moral and emotional support of my family and progressive friends in Johannesburg. But they left Johannesburg for Bloemfontein as soon as Timothy was discharged from the Johannesburg Children's Hospital to the care of Dr. Maxine Stillwell, the local plastic surgeon whom I had yet to meet, thankfully with no damage to his eyes or face, and in time for the older children to start school. Heather and Jenny were enrolled in Eunice, an old and highly regarded English-speaking school for girls. Andrew had been admitted to the Christian Brothers College, another well-established and first-rate English-speaking school for boys in Bloemfontein. They started school almost as soon as they arrived and settled in remarkably quickly.

I had been noticing that several Africans had started to come to our main service of worship on Sunday evenings.

Among them were a physician and her husband whom we later came to know socially. It was impossible to miss the fact that, whenever persons of color came to worship at Trinity, several white members of the congregation would pointedly stand up, move out to the center aisle, and angrily leave the church. I was not the only person to observe this happening.

At the first congregational Leaders' Meeting that Methodist polity requires to be held every quarter, one of the leaders stood soon after the meeting began and angrily asked me, as chair, if it was my intention to fill the church with blacks.

I responded to his question with a couple of my own: "There is a large sign outside your church. I did not put it up. It was there when I arrived. It proclaims that this is *The Church of the Friendly Welcome*. Would you please tell me what this sign means? Does it mean you welcome only people who are white but not black or colored?[125] If so, I need all of you, as leaders, to say so right now because I refuse to serve a church that excludes persons of color and expects me to minister only to those who are white. The Conference appointed me to have pastoral oversight over and concern for *all* Methodists in Bloemfontein."

The person who had asked the question sat down without saying another word. I waited for any of the other forty or so leaders to respond. Slowly, a few began to express their

---

[125] The term *colored* had traditionally been applied to mulattos, those born of mixed black-and-white unions. In the opening chapter of this memoir, I placed the word in quotation marks or qualified it with the prefix "so-called" only to draw attention to the fact that from the time whites settled in South Africa that was how mixed-race people were described. Centuries later, South African governments had an obsession with race (itself a concept I try seldom to use) and classified people as European (white), African or Bantu (black), colored, or Asian (Chinese, Japanese, and Indians). These were the terms in use at the time. This is why I have since dispensed with quotation marks and the prefix.

support, not only for me, but for the Methodist Conference's unambiguous declaration that the church was multiracial and could not exclude those whose color was other than white. It was a small but significant victory. I had reason to believe that, among my leaders, there were some who indeed wanted to do the right thing and that, together, we could make a difference. Over the course of the next two years, for the most part, this nucleus would stand with me.

My next required quarterly meeting at Trinity was of the Trust, a smaller group of about twelve, among them the two circuit stewards, Arthur Nell and Albert Cordiner;[126] the trustees were in charge of the church's finances. Two events from that first meeting remain indelibly fixed in my memory. First, in the minutes of the previous meeting (the final meeting of the Trust presided over by my predecessor) that had formally to be approved and entered into the church's records; there were repeated references to the church's "boy." Apparently, this "boy" was the janitor as well as the gardener and generally in charge of the upkeep of the church buildings. I asked the name of the "boy" and also how old he was. His name (not recorded in the minutes) was "Harold", and he was thought to be more than eighty years old. He had been mentioned in the minutes because of a previous discussion about giving him a small increase in salary. With pretended innocence (to mask my dismay), I asked whether we might amend the minutes to accord Harold his name and remove the demeaning description of him as a "boy," replacing it with the term "janitor." The members of the Trust agreed to my request. But to my chagrin, even in the next two or three meetings of the Trust, the recorder of the minutes reverted to calling him the church "boy." Only after making my point repeatedly over the course of the next nine months was he accorded the respect due to him, at least in the church's records.

---

[126] Both of these good men are now deceased.

Second, in reporting on the church's finances, the trustees introduced a more substantial and contentious topic of discussion. The church's finances were robust. There was no church debt. All the buildings were fully paid for, and there was a considerable amount of money in various savings accounts. However, a small number of trustees were eager to point out that several formerly DRC families were now leaving the church and were taking with them their "pledges" or actual financial contributions. They expressed concern that my determination to make Trinity an inclusive congregation would cost them money.

Choosing my words carefully, I decided that this was another crucial moment to let them know who I was and for them to tell me who they were. "I am prepared to begin my ministry here regretfully watching those leave this church who do not want to accept, let alone stand by, the pronouncements of our Annual Conference, year after year, that we are a multiracial church, an inclusive community of God's people. They are free to take their money with them. I will then start building a new congregation of those who are serious about bearing witness to the inclusiveness central to the Gospel message and the stated policies of the Methodist Church. Are you with me, or against me?"

I doubt that sort of question had been put to the members of the Trust in the history of Trinity, but to their enormous credit, by the end of the meeting a few of the trustees had expressed their support. I went home that night believing that there were trustees as well as leaders who could become my allies in making Trinity truly more inclusive—in fact, the church of the friendly welcome.

Soon after Margaret arrived, we decided to invite all the Methodist ministers (many of whom I had yet to meet) with their wives and families to Sunday afternoon snacks and tea at our manse. About a hundred people responded to our invitation. The majority was black. Those of us who were colored or white were in a distinct minority. It turned out to be the most marvelous afternoon. The children all played together. Our guests mingled with one another on equal terms, and all of us celebrated something that had probably never happened before in Bloemfontein—a social event in a white minister's manse when the artificial barriers of race[127] were temporarily forgotten and transcended. But there were inevitable repercussions. Our neighbors had noticed the comings and goings of dozens of dark-skinned people to and from our house and had heard the children's laughter in the backyard. Looking over the fences between their properties and the church's, they had seen a multiracial crowd of people having a good time. From that day forward, they would not return our greetings whenever we encountered them. They turned their backs on us and hurriedly went indoors. They would not allow their children to play with ours. Only one couple farther up our street continued to treat us in a neighborly way. It is interesting to note that immediately next door to us on one side were a Lutheran "missionary" minister and his wife and on the other side a deacon of the Hervormde Kerk. Converting the African was one thing—consorting with him quite another!

Sid Modell,[128] a Jewish pharmacist in Bloemfontein, asked to see me after the *Friend's* article had publicized my intention to start a branch of the Progressive Party in Bloemfontein. He,

---

[127] Although for convenience I use the word *race* throughout, I want again to make it clear that I simply do not believe in the concept of different races. Certainly, there are different ethnic and cultural groups, but to call them *races* is erroneous. There is no Jewish *race*; there are those who are ethnically, culturally, or religiously Jewish. Whenever I have to fill out a government form describing my *race* I respond with the word *human*. We are all members of the human race and genetically 99.9 percent identical to one another.

[128] A pseudonym used to protect his identity. He left South Africa at the time we did and now lives in another country. I do not know where.

too, was a progressive. He wanted to help me establish a branch of the party in this city, offering to serve as treasurer if I would assume the role of chairman. I welcomed his offer, but I told him I couldn't accept the chairmanship because of the difficulties it would cause in my congregation. We agreed to launch the party with the support of Colin Eglin, the national chairman, who gave us names of people in the Bloemfontein area we could contact. We would appoint a chair at our inaugural meeting. Sid made most of the calls, and when we held our first meeting, about two hundred people showed up. We elected a chairman, and from that time on, I worked in the background, glad that others would more visibly take the lead.

Among those who came to that memorable inaugural meeting were Richard (Dick) Howell,[129] a veterinarian from Westminster, a fertile farming area about sixty-five miles east of Bloemfontein, and his wife Joan. They were both Anglicans and were a striking couple, very much in love, with three children: Carolyn, David, and Moira. We felt an immediate kinship with them, and not long afterward, they asked us to help them with a problem regarding David's schooling.

There were no English-speaking schools in the Westminster area. The Howells had enrolled Carolyn as a full-time boarder in a Roman Catholic girls' school in Bloemfontein, and Moira, the youngest, as a weekly-boarder in the same school (meaning that she could go home every weekend). But there was no boarding school for boys. They wanted David to go to the Christian Brothers College that Andrew attended and asked if he could live with us during the week and then go home with Joan when she came to collect Moira every weekend. Joan would bring both David and Moira back to school on Monday mornings. We were delighted to be able to do this for them and readily agreed to take David in. Coincidentally, he was born on

---

[129] Dick is no longer alive. We have visited and kept up a correspondence with his son David, now married with a family of his own.

the same day as Andrew and Margaret (April 29th). So it was that we added a fifth child to our family.

Every Friday afternoon, Joan would drive in from Westminster to meet David and Moira after school closed, come to our house for David's laundry, and take them back to their home for the weekend. On Monday mornings, she would bring them in to school, stop by our house with David's laundered clothes, and have a cup of tea with Margaret before returning to Westminster.

Early every morning I routinely went for a five-mile run. One Monday morning, Margaret greeted me ashen-faced as I came in from my run in my sweaty clothes shortly before eight o'clock. "There has been a terrible accident," she said, "and Dick needs you to call him immediately." When I got through to Dick on the telephone, he was sobbing and could barely speak. It was obvious that he had had a tremendous shock. Through his convulsive sobs, he told me that a truck going in the opposite direction had crossed the median onto Joan's side of the road and had collided head-on with the Volvo station-wagon she was driving. Joan and Moira had been killed outright. David was badly injured and had been taken to the national hospital. Dick couldn't trust himself to drive in on the same road past the spot where Joan and Moira had died little more than an hour earlier, and he asked me to go to the hospital to take care of his little boy.

The nurses on the unit at the National Hospital where David had been admitted reassured me that his injuries were not life-threatening. Fortunately, he had been on the back seat of the Howells' station-wagon. Moira had been in the front seat next to her Mom. Both died instantly. But when the truck collided with the Volvo, the back of the seat where David was sitting flipped forward, sandwiching him between two upholstered layers of protection. Despite the fact that the impact had completely crushed the roof of the station-wagon, David was unharmed except for a broken ankle. However, the child had been profoundly traumatized emotionally. Whenever he asked about his mom and sister, the nurses responded vaguely with the half-truth "They are in another part of the hospital." They were indeed—in the morgue.

As I sat down next to his bed, he looked at me and anxiously asked, "Where's Mommy?" Taking his hand, I told him she had died in the accident and then held him as he wept uncontrollably. After what seemed like a couple of hours, he again asked, "Where's Moira?" I had to tell him that she had died in the collision as well. For eight hours, I sat with little David, doing what I could to comfort him in his anguish. Then when his ankle had been encased in plaster of Paris and he was ready to be discharged, I took this grief-stricken child to our home.

Margaret was able to hug and comfort him far better than I could. For the next year that he lived with us, invariably two or three times a week he would start screaming in the middle of the night as he relived the terrible crash that had robbed him of his mother and younger sister. Margaret was absolutely outstanding in the way she always took him into her arms as she had taken him into her heart, gently soothing him back to sleep and trying to assuage his grief with her unbounded love.

My colleagues in Johannesburg, John Rees, general secretary of the South African Council of Churches (SACC) and Fred van Wyk,[130] director of the South African Institute of Race Relations, tried to reinforce what I was doing in Bloemfontein by including me in their own organizations. John had me fly up to Johannesburg regularly for meetings and appointed me the chair of the SACC's Committee on Justice and Reconciliation, in which capacity I later represented the South African Council of Churches at meetings of the World Council of Churches in Geneva. It was after one of these Geneva meetings that I returned to South Africa through London, stopping over to see my old mentor and friend, J. Clark Gibson, then in his nineties

---

[130] Both are now deceased.

and living in a retirement home in Worthing. It was the last time he and I would be with one another. He died three weeks after my visit. I have the feeling that he had hung on to life knowing that I was coming to visit him, after which he was content to let go.

As already mentioned, I had also been appointed to the editorial board of the *Journal of Theology for Southern Africa*, which published two of my articles surveying what was going on in the country from the perspective of an opponent of apartheid. These meetings provided me with a community of progressive people away from Bloemfontein with whom I shared the same values, encouraging and strengthening me for the work I was doing there.

Fred van Wyk told me that there was a branch of the Institute of Race Relations in Bloemfontein (as there were in all major South African cities) but that for many years it had been moribund. He invited me to revive it by assuming the chairmanship. He, as national director, had the prerogative to make this appointment. I agreed, pleased to be able to extend the work of the Institute in my new field of endeavor. In addition to my friends in the Progressive Party, I found myself leading another multiracial group of liberal-minded people in the heart of this racist city. There were about thirty members on the committee, mostly either African or colored. As will be seen, it is important now to mention that many of them were professionals—schoolteachers, social workers, nurses, and physicians— whose salaries were paid by the provincial government. The role of the committee was to identify social problems and then attempt to find solutions for them. Three examples come to mind.

The first involved us in extensive discussions with the commissioner of the South African Railways in the Orange Free State. In terms of the Natives [subsequently termed black] (Urban Areas) Consolidation Act of 1945, Section 10(1), it was stipulated that Africans who had been born in and resided continuously in urban townships (prescribed areas), had worked for ten years continuously for one employer, or had been there continuously and lawfully for fifteen years, were allowed to apply for housing in these townships adjoining Bloemfontein. For the vast majority, this was almost impossible given the way white employers fired senior workers in order to hire junior and therefore less-well-paid replacements. These were compelled by law to live seventy-five miles away in a Bantustan named Thaba 'Nchu.[131]

There was a single commuter railway line between Thaba 'Nchu and Bloemfontein. The train was so crowded that there was standing room only, and the journey took two-and-a-half hours each way. The problem our committee identified was that there were two villages where the train did not stop, five miles and ten miles from the end of the line in Thaba 'Nchu. Those living in these small Bantustan villages who worked in Bloemfontein had to walk five miles or ten miles to the station, board the train for the two-and-a-half-hour commute, work for eight to ten hours in the city, return on the train taking another two-and-a-half hours, and then walk either five or ten miles back to their homes—adding up to a workday of about twenty hours! Additionally, the trains were so crowded that most passengers had to stand all the way into Bloemfontein and then back to

---

[131] The term *Bantustan* was applied to about fourteen so-called tribal homelands—Zulu, Shangaan, Sotho, Tswana. Xhosa, Pedi, and so on—so-called because it is doubtful that these nomadic tribes had ever truly settled in these remote areas. In accordance with the government's policy of apartheid, those who were not entitled to live in the townships surrounding the major cities in South Africa that provided the principal opportunities for employment were legally compelled to reside in Bantustans. To move outside of one's Bantustan required a hated reference book, or pass, without which one could be arrested and imprisoned. Despite the fact that these were designated tribal homelands, the government retained title to all mineral and water rights.

Thaba 'Nchu. Not infrequently, their employers would berate them for being lazy or for falling asleep on the job!

As chair of the committee, I spent two years making a case—in Afrikaans[132]—to the regional railway commissioner in support of our request that the train should be allowed to stop at these two villages. We asked not that a station or even a platform be built but merely that the train might be allowed to halt at each village to allow passengers to alight or exit. I—and others from our Institute for Race Relations Committee—must have had a dozen meetings with this man. After two years of pondering the matter, our request was turned down because "it would disrupt railway timetables and services throughout Southern Africa". This was patently a lie."

A second egregious example comes to mind. A black man living in Bathu Township on the outskirts of Bloemfontein married a woman who lived in the nearby Botshabela Township for coloreds only. Once married, in terms of South Africa's laws on racial identity, she was reclassified as Bantu or black and was allowed to live with her husband in Bathu. They had three children before her husband died. After his death, she was immediately reclassified as colored and was ordered to leave Bathu for Botshabela. Her children, whose father had been black, were deemed black as well and were not allowed to live with their mother in Botshabela. For two years, our committee met with the white man responsible for administering these racial laws in Bloemfontein, pleading for the three children to

---

[132] I should mention that most English-speaking South Africans were completely bilingual. Although the medium of instruction in our schools was English, we had classes in Afrikaans and had to pass national examinations, the *Laer* (lower) and *Hoer* (higher) *Taalbond* tests, as a condition for graduating from high school. From my experience in Bloemfontein, Afrikaans-speaking people were not equally proficient in English. Perhaps this was because the nationalist government's long-term intention was to impose Afrikaans on the entire population in addition to those who were non-white.

be allowed to live with their mother in Botshabela. Again, all these discussions took place in Afrikaans. Finally, the official turned down our committee's request with a shrug and the pathetic statement "Die wet is die wet" ("The law is the law"). "Maar wat of die wet selfs sleg is?" ("But what if it is a bad law?") I asked. In a rare moment of honesty, the administrator shrugged and ruefully and told us that he was due to retire in a few months' time and that he was not going to do anything "to rock the boat" lest he lose his pension. However pathetic, this was at least a straight answer.

Here is a third instance of the work attempted by our branch of the Institute for Race Relations. Bloemfontein's railway station was a half mile from the city center. There were (separate) toilets at the railway station for blacks and coloreds, but there were none in the city center itself. Nor would any of the department stores in the city allow blacks or coloreds to use their restrooms. (Not so incidentally, they would also not allow blacks or coloreds to try on shoes or clothing before purchasing these items.)

Our committee learned that architectural plans had been drawn up to beautify and remodel a plaza in the city center. We were able to obtain a copy of the plans for this renovation and noticed that although there was a park and several fountains, as well as toilets for whites (only), no provision had been made for restrooms for blacks or coloreds.[133] Since construction on the beautification of the city center yet to begin, we asked

---

[133] Such were the laws under apartheid that all public conveniences, for example toilets, water fountains, or park benches, had to be segregated. Such facilities were all clearly marked "Slegs vir Blanke" ("Whites only") or "Slegs vir nie-Blanke"—"Non-whites only". The Japanese were classified as non-whites. Yet with sublime hypocrisy, twenty of them were reclassified as "honorary whites" when the South African Rugby Union was scheduled to field a team against the Japanese in one of the few international events still taking place in South Africa at the time. Rugby in South Africa, particularly among

permission to appear before the city council to request that the plans be amended to provide for black and colored toilets as well. Again, this request was eventually turned down for what specious reason I cannot remember. I do recall clearly that the white citizens of Bloemfontein would piously denounce African men seen urinating on street corners for being such primitive and uncivilized people.

It was clear that the activities of our committee were being watched by the Special Branch (the secret police) and that they had bribed or intimidated some of our committee members to report back on what we were saying and doing. On at least three occasions, I received telephone calls from members regretfully telling me that they were resigning from the committee. When I asked why, the response each time was that they had been contacted by the Special Branch. The Special Branch instructed them to put certain "communist" items on the agenda of our next meeting. The threat was that if they did not do this, they would lose their state-appointed positions, which entailed the loss of their government salaries. Because they could not afford to forfeit their income and equally would not betray me, they regretfully felt they had no choice but to withdraw from the committee.

These were the sort of "communist" activities I was engaged in. I put the word "communist" in quotes because it has an intrinsic bearing on the following episode.

One evening, Dr. Maxine Stillwell, who by then had become a close friend, came to me with an urgent and dire warning. "I cannot tell you who this person is," she said, "because I promised him confidentiality. But there is someone in the church who has been given keys to your office and is going through the books in your library by night to provide evidence to the Special Branch that you are a communist."

Afrikaners, had the status of a secular religion, much as professional football does in the United States today.

In his book, *Law, Order and Liberty in South Africa,*[134] Professor Mathews, dean of the Department of Law at the University of Natal, Durban, has an extensive analysis of *The Suppression of Communism Act* and *The Unlawful Organization Act.* In a chapter on these statutes, he writes:

> An organization does not have to be communist, either in its aims or activities, to become the victim of a ban under the Act. A man who joined the organization for a non-communistic and entirely lawful purpose, and whose activities were equally lawful and free from communist taint, has no right to claim removal from the list [of those to be banned, that is, arrested or placed under house arrest.][135]

Considerably more than a "life" sentence may thus be imposed upon a person who does not believe in, and has never committed, an act of violence or even a criminal act other than the act made criminal by the [statute] itself.[136] [In essence, the definition of a communist is anyone whom the state says is a communist], and "The cumulative effect of this legislation ... is the annihilation of the right to personal freedom which, though previously hedged in by many restrictions, was the common-law possession of the most humble South African subject."[137]

---

134 Anthony S. Mathews, *Law, Order, and Liberty in South Africa.* Cape Town: Juta & Company, Ltd., 1971.

135 Ibid., 64.

136 Ibid., 61.

137 Ibid., 134.

Most of the criminal offences created by the Act are unrelated to communism ... The crime of furthering the aims of communism may be committed by non-communists or even anti-communists who launch or encourage anti-government programmes of disobedience ... There is not a single provision of the Act which makes proof of communist convictions or activities an essential precondition precedent to administrative or criminal action against a person or group of persons.[138]

In other words, the definition of a communist in terms of this legislation is tautological: whomever the minister of justice alleges to be a communist is, *ipso facto,* a communist. Maxine Stillwell's warning, therefore, was something I had to take seriously. The pernicious effect of a red flag like this was to make me less trustful and more suspicious of everyone in the congregation. Even in the most innocuous pastoral encounter, whether it was a parishioner coming in for counseling or a couple planning a wedding, there was at the back of my mind the unspoken question: "Are you or one of you the person who is working for the Special Branch?"

Some months later, I was driving to Kroonstad for a circuit quarterly meeting. Arthur Nell, our circuit steward and an accountant, was with me. One of his responsibilities was to examine the financial statements of churches in the circuit. Almost casually, on the way back to Bloemfontein, Arthur asked, "Do you know that "so-and-so"[139] (the name of someone in the congregation) is spying on you for the Special Branch?" I was stunned. I told him what Dr. Stillwell had related to me

---

[138] Ibid., 109.

[139] This event actually happened and was crucially important in our eventual decision to leave South Africa before I was placed under house arrest. The name of the person coerced into spying on me has been omitted entirely. Other salient details have been altered to make it impossible to identify this young man used by the Special Branch as an unwilling tool. I have no idea whether he is still alive, or, if so, where he lives.

months earlier that had made me aware this was happening. But because she had promised this person confidentiality, I had no idea who it was. The young man Arthur Nell now named, twenty-two years old, had recently been transferred by his firm from Bloemfontein to Kimberley, a city a hundred miles away. This must have been the individual about whom Maxine had warned me. Dr. Stillwell subsequently confirmed that this was indeed the case.

His parents still lived in Bloemfontein, and he would come home for the weekend periodically and join them in worshipping at Trinity. One Sunday evening, he was in the congregation. After the service, as I stood at the door shaking hands with people as they left the building, he was next in line. Looking him in the eye, I quietly asked, "Are you still working for the Special Branch?" He blanched. Putting my arm around his shoulder, I invited him to come back to the manse for a cup of coffee to tell me what he had done and why. With a look of inexplicable relief on his face, he agreed.

This is the essence of the confession this young man made that night in our living room.[140] By profession, he was an accountant, working as an auditor for a national chartered accounting firm. The Bloemfontein branch that employed him regularly sent him to various businesses to audit their books. One of these companies was the largest locksmith in the city. This company had installed the locks in all the Trinity Church buildings as well as the safe in the secretary's office. Usually he did his audit in an office shared by several of the employees, but shortly after I arrived in Bloemfontein, the owner invited him into his private office in a back room. With the locksmith was a man who introduced himself as the head of the Special Branch in the Orange Free State. This person began by asking

---

[140] The names and nature of the firms he audited as well as other details in this paragraph have been altered to such an extent as to make identification of this person impossible.

the youngster if he loved his country. When told that he did, the policeman continued, "Then we have an assignment for you. We have reason to suspect that this new Methodist leader in Bloemfontein is a communist. This is why we are already tapping his telephone and opening his mail. But we need you to go through the books in his library, looking for notations or passages he has underlined that will give us the evidence we need to take action against him. Mr. Van der Walt (the locksmith) will provide you with keys to all the church offices. You will have no difficulty gaining access to his books after he has gone home for the night. Furthermore, if you breathe a word of this to anyone, we will arrest you under the Official Secrets Act."[141] Terrified, for it was made clear that this was anything but an idle threat, he agreed to do what was asked of him.

About six months later after listening to my preaching Sunday after Sunday, the young man became convinced that I was anything but a communist and that I was simply interpreting the Christian message in a way he and the members of Bloemfontein's white Methodist churches had not heard before. He found himself facing a moral quandary. He could no longer in good conscience do the underhand work of the Special Branch, but he was terrified that they would bring criminal charges against him if he refused to continue his spying. He went to Dr. Maxine Stillwell, one of the most mature and trustworthy people in the congregation he knew, and asked if he could unburden himself confidentially. After doing this, Dr. Stillwell advised him to put in a request to his accounting firm to be transferred from Bloemfontein to its Kimberley branch. It was then that she had given me her warning without breaking her promise of confidentiality by naming him.

---

[141] Matthews writes about the Official Secrets Act and the penalties for contravening it on pages 196–203 of *Law, Order, and Liberty in South Africa*.

But before acting on Dr. Stillwell's advice, the frightened young man decided to seek counsel as well from Brian Brutus, the chaplain to the armed forces on my staff whom he had come to know when he did his compulsory military service at the military base in Bloemfontein. When Brutus learned of his assignment and his moral dilemma, he picked up his telephone and called the head of the Special Branch, apparently a personal friend because they were on first-name terms. This person (whom I never met) assured Chaplain Brutus that this assignment was necessary for the security of the country and urged him to do everything he could to persuade the young auditor to continue searching for the evidence they needed. Brian Brutus did this. He encouraged the young man to carry on with what he too now believed to be a crucially important patriotic duty.

It was then that the young man decided that the only way to cut the Gordian knot was by following Dr. Stillwell's advice and asking his firm to transfer him to their Kimberley branch, which in due course they did. He was obviously relieved to get this shameful story off his chest. I had enormous empathy for him. We parted company that night genuinely on the best of terms. I was as relieved finally to know who it was that Maxine had warned me about as he was to make his confession. But I was dumbfounded and disappointed that I had been betrayed by Brian Brutus whom I had befriended and treated as an equal with those appointed to my circuit by the Annual Conference. I decided it would be imprudent to let him know what I had discovered and to bide my time before confronting him— something I did eighteen months later before leaving South Africa permanently. All my subsequent dealings with him were extremely guarded.

The two years we spent in Bloemfontein were difficult not only for Margaret and me but also for the children. With one exception, our neighbors would not allow their children to play with ours. At school, they were stigmatized and ostracized because of what their father was doing and sometimes for their own plucky actions. Heather, for example, had been taught at her schools in Johannesburg always to stand when an adult entered the classroom. One day, an African messenger came into the classroom at Eunice with a message for Heather's teacher. Heather alone stood up. The teacher turned to her angrily asking why she was standing. When she reiterated what she had been taught at her previous schools, the teacher said, "Hy's nie 'n mens nie. ("He's not a human being"). Hy's mos 'n…, 'n 'kaffir'" ("He's just a … a kaffir")—a South African racist epithet as obnoxious as the word *nigger* is in the United States. After that, she was known in the school as a "kaffir-boetie," a derogatory Afrikaans term for anyone who associated with the blacks they despised.

We were not the only whites singled out for the attention of the Special Branch. Early in 1972, a young academician named Johann Maree, a graduate of Rhodes University (BSc Honors in mathematics) and Oxford University (BA in philosophy, politics, and economics) and still finishing his master's in development economics at Sussex University, arrived at the University of the Orange Free State after being appointed temporary lecturer in the department of economics until the end of the year. He was to teach econometrics,[142] to third-year economics students—with the understanding that his position could become permanent. He was one of three economists in South Africa with this qualification.

Then, no doubt because of surveillance by the Special Branch while a student at Oxford, it was reported in the *Friend* that he was one of twenty-two South African students at that university who had put their names to a letter to the London *Times* to

---

[142] Econometrics is the application of mathematics to economic data or theories and is of vital importance in helping advance developing countries. The proximity of Lesotho to the University of the Orange Free State made the appointment of an instructor in econometrics both timely and necessary.

protest an upcoming rugby match between the Springboks and the Oxford Students' Rugby Football Team. They did this, they said, on moral grounds, expressing their concern that allowing this match to be played would give tacit support to the Nationalist government's racial policies and would undermine the growing worldwide censure of the country in general and of its ideology in particular.

As a result of this disclosure, Johann Maree was summarily dismissed from his appointment. The university undertook to pay his salary until he could find another teaching post[143] but forbade him from having any further contact with his students—who themselves protested his dismissal stating that he had never advanced his own moral, religious, or political beliefs in the classroom. In a letter to *Die Volksblad,* Maree admitted signing the letter and added that he had protested against the Springboks versus Oxford rugby match on the basis of his Christian conviction that the commandment to love one's neighbor includes the neighbor whose color is other than white. On March 22, 1972, I wrote a letter to the *Friend*[144]

---

[143] No sooner had Johann Maree been dismissed by the *verkrapmte* University of the Orange Free State than he was offered a teaching post in the department of economics at the University of Cape Town—a far more liberal institution. He introduced econometrics as a subject (it had not been taught there before either) and went on to a distinguished academic career at UCT, first in the department of economics and then, after earning his PhD in the department of sociology, as a tenured professor in that department. He also co-founded and co-directed the Western Cape Workers' Advice Bureau (a euphemistic title for a trade union, something which would have further interested the Special Branch in his activities). Despite this innocuous name for the organization, five of his fellow organizers were arrested and taken into police custody. One of them, Storey Mazwembe, was found hanged in his cell a few hours after his detention.

[144] Letter to the Editor, *The Friend,* March 22, 1972. University's Function is to Pursue the Truth. Sir—It was with real regret that

in support of Johann Maree. Having lost touch with him once he left Bloemfontein, I was reminded of this episode after reading about it in Helen Zille's book *Not Without a Fight*.[145] As a result, I wrote to Johann, and we have since been in correspondence with one another. Johann provided me with a copy of this letter.

Helen Zille and Johann Maree were married in 1982. Helen has had a distinguished career in journalism and in the Democratic Alliance, the only viable political party in South Africa strong enough to provide an opposition to the ruling

---

I read in the *Friend* of the dismissal of Mr. Johann Maree from his temporary teaching post at the University of the Orange Free State. No reasons were given for this abrupt termination of his services. It seems reasonable, however, to assume that what prompted the university authorities to take this action was Mr. Maree's protest, while at Oxford, against South Africa's policy of racial discrimination in sport on the basis of his own Christian convictions. Despite the fact that the welcome move towards multi-racialism in sport is, in part, attributable to the protests of persons such as Mr. Maree, and that what was done was done in the light of his Christian understanding and as an individual, not as a member of any organized pressure group, Mr. Maree's offence appears to be that of failing to conform to the ideology of those presently in power in this land. That this should be punished with the action taken seems to me to be a denial of everything a university stands for. For surely, in any university worthy of that name, what is sought in both students and teachers is the critical pursuit of the truth—wherever that pursuit may lead, and however unpalatable the truth finally arrived at may be—rather than a spirit of craven conformity to any ideology. And it is such action which gives credence to the claims of South Africa's critics overseas that many of our institutions for higher learning are no longer universities but merely tribal colleges. For the sake of South Africa's good name abroad, as well as for Mr. Maree personally, I appeal to all who believe in freedom of conscience to protest solidly against his arbitrary expulsion from this particular academic community. Better by far that the protest should come from within South Africa than from countries further afield. (Dr.) Ernlé W. D. Young, Bloemfontein.

[145] Helen Zille, *Not Without a Fight*. Penguin/Random House, South Africa, 2015.

African National Congress. She is currently premier of the Western Cape. Though now emeritus, Johann is still active in trying to create jobs through skills development, having shifted his concern to the eight million unemployed people in South Africa after the union he helped found was absorbed into the powerful COSATU (Coalition of South African Trade Unions).

In spite of our own difficulties, there were small victories. There was a growing number in the congregation who understood and responded to the message I was preaching and were willing to make Trinity a more inclusive community. Particularly gratifying was the support of the Paardekop congregation, sixty miles west of Bloemfontein in a predominately farming area. There were perhaps only a dozen families in this Methodist community. The vast majority of the residents of this outlying rural area belonged to one or other of the Dutch Reformed Churches, and their dominees (ministers) wielded enormous power over them. Stories abounded of congregants being publicly excommunicated because they had been seen dancing on a Saturday night (the night of *Sha'bat*). Leon Pretorius and John Harris were the two stalwarts of the tiny Methodist Church. I was to travel to Paardekop once a month to lead worship and administer the sacraments at the morning service.

It was the custom at Paardekop to invite the minister and other congregants to one of the farms for a midday meal after the service. My first such invitation was to the farm of Leon Pretorius. And what a midday meal it was! The table was laden. Practically everything on it came from the farm itself—from the meat and vegetables to the pies with rich cream that followed. At my first such meal, I was asked to say grace, and then we settled into a rather stiff and stilted lunch at which I was interrogated about my background and our time in America. It was not what one would call a relaxed and convivial gathering. After a couple of hours, the meal long ended, Leon (who had a tennis court on his farm) got up from the table asking if some of the men could be excused to play a few sets of tennis. "Certainly," I replied. "In fact, if you could find me a racquet, a pair of shorts, and some old tennis shoes, would you mind if I joined you?"

There was a look of stunned then delighted surprise on the faces of those at the table. Leon scurried around and found me some kit. We all changed and went out to the tennis court. I hadn't played for some time, but I quickly began to see and hit the ball with something of my old assurance. At first, they were calling me "Dominee," but before long, it was Ernlé. The atmosphere changed rapidly from guarded, to warm, to intimate, and we had one of the best afternoons of tennis I can remember. That spontaneous gesture on my part won the hearts of the men, and then their wives, in the Paardekop congregation, and from that time forward, they were among my most devoted allies. Every Sunday I preached there, I took my tennis gear with me, and we played regularly in the afternoons—something that later was to cause major trouble with one of my ex-DRC leaders at Trinity.

One other anecdote from Paardekop is worth recounting. John Harris was engaged in mixed farming. That is to say, instead of concentrating solely on one crop or farm animal, he had livestock, poultry, fruit orchards, and wheat fields—among other things. Most of the Afrikaner farmers in that area paid their laborers poverty wages and gave them a sixty-pound sack of mielie meal (corn meal, a staple of the African diet), milk, occasionally meat, dilapidated accommodation, and a pair of boots. John Harris had built clean, modern dormitories for his workers and their families and a school for their children, paid them a living wage, and gave them meat regularly as well as other vegetables besides mielie meal, clothing, and boots. He had little or no turnover in his labor force, and there was no shortage of farmworkers waiting to join his team.

Being engaged in mixed farming, John could not justify the purchase of a highly expensive combine harvester of his own, to be used only once or twice a year. Instead, he contracted annually with someone who owned a combine harvester to reap his fields when his wheat was ready. The first year I was there, he had a particularly abundant wheat crop and called for the man with the combine harvester, as previously arranged. The man never came. First there was one excuse, then another. Eventually, John's wheat rotted in his fields. Rumor had it that other farmers in the area had organized a boycott of the Harris farm "because he was spoiling the kaffir."

Another minor triumph was the class we offered in the Sesotho language. The tribe most of the Africans in our part of the country belonged to was Sotho. They were thus Basotho, and their language was Sesotho. Whereas most whites spoke only English and Afrikaans, the Basotho were fluent in their own language, one or more of the other African languages, as well as in English and Afrikaans. I learned of and contracted with a Basotho man, a high school teacher, who was willing to come to Trinity to give classes in Sesotho. About thirty of us enrolled in his courses. He was a brilliant educator, teaching us not only the language but also a great deal about Basotho culture. Perhaps even more importantly, it was the first time in our lives that we whites had sat at the feet of an African instructor—an interesting reversal of traditional roles. He held us spellbound and sometimes in stitches of laughter every week for the eighteen months before we finally departed Bloemfontein and South Africa. Heather still has her notes from his classes.

I had brought back from the United States a long-playing record of Dr. Martin Luther King's speeches—including the famous "I Have a Dream" speech he delivered from the steps of the Lincoln Memorial. These speeches were banned in South Africa. It was a criminal offense to own this record. I took the precaution of taking it out of its original jacket and kept it in the jacket of a recording of a Mahler symphony, playing it to all who would listen—especially to young people in the church. There were none who heard Martin Luther King Jr. speak who failed to be profoundly moved. He was one of the most eloquent, articulate, impassioned orators any of us had ever heard—one who instantly dispelled racial stereotypes about the inferiority of blacks.

Whenever we wanted to take young people away for an interracial retreat, we would travel to Maseru, capital of Lesotho, the tiny Basotho nation sixty miles from Bloemfontein, previously a British protectorate but now an independent nation. It was illegal in South Africa for people of different races to sleep under the same roof—but not in Lesotho.

I made arrangements with a Basotho pastor in Maseru, the capital, to accommodate us in the fellowship hall of his church where we could all lay out our sleeping bags. It was at one of these retreats that we saw the Andrew Lloyd Webber and Tim Rice musical, *Jesus Christ Superstar*—banned in South Africa because it suggests that Mary Magdalene was in love with Jesus. These retreats were life-changing experiences for many of our young people.

Despite our ethnic and cultural differences, we came to know each other as fellow human beings. My only concern was that without my knowledge someone intent on silencing me would slip a copy of *Playboy* magazine—also banned in South Africa—into the trunk of our car, that on returning to South Africa it would be found by customs officials at the border, that I would be arrested, and that front-page news headlines would dramatize my being discovered in possession of forbidden pornography. This had been known to happen before. Thankfully, it never happened to me.

Another positive development was the rather impressive growth of the Progressive Party. When we started, we had perhaps two hundred members. Two years later, two thousand were enrolled, and the party had made it possible for liberal-minded people legally to express their political views and their opposition to the policies of the ruling Nationalist government and to vote accordingly.

And as a final example, there was the "Mission to Methodism." Some of the more evangelical members of Trinity had approached me wanting me to organize a mission to recruit new (white) members for the church. I undertook to do this with the stipulation that it should be a weeklong mission to all in our city—black, white, and colored—and that the leadership of all our various congregations should be involved. Thus began one of the most inspiring projects of interracial cooperation in which it has been my good fortune ever to participate.

The choirs of all our churches were enlisted, most of them African—and listening to the singing of an African choir is in and of itself a sublime spiritual experience. We invited Norman Hudson, general secretary of the Methodist Missionary Department, to be the principal evangelist. But since he was white, I insisted that all of our African and colored ministers also participate to present "mini" messages prior to Norman's main exhortation each night of the mission. Volunteer counselors from all our churches were trained to guide those who came forward to begin their Christian journey anew or for the first time, and these volunteers were also trained to act as spiritual guides in follow-up groups continuing long after the mission had ended. This was deliberately in contrast to a typical evangelical rally. And the overall theme of the mission was to be the costly challenge of living as a Christian in a racially divided country under an unjust and inhumane system of government.

Hundreds of people of all ethnic groups were involved in preparing for the Mission to Methodism, during the mission itself, and in the months following. Our careful planning bore fruit beyond our wildest expectations. Each evening during the week of the mission, Trinity was packed to overflowing. A different African choir led the singing each night, and on the final Sunday night, a huge combined choir played a major role in our worship.

Norman and the "mini" missioners stuck succinctly and powerfully to the challenging theme, highlighting each evening a different facet of the diamond of costly discipleship. Many whites who had never sat and listened to a black preacher shed tears of repentance and joy. White women came forward at the end of each service to be counseled by their African domestic servants. The culmination of the mission was a communion service in which our entire interracial team of ministers served Communion to an equally interracial congregation kneeling side by side, one communion rail at a time while the choir quietly sang its majestic harmonies, and then with us all holding hands as together we sang the final hymn.

Following the concluding service, we shared a simple supper in the adjoining hall, and it is no exaggeration to describe this meal as truly a foretaste of the heavenly banquet. As a result of our Mission to Methodism, all our congregations were enlarged and reenergized, and a new vision of one Methodist church in an apartheid society animated us all. For the first time since coming to Bloemfontein, Trinity truly began to become "The Church of the Friendly Welcome."

There was only one jarring note. Each evening, one or other of my African colleagues would point out to me two or three men from the Special Branch (in plain clothes) standing at the back of the church, not participating in our worship and writing conspicuously in their notebooks. My colleagues recognized them from bitter personal experience long before I did. Without question, they were reporting on what we were saying and doing to their superiors, gathering trumped-up evidence later to be used against us.

On the negative side of the balance sheet, I must mention Mr. van der Merwe (now deceased) one of the leaders of Trinity Church. Despite my visiting him in his home several times, he had never warmed to me. One Wednesday evening, months before I learned of Brian Brutus's role in urging the young auditor to continue spying on me, he and his wife and Margaret and I had midweek tickets for a rare theatrical performance in Bloemfontein. When they came to fetch us on the way to the theater, Brian Brutus brought me a leader-page letter to the editor that had appeared in the *Friend* that morning, which I had not yet seen. The letter was written by Mr. van der Merwe, identifying himself as one of the Trinity Church lay leaders, and the sensational headline, in bold letters, read: **"Methodist Leader Resigns from Trinity—Says Minister Is the 'Antichrist.'"** Mr. van der Merwe gave three reasons for his assertion that I was the Antichrist: I played tennis on a Sunday, I allowed guitars to be used in church at young people's services, and I encouraged blacks to worship in a white church.

Urging the others to go on to the theater, I said I would join them after going to see Mr. van der Merwe but that I had to speak to him first. I did not make it to the theater. I went straight to his home, was invited in, and was there for the next three hours. I tried to address the three points made in his public letter of resignation—from Scripture and from the Methodist Book of Discipline—to no avail. Mr. van der Merwe's mind was made up, and nothing I could say could change it. His resignation was firm, and sadly I had no choice but to accept it.

There is, however, a poignant addendum to this incident. A month or two later, Mrs. Van der Merwe (who had remained silent that night when I had tried to reason with her husband but whom I sensed was more persuaded by what I had said than he) was admitted to the national hospital with an inoperable metastatic brain tumor. I went to visit her immediately and did so every single day in the seven or eight weeks preceding her death, ministering to her with prayer, spiritual counseling, and holy communion—as I would to any other stricken human being. On occasion, her husband was there when I arrived. Without referring again to his resignation from the church I ministered to him as well—offering him and his wife communion and praying for both him and her. He did not return to Trinity, but without saying as much he gave me the impression that he was both deeply appreciative of what I had done for his wife and not a little ashamed at the way he had treated me.

Three developments, each now to be described, precipitated our hurried departure from Bloemfontein at the end of 1973.

The first was the arrival in Bloemfontein that July of Robert Hamerton-Kelly. As already mentioned, Bob and I were friends from our days at Rhodes. His mother, Joan Hobbes, was a member of the Trinity congregation, and he had come out to South Africa to see her before assuming his new position as Dean of Stanford University's Memorial Church, one of the most prestigious ecclesial appointments in the United States.

Bob immediately contacted me. I invited him to preach the following Sunday, and I spent two or three days taking him around the suburbs and townships surrounding Bloemfontein, showing him some of the things we were doing in our various Methodist churches, in our branch of the Institute for Race Relations, and in the Progressive Party, and introducing him to many of my colleagues in the churches and other organizations. To say the least Bob, returned to California tremendously impressed, and each of us went back to our assignments, thinking no more of this happy reunion.

The second development was a warning to leave the country before I was placed under house arrest. A Dutch immigrant couple, whose children were much the same age as ours, had befriended us socially. They had a swimming pool in their backyard and would occasionally invite us over for a Saturday afternoon swim and a barbeque. On one such occasion, Hans, as I shall call him,[146] took me aside. He lived next door to the Chief of the Special Branch in the Orange Free State, and this neighbor had casually mentioned to Hans when they bumped into each other earlier that week that I was about to be banned—placed under house arrest in terms of the Suppression of Communism Act. This always happened without

---

[146] I do not recall the full names of this Dutch couple or their children. I do not know whether they are still alive or if they are, where they live. His warning to me was an act of kindness for which I will always be grateful.

the benefit of a trial and would be in effect for five years, subject to repeated renewal at the discretion of the minister of justice.

Once banned, one was not allowed to meet with more than one person at a time, nor write (not even in a private journal), teach, preach, or publish. One could only leave one's home between 7:00 a.m. and 7:00 p.m. to work (subject to the above restrictions) with the additional restrictions of not being allowed to work where there was a printing press—a photocopying machine was classified in terms of the act as a printing press—or leaving the magisterial district where one resided without explicit magisterial or ministerial permission, which was almost never granted. Hans told me that my banning order was imminent and urged us to leave South Africa while there was still time.

To underline the drastic, authoritarian nature of the government's powers under the Suppression of Communism Act, let me briefly recount the stories of three courageous individuals, one of them a prominent dominee I befriended after he had been banned, and two of them friends from my days at Rhodes.

Dominee Beyers Naude was pastor of one of the largest Dutch Reformed Churches in Johannesburg's Northern suburbs. He had been a lifelong member of *Die Broederbond.* Dismayed and disillusioned by the way this secret organization was shaping South African society and its racial policies he publicly resigned and became an outspoken critic of apartheid. He founded the Christian Institute, a progressive Christian organization. As a result, he was dismissed from his church and was then served by the government with three successive five-year banning orders. He spent fifteen years under house arrest—effectively silenced as an opponent of Afrikaner nationalism. It was during these years that I came to know him as I visited him from time to time in his home.

A friend from my days at Rhodes, a Methodist minister then in Kimberley was also a fierce critic of apartheid. He was actively working for change in a new political party that the government later classified as subversive. He was then banned. He applied for and was granted an exit permit—which allowed him to leave South Africa but never return. But there was no international airport in Kimberley. The nearest was Jan Smuts Airport in Johannesburg, five hundred miles away. Under the terms of his banning order, he was not permitted to leave the magisterial district of Kimberley to go to Johannesburg in order to depart the country on the strength of his exit permit.

As Professor Matthews puts it:

> Notices [of banning] by the Minister very commonly confine a person to a magisterial district. The restricted person may only leave the district with magisterial or ministerial permission, which is rarely granted and then under very stringent conditions.[147]

My friend remained where he was, until, during his second sequential five-year term as a banned person, he managed to arrange to be smuggled out of the country secretly and in disguise.

Yet another fellow Methodist minister, Mark,[148] whom I had also known at Rhodes, served a church in Odendalsrus, in the Orange Free State. He was a fierce opponent of the government's racial policies and "security" measures. Under the Terrorism Act of 1967, he was imprisoned in solitary confinement for two consecutive 180-day periods—without the benefit of a trial. Professor Matthews describes this statute thus:

---

[147] Matthews, ibid., 87–88.

[148] Mark is the pseudonym I am giving him to protect his privacy. I do not know where he lives or even if he is still alive.

> This enactment ... authorizes the arrest and detention of persons without trial and the interrogation of such persons in conditions of solitary confinement. ... The detainee may now be held without trial for life. His isolation from the outside world is made absolute by the provision that no person is entitled to information relating to or obtained from the detainee.[149]

Mark was released years later after we had relocated to California and after Nelson Mandela had been elected prime minister of the new South Africa. Some months after his release while traveling in the United States he took the opportunity to visit and stay for a few days with Margaret and me. He then told us in detail of his ordeal. His cell was tiny, six feet by eight feet, and had no windows. The overhead light remained on, night and day. Raucous music was played incessantly over the prison's loudspeakers. He was interrogated repeatedly, at all hours of the day or night. He was locked in his cell for twenty-three hours at a time and was only allowed out into a small exercise yard for an hour. In plain view, on a board in the fence surrounding the exercise yard, his guards had placed razor blades—tempting him to use them to commit suicide.

Given the seeming hopelessness of his situation and his consequent state of depression, Mark said that ignoring the razor blades and not giving his guards the satisfaction of knowing they had caused him to kill himself was the most difficult thing he had ever done. To place one under house arrest, restrictive and punitive as it was, was not necessarily the last or the worst of the draconian measures the South African Nationalist government could take against an individual.

The third development, the straw that broke this camel's back, was most unpleasant. It involved an Afrikaans woman

---

[149] Matthews, ibid., 147

who was nominally a member of the Trinity congregation but whom I had never seen in church—although I had made pastoral visits to her and her husband in their home. Hattie Minnaar[150] was a member of our circuit quarterly meeting and showed up for the first time at the September meeting of 1973, twenty-one months after I had arrived.

I opened the meeting in the routine manner with a prayer, a welcome to all present, and the reading of the minutes of the previous meeting. I asked that approval of the minutes be moved and seconded and that they be amended or entered into the record as read. Before we could move on to new business, Hattie Minnaar stood up, saying that she had something important to read to the members of the quarterly meeting.

Permission granted, she proceeded to read a long, rambling, prepared speech from a typewritten manuscript about twenty pages in length. This was a hate-filled condemnation of me and my leadership. She did not mince words. I was a communist. I preached a social gospel dictated by the World Council of Churches, which everyone in South Africa knew was a terrorist organization because of its support for the armed struggle against apartheid in Namibia (formerly German South West Africa, administered by South Africa under a mandate of the League of Nations). I was a traitor for opposing the policies of the government. I should go back to America, my native country (this despite the fact, as mentioned in chapter 1, that my South African roots went back to the early eighteenth century). Further evidence of my communist activities was the campaign I had launched in Bloemfontein to raise the minimum wage for domestic servants from an average R10 ($5) a month to R25 ($12.50).[151] On and on went her harangue.

---

[150] Hattie Minnaar is a pseudonym for this ex-Dutch Reformed Church woman who is now deceased.

[151] Domestic servants in Bloemfontein typically worked long, fourteen-hour days, six days a week. They were provided with accommodation

When she sat down almost a half an hour later, the room was completely silent. Quietly, I asked, "How is it that you know so much about my preaching without ever having heard me? I don't recall ever seeing you in church in the year and nine months I have been here."

Furiously, she shouted, "No, I have never heard you—and I never will. I have my own informers." Looking back, I am certain that her informants and those who provided the details of her invective were members of the Special Branch.

I glanced around the room, waiting for those who knew me and who regularly had heard me preach to speak up and counter her accusations and allegations. No one said a word in my defense. Silence reigned. Finally, I rose and announced that I was closing the meeting and that I would be resigning my appointment at the end of the year. I went home with a heavy heart, shaken both by Hattie Minnaar's vicious and mendacious diatribe and because not one leader had found the courage to set the record straight.

Not long after arriving home, the two circuit stewards, Arthur Nell and Albert Cordiner, were at the door. I invited them in. They entreated me to stay on for the full term of my five-year appointment, additionally saying how wide of the mark Mrs. Minnaar had been. In response I said to them. "I wish you had spoken up and confronted Mrs. Minnaar during the meeting. Instead, you chose to remain silent. Surely you need no reminding that it was the silence of good people in Hitler's Germany of the 1930s as much as the vociferous endorsement of his racial and political ideologies by others that allowed Nazism to metastasize, eventually taking the lives of millions upon millions of innocent people?"

---

and sometimes uniforms. Many had left their children with their own mothers back in the villages from whence they had come and sent home what meager savings they could for the children's schooling, clothing, and feeding.

I did not mention to Nell and Cordiner the Dutch couple's warning, but it played a major part in the firm decision that Margaret and I came to that night to leave Bloemfontein and South Africa permanently. Hans's somber recent signal that my banning was imminent; the earlier incident involving the young auditor, the Special Branch, and Brian Brutus; and now this attack by Mrs. Minnaar, which clearly had been drafted by the Special Branch, all pointed to the shortening of my leash. We realized that we had to leave while we could. At the time, we honestly believed that only a violent uprising by Africans themselves could bring an end to apartheid. However active we were in nonviolent direct action, we could not bring ourselves to participate in violence. (Who among us could have foreseen the astonishing nonviolent transformation in South African politics wrought twenty years later by Nelson Mandela?) If and when I was banned, where were we to live—since we had no house of our own and could not hope to stay in the church's manse indefinitely? And how would we be able to provide for our children once I had been placed under house arrest? We concluded that our only option was to prepare for our departure while getting out of the country still seemed possible.

That October, at the Methodist Annual Conference, I formally declared my intention to relinquish my post and emigrate from my native country. Curiously, once I had made this announcement to the congregation, the undercurrent of criticism died down. However, we subsequently learned that Jack Scholtz, appointed by the Annual Conference as my successor, had an even briefer tenure in Bloemfontein than ours. Apparently he had tried to take up the cause of integration where I had left off. While he and his wife were asleep one night an improvised explosive device was detonated against the outside wall of their bedroom. Thankfully, apart from being badly shaken, the couple was not injured in the blast but windows were shattered and the manse sustained major structural damage. This violent act on the part of the regime precipitated their premature departure from *verkrampte* Bloemfontein as well.

For us at the time it was one thing to decide to leave; it was quite another to know where we were going. We still had our United States green cards, but our South African passports had expired. We would have to apply for new ones. Whether they would be issued was an open question, but the most pressing problem was finding a job.

I decided to write at once to Robert Hamerton-Kelly, apprising him of our predicament, seeking his advice, and asking him to approach the Methodist Bishop of the California-Nevada Conference on my behalf to inquire if there was any prospect of my being given an appointment to a local church. Bob did better than that. He wrote back saying that he, the vice-president of the Stanford Medical Center (Peter Carpenter), and the Administrator of the Stanford University Hospital (Paul Hoffman) had recently agreed to create a new position—and a national search was underway to fill it. The person appointed would have three areas of responsibility: associate dean of Memorial Church, chaplain to the Stanford Medical Center, and senior lecturer in medical ethics in the Stanford School of Medicine. He invited me to submit my name to the search committee and to come early in 1974 to assume this position in an acting capacity, also promising to introduce me to the bishop in case there were other pastoral opportunities in the California-Nevada Conference.

Margaret and I were ecstatic. In one stroke, Bob had provided us with a way out of South Africa and an immediate and highly attractive temporary job opportunity beyond our wildest dreams.

Ernlé aged about 5 dressed for Mrs. Bennett's Oak Tree Kindergarten

Winston Weldon (left) and Justin Thomas (right),
my brothers, about 18 months old

Rhodes University, Livingstone House, theologs
with Professor Leslie Hewson, 1958

Margaret and Ernlé during Spring break from Rhodes, with the old Austin
Ten Winston gave us after he and Jean left South Africa for England

From left Justin and his first wife, Judy; Ernlé and Margaret
(not yet married); Winston and Jean (just married)

Uncle Tom, Mom's younger brother

The Reverend Dr. Joseph Benjamin Webb (JB Webb)

November 21st, 1959, Margaret and Ernlé's wedding day

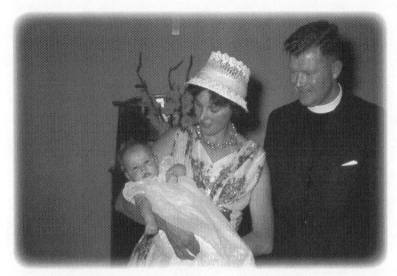

Heather in her baptismal robe and with her proud parents

From left Back row Gillian Rowe, Aunty Gwen, Sheila Rower, Margaret, Aunt Elizabeth, Ken, Uncle Harry, Uncle Dick. Front Row Gran, Mavis holding Heather, Cecil Rowe sitting, Peggy and Alan Rowe sitting, Weldie

From left: Peggy, Heather, Gran, Weldie with
Bess, Uncle Dick, and Margaret

Heather looking apprehensively at the kippies at Bedfordview

From the left Aunt Elizabeth holding Andrew Ken
Mavis with Jenny Margaret Matt with Heather

Heather on her way to Kindergarten at St. Francis
Anglican Church, Parkview, Johannesburg

Back row from left: Ernlé, Matt, Winston, Uncle Dick, uncle Tom. Middle
Row: Margaret, Aunt Ivy, Peggy, Mavis, Jean. Front row: Barry, Robin,
Gavin, Gran, Gillian Young holding Jenny, Heather, and Andrew

Assistant Minister at Kessler Park Methodist Church, Dallas, Texas, 1970

New SMU Ph.D. Graduate, 1972

Andrew, Timothy, and Jenny surfing down the sand dunes at Great Brak

Andrew, Timothy, Heather, and Jenny, 1972

August 7, 1974 first night reunited - at one of our camp sites
after meeting Peggy, Heather, and Andrew in New York

Andrew with Jenny in front of him, and Heather with Timothy

Biomedical ethics seminar at Stanford University

Crossing the finish line in the Paul Masson
Champagne Marathon, January 17th 1980

From the left Andrew Mavis Matt Timothy Heather Margaret and Jenny

Timothy demonstrating his early aptitude for music

Peggy and her little VW Bug

Timothy, age 6, and me on one of our many high Sierra back-packing trips

Margaret, Ernle, and Jess back-packing in the high Sierra

Margaret, high Sierra chef par excellence

April 29th, 1988 Margaret 50th Birthday

With Wits Medical School faculty as visiting professor in 1980

The first time Timothy saw his grandfather and his Uncle Justin, and the last time I saw my father and brother in 1980: Justin died in an automobile accident shortly afterwards, and my Dad died in 1994.

Heather graduating from the University of Washington
with her Ph.D. in nursing science in June, 1991

Laphroiag Twins

Peggy in her eighties

Fifty years later our 50th wedding anniversary, November 21st, 2011

With all our children and their families on our 50th
wedding anniversary, 2011(Michael not pictured)

Fritz Kalhammer and Sabine Biedenkopf at our home in Woodside

Daniel and Judy Dugan, hiking in the Cotswolds, England

Robert Hamerton-Kelly, instrumental in getting us
out of South Africa in our home in Woodside

Clockwise from left Alex, Andrew, Christi, Mara, Margaret. Gaudaloupe catamaran cruise, 2016

From left Margaret, Ernle, and Jean Smythe in Talent, Easter 2014

Peter Quinby and Heather, 2014

Andrew and Alex high school graduation

Timothy trying out his new guitar from Young's Woodworking

Two musicians Levon and Timothy

Peter Quinby and the bass guitar made by Young's Woodworking

Jenny and Gino, El Dorado Hills, 2017

Back row Heather and Pete; front row Eryn, Timothy
with Levon, Margaret, and Ernle, Christmas 2016

at home in Talent

PART 4

Professor, Clinical Ethicist, Cofounder/Codirector of the Center for Biomedical Ethics, Ethics Consultant

9

Stanford University, Palo Alto, California

After the Christmas services we left Bloemfontein without delay and traveled to Johannesburg. Before confronting Brian Brutus to let him know how bitterly disappointed I had been by his betrayal and even more by his apparently being seduced, if not brainwashed, by Nationalist propaganda and ideology, I had waited until our passports arrived—which they did only at the very last minute and after repeated inquiries. He didn't apologize, but he certainly looked ashamed. I had bided my time in case his friends in the Special Branch sabotaged our passport-renewal applications. With no unfinished business, we departed from Bloemfontein—the fountain of (now seemingly wilted) flowers and had our family celebration of Christmas in Johannesburg on Boxing Day with Margaret's Mom and Dad and my Mom.

In the shortest possible time between hearing from Bob Hamerton-Kelly and leaving Bloemfontein, major decisions had to be made. The question of Heather and Andrew's schooling had to be discussed. My Mom's emigrating to join us in California was another topic high on our agenda. And flights had to be booked.

The question of schooling was complicated, and it affected the two older children particularly. Once again, we were faced with the fact that whereas the school year in South Africa ran from January through December, in the United States it went from September through May. Had Heather and Andrew come with us in January, they would have had to repeat work done in 1973. If they waited until August before joining us, they would move up a grade in September. I cannot remember whether they were involved in what would have been for them a wrenching decision (and in any case, I now ask their forgiveness), but it was deemed best for their education to complete most of the South African school year for the sake of then advancing to the next grade in the United States in September. The arrangement we made was for them to stay with Matt and Mavis, Margaret's parents, and to go to the school in Halfway House close to where the Eddys were building their new home, until their August departure for California.

We wanted my Mom to join us and make her home in California, principally for her own sake. She would soon be seventy years of age and was still working at Lawson's car dealership in Johannesburg. Practically every penny she earned was spent on the twins, Winston and Justin, paying off their debts, advancing loans that were never repaid, and worrying constantly about where they were and what they were up to.[152] She had taken care of Gran and Uncle Dick in her home until the day each of them had died. She was exhausted and a nervous wreck. She looked as if she herself could drop dead at any time. We urged her to put her little home in Parkhurst on the market, bring Heather and Andrew over with her in August, and make her home with us permanently. She didn't need much persuading. Margaret and I are sure that she was relieved to think of cutting the emotional umbilical cord that had bound her to the twins for so long and of finding a modicum of tranquility in her final days.

---

[152] My brothers had both become alcoholics, a serious occupational hazard in the printing trade.

On this basis, we booked four airline tickets to San Francisco International Airport to arrive in the third week of January, 1974, making it possible for Jenny, Timothy, and ourselves to have a much needed week-long vacation in Luxembourg where we had to change flights.

From Mountain View to Atherton

Bob and Rosemary Hamerton-Kelly met us and took us and our four suitcases (almost all our worldly possessions)[153] to their home on the Stanford campus and then to the Holiday Inn in Palo Alto where we were told the university would accommodate us while we were looking for an apartment. They lent us one of their two cars until we were able to buy one of our own. I remember vividly how impressed we were with their gracious welcome and with the magnificent campus and the stately orderliness and beauty of the tree-lined streets of Palo Alto. The contrast with Bloemfontein was dramatic. The difference between the two cultures, that of the *verkrampte* Orange Free State and that of progressive California, which we were yet fully to experience, was even more so.

Feeling that we had to find a place to stay as soon as we could because Stanford University was footing the bill for our accommodation and meals at the Holiday Inn, we enlisted the help of a realtor who specialized in rental properties. My starting salary at Stanford was to be $14,000 annually. Anything available for rent close to the campus was beyond our means.

In less than a week, the Realtor showed us around an affordable two-bedroom unfurnished duplex apartment in Mountain View, eleven miles from the campus. We signed a six-month lease at once. We opened a banking account, bought

---

[153] A packing crate with larger items such as Margaret's sewing machine, my typewriter, books, tools, and the one piece of furniture made by Chilli that my Mom had given us was sent by sea and arrived the following March.

some pieces of foam to serve as mattresses, went to Sears Roebuck, purchased bedding, pots, pans, dishes, and tableware, and moved into an otherwise bare apartment within a few of days of our arrival. One of our neighbors in the duplex lent us a card table, and Bob Hamerton-Kelly donated a broken chair that had been discarded from Memorial Church.

With only borrowed tools and no workshop, working on the concrete walkway leading into our duplex, we took the one hundred-year-old chair apart, sand-papered it, made two new back legs to replace those that had broken, put it together again, and refinished it—our first piece of furniture. For sentimental reasons we hope never to have to part with it and have it in our Oregon home today. Having opened a banking account in Palo Alto, we were able to take out a loan and buy a new Chevrolet van, large enough for all six of us and my Mom—with plenty of room to spare. That enabled us to return the car Bob and Rosemary had lent us. Our next purchases of second-hand bicycles, small tables, lamps, and other household items were made at Goodwill and various rummage and garage sales. Within a week, I had started my new job.

Until space could be found in the hospital to house the acting chaplain to the medical center, my temporary office was in an old building on campus known as the Clubhouse. The Clubhouse had office space for the various campus ministries that served students at the pleasure and under the aegis of the Dean of the Chapel (as Memorial Church, or Mem Chu, was popularly known). I shared an office with Chuck Familant, Hillel Rabbi to the Stanford Jewish community, and he and I soon became close, both as colleagues and friends. The secretary to all the campus ministries in the Clubhouse was Louise Melle.

Eventually, when an office was provided for me in the hospital and I moved out of the Clubhouse, I invited Louise to join me in setting up the new Chaplaincy Department. Having worked with campus ministers for many years, Louise knew practically all the clergy in the local communities and this background was invaluable since we wanted to work cooperatively with them. In June 1974, Father John Hester was appointed by his diocese to minister to Roman Catholic staff, patients, and families in the hospital, and he joined Louise and me. The three of us soon became friends as well as colleagues. Long after my retirement from Stanford, John continued as Roman Catholic chaplain, leaving his assignment only early in 2015.

As I was setting up the hospital's chaplaincy department, I had to lay down some guidelines for local clergy visiting patients and families in the hospital. I formed a Chaplaincy Advisory Committee, composed of select local clergy, physicians, and nurses from the medical center, a hospital administrator, and representatives from Mem Chu. We began to formulate various policies; among the first was that patients and families were not to be proselytized. They themselves were to set the agenda for any visits by chaplains or community clergy. This policy became important in light of the fact that there were several fundamentalist, evangelical faith communities in the Palo Alto Area (Peninsular Bible Church was one) who were all too eager to use patients' illnesses and consequent vulnerability as an opportunity to convert them to "the true faith" as they saw it according to their lights.

My work at Mem Chu began at the same time. Bob did most of the preaching, but I occupied the pulpit at least once a month and sometimes more. When I was not preaching, I was assisting in the liturgy. Our styles complemented one another, and we began to attract more and more people to the Mem Chu congregation. Bob asked me to organize and conduct a Sunday evening study and fellowship group for Stanford students and celebrate Communion early in the morning for students, faculty, and staff one or two days a week. He (being a New Testament scholar) led a midweek evening Bible study.

My third responsibility was to begin teaching medical ethics in the medical school. I had an academic appointment as senior lecturer in the Department of Community, Family, and Preventive Medicine. Count (his first name) Gibson was chair of the department, and after my arrival, he proved himself to be a staunch ally and advocate in the work of integrating medical ethics into the medical school curriculum.[154] Fortunately, in addition to my graduate studies in ethics, I had had an exposure to medical ethics through Margaret's training as a nurse. She commonly brought home instances of ethical conflicts in the units where she had worked. I had also consulted with physicians at Methodist Hospital in Dallas, in Johannesburg, and in Bloemfontein.

But now I needed to immerse myself more thoroughly in medicine. I began by enrolling in the gross anatomy course. At that time, the anatomy course stretched over an entire year, meeting in the anatomy lab for three hours, three afternoons a week.[155] I joined various ethics forums and societies and started auditing as many of the classes as I could in the medical school—a practice I continued over the years. I began reading voraciously what bioethics literature there was at the time, consisting mainly of books, articles, and *The Hastings Center Report*. I began attending conferences on biomedical ethics wherever and whenever I could.

---

[154] Count Gibson had come to Stanford from Boston. A native of Georgia, he was extremely sensitive to and concerned about matters of racial and social justice and was a courageous civil rights activist. In Boston, he had cofounded the Columbia Point Health Center, the country's first community health center for low-income families. In so doing, he launched a network of nearly nine hundred community health centers that now provide health care to roughly ten million people. In the early 1990s, the Columbia Point center was renamed the Geiger-Gibson Health Care Center.

[155] Professor Mortinson impressed me at the beginning of the course by warning us that no joking with body parts would be tolerated and that any such betrayal of the trust reposed in us by families who had donated the bodies of loved ones for medical teaching and research would result in instant dismissal from the medical school.

From the start, two guiding principles informed my teaching of biomedical ethics. Each warrants separate description. Firstly, I wanted to establish the fact that the field of biomedical ethics is definitely not intended furtively to monitor the behavior of physicians and other health care providers so that one could then instruct them on how they should and should not behave. My working definition was that ethical issues in medicine and the life sciences arise whenever there is either *disagreement* about what to do or *uncertainty* about the right course of action. Disagreements may arise between professionals (which is why it is usually a good idea to get a second opinion on any important medical issue), between members of the same family (with the guilt-ridden "black sheep" who has neglected an elderly parent, for example, riding in on a "white horse" insisting on aggressive treatment long after those who have been actively involved in the care of their parent have realized that the time has come to switch to palliative care), and between the professional team and the family. In situations of disagreement, the ethics consultant is more often than not involved in conflict management.

And new technologies spawn uncertainty about their use. The advanced reproductive technologies, for example, generate questions such as: Is the fertilized egg a person, to be accorded full human rights? What is to be done with so-called "spare" embryos stored in liquid nitrogen, once the couple who brought them into being has achieved a pregnancy and no longer wants them? May they be destroyed or used for research purposes? Or must they be implanted, gestated, and brought into the world as newborn babies? And if so, whose babies will they be? Who are a child's parents, those who contribute the gametes, the woman who assumes the burden of pregnancy, labor, and delivery, those who nurture the child, or all of the above? How, if at all, should sperm banks be regulated? The capacity to modify genes, both in somatic cells and in the germ line, raises other questions: Where, if there is one, lies the boundary between treating a disease or disorder and seeking to enhance or improve on nature? Ought germ-line therapy or cloning ever be attempted in humans as has been done in animals? The questions continue, *ad infinitum*.

In situations of uncertainty, the ethics consultant is often in the role of an investigator: Are there any facts—medical, legal, environmental, demographic, or otherwise—that can provide some basis for a responsible decision? What are the core operative values of the parties involved? How do the classical ethical theories—deontological, utilitarian, or ethics of virtue—apply? What are the economic, legal, and professional constraints extrinsic to the clinical situation that yet may drive the eventual decision? Is there anything in the bioethics literature to inform topical opinion?

The second principle I wanted to make foundational was that my teaching would begin with case studies and that the didactic material would arise out of real-life clinical cases rather than the other way around. Being chaplain to the medical center gave me access to clinical cases on a daily basis. I had an abundance of material to work with as a result of simply doing my daily rounds in every department of the medical center—from the delivery room to the operating room, from the Alzheimer's unit to the neonatal intensive care unit, from the oncology and hematology unit to the orthopedic service or the neurological floor—an advantage I had over most physicians themselves, who in the main were restricted to their own departments. Starting with cases seemed the natural way to initiate a Socratic discussion of how to work constructively through disagreements or how best to handle uncertainty.

With the Spring quarter approaching (Stanford was and still is on the quarter system) I had to draw up a syllabus for my first course in time to get it included in the book of curriculum offerings, find a slot for it (being an elective, it could only be offered in the evenings, and we settled on Tuesdays), and reserve a conference room. Limiting the course to twenty-five students to maintain the give and take between instructor and students only possible in a seminar, I asked for and was granted permission to use the dermatology conference room, a comfortable and intimate space close to the lecture theaters in the medical school.

Late in April the search committee was scheduled to announce its final selection among the candidates for the position I now held in an acting capacity. So early in March, Bob and I traveled by train to San Francisco to meet with Marvin Stuart, bishop of the California-Nevada Conference of the United Methodist Church. Bishop Stuart had come to know Bob and received him and me warmly. After reading my credentials and letters of recommendation, he agreed immediately to my transferring from the South African Methodist Conference into his. He also offered to appoint me pastor of the Twin Towers United Methodist Church on Alameda Island in the San Francisco Bay. I thanked him profusely, but told him about the position I now filled in an acting capacity and said frankly that my preference would be to stay in academia if at all possible. Once the search committee had made its selection known, I would advise him of my decision one way or the other. Whatever happened, I was now certain that I would have a job in California—something I had hardly dreamed could happen five months earlier.

In April, I received the good news from Bob Alway, dean of the medical school, that from a national and international field of applicants, I had been selected as the permanent occupant of the position I had been filling in a visiting capacity. We were jubilant. This was the opportunity of a lifetime, and at the age of forty-two, I seized it eagerly. I immediately let Bishop Stuart know, and he graciously accepted my decision to remain at Stanford. He and I subsequently became the best of friends.

On the home front, Margaret was not having an easy time of it. We discovered that our duplex was in a dormitory community. During the day, there was no one there except for Hal and Janet Young, the retired couple who had lent us the card table. Once

Jenny started school and I was at Stanford, Margaret and two-year old Timothy were on their own. In this completely new environment she did not want to leave him in day-care to go back to nursing, either part-time or full-time. There was no housework to be done; apart from our foam mattresses and few pieces of furniture, the apartment was bare. She missed Heather and Andrew terribly. The fact that she had irrevocably left South Africa, not knowing when, if ever, she would see her parents, family, and close friends again, gradually sank in. She became extremely homesick, sad and lonely to the point of becoming depressed.

One particularly poignant incident is illustrative of her difficulties. It was a day I had taken the car to Stanford because I had an evening meeting. (Usually, I rode my bicycle to and from the campus.) Margaret set off for the grocery store and the Laundromat close to it with Timothy strapped into a child's seat on the back of her bicycle and with the laundry in a basket at the front. After putting her washing into a machine, she went to the grocery store, leaving her bicycle outside and locking it with a combination lock. When she came back to the bicycle with sacks full of groceries, she couldn't remember the combination to open the lock. She then had to collect her washing from the Laundromat and walk two miles back to the duplex with the groceries, the laundry, and Timothy—while holding the locked rear wheel of the bicycle off the ground. When I got home later that evening, she was still in tears. Once the extent of her disorder became apparent, we sought professional help. It took many months, but with treatment she eventually pulled out of her depression.

With her indomitable spirit, however, Margaret set herself one crucial task: finding a home for our reunited family and my Mom once she, Heather, and Andrew arrived in August. We had a few important selection criteria. Because I was on call at the hospital seven days a week, twenty-four hours a day, it had to be within easy reach of the campus. It had to be affordable on my salary at the time. It had to have four bedrooms: one for Mom, one for the girls, one for the boys, and one for us. And it had to be accessible to good primary, middle, and high schools. After selecting a real estate agent, Margaret began her search, going house hunting two or three times a week. The task was discouraging. Almost all of the houses she was shown were on the market for at least $110,000, an amount we considered way beyond our means. Finally, in early May, she had narrowed the possibilities to three and wanted me to join her and the realtor on a Saturday afternoon to make a final selection. One of the homes we looked at was in Palo Alto, but the asking price was $125,000; two, just above $110,000 were in Menlo Park on Valparaiso Avenue, a busy major thoroughfare, which we thought unsuitable for small children.

Disconsolate, we discussed what seemed like our bleak situation with the realtor. I suddenly remembered and mentioned to her that I had seen in the paper the night before an advertisement for a three-bedroom home in Woodside on three acres for $68,000. She immediately pricked up her ears and put a call through to her office. Minutes later, she came back with the news that there had been a typographical error in the advertisement I had seen. The price was in fact $168,000. "But this gives me an idea," she said. "If you like trees, there is a house on an unpaved cul de sac in unincorporated Atherton that has not yet been listed as up for sale for which the owners want $62,000. Should we go and look at it?"

On May 18, Peggy's birthday, we went to look at 348 Camino al Lago in Atherton. At first sight, we both decided that it was exactly the right home for our family. It was on two-fifths of an acre with beautiful, mature pine and hawthorn trees. The house had a living room with high, beamed ceilings, a dining room leading out on to a small deck, a kitchen, two bathrooms, and three bedrooms—one each for Peggy and Margaret and me downstairs—and upstairs in the attic, an additional divided bedroom with two built-in bunk beds on either side, perfect for Heather and Jenny on the one side of the partition and Andrew and Timothy on the other. There was a double garage and plenty of room to add on another, larger bedroom for my mom and eventually a swimming pool for the children. La Entrada Elementary School was three minutes away; Las Lomitas Middle School and Woodside High School were each only minutes from the house, and the Stanford campus was less than two miles to the south!

It took us about five minutes to make an offer at the asking price, and we wrote out a check for $500 to secure the deal, dependent on our ability to come up with the $10,000 down payment which the realtor advised us the mortgage company would require. We called Monty and Marlee Stewart in Texas (our former colleagues at Kessler Park). They had offered to help us in any way they could, and we asked them whether would consider taking out a $10,000 loan in their names from the Texas Methodist Savings and Loan Society of which I was not a member, promising to repay them with interest as soon as Mom sold her Parkhurst home in Johannesburg and could lend us the money. This they immediately agreed to do—an amazing act of trust on their part. By mid-June, Margaret and I had bought the first home we had ever owned. We gave notice to the landlord of our Mountain View duplex, and at the end of the month, Monty and Marlee drove from Texas to California to help us move our few belongings and paint the inside of the house before we began to settle in.

One of the secretaries at Mem Chu was a young woman named Hilary Lasch. She and her boyfriend Joe, who did odd jobs around the church, became our close friends. We bought Joe's beautiful little upright piano for $300 and installed it in our living room.[156] In the evenings, Joe helped me turn one half of

---

[156] We later replaced it with an old grand piano for which we paid $2,000. The piano had an interesting story behind it. It belonged to a journalist who had come to Stanford as a Knight Fellow in Journalism

our double garage into a study where I could shelve my books and work on sermons and lectures at home. The other half of the garage was sufficiently large to accommodate our van and allow me space for a workshop at the far end. A window looking out onto our backyard provided plenty of natural light for the bench. I could begin to accumulate power and hand tools and start making furniture for our new home.

By the end of June, I had completed my first course in biomedical ethics.[157] The work at Mem Chu and in the hospital was going well. And we were readying ourselves and our home for the long-awaited arrival of Peggy, Heather, and Andrew at the beginning of August. They were flying from Johannesburg to Heathrow and then boarding the *Queen Elizabeth II* in Southampton for the Atlantic crossing. We bought a tent large enough for the seven of us and planned to drive to New York to meet them and bring them to our new home, camping along the way. We set off for New York at the beginning of the last week in July, driving about five hundred miles each day, camping in

---

and who had audited two of my courses in the medical school—as Knight Fellows did regularly each year. While working for a well-known national newspaper, she had interviewed in prison a man serving a long sentence for murder who had become a Buddhist and had turned his life around. After her article was published, they corresponded faithfully and discovered they had fallen in love with one another. When he was finally released from prison during her time at Stanford, she asked permission to bring him with her to my class. I was most impressed with him. They later asked me to perform their marriage ceremony, which I was delighted to do. Going back to Texas after her year at Stanford, she had to sell her piano. I was given the offer to buy it before she showed it to anyone else.

[157] One of my first students, Bill Mobely, later became a distinguished neurologist, and for many years, he chaired the Neurology Department at Stanford. Another was William Hurlbut, who later became a member of President George W. Bush's Council on Biomedical Ethics.

the most scenic campsite we could find each night, and arrived at the dock in time for the arrival of the *QE II*.

What a joyous reunion we had! Heather, now almost fourteen, and Andrew, twelve, seemed to have grown impossibly in size and maturity. They had had the cruise of a lifetime. Both had learned ballroom dancing on the beautiful liner. Mom, on the other hand, looked desperately ill and was almost unrecognizable. The strain of selling her little home, ridding herself of most of her possessions, and saying a final goodbye to Winston and Justin, Uncle Tom and Aunt Ivy, Gillian and Ronald, Jean, Gavin, Barry, and Robin, other family members, and numerous friends had taken its toll. She was physically and emotionally spent, and Margaret and I seriously doubted that we would get her back to California alive.

Nevertheless, we packed their luggage into the back of the van and made a comfortable bed above it where Mom could lie down if she wanted to sleep. We set off at once, planning to do about five hundred miles each day as we had on the way to New York, camp out at night, and have as much fun as possible along the road. On August 8, 1974, we were in a state park campground in Minnesota, pitching our tent and listening to the radio broadcast coming from the van when there was the dramatic announcement that President Richard M. Nixon had just resigned in the wake of the Watergate burglary scandal. He was the first president in American history to resign. That date and this sordid event are unforgettable.

Our trip home was otherwise uneventful. We chatted nonstop, and Mom began to perk up noticeably. We arrived back at Camino al Lago in time to celebrate Heather's birthday on August 20. Heather and Andrew were thrilled with their new abode, especially the little bedrooms, as was Mom. All thought our neighborhood and surrounding environment quite splendid. And we immediately made plans to build an additional large bedroom for Peggy as well as remodel the bathroom adjacent to the bedroom we would add so that Heather could eventually move into the bedroom temporarily allocated to Mom, and put in a swimming pool in our spacious back yard.

By September, we had all settled more or less into our new and various routines. Timothy was enrolled at La Entrada Elementary School, Jenny and Andrew had entered Las Lomitas Middle School, and Heather was at Woodside High School. Heather and Andrew, in particular, were teased unmercifully because of their accents. Schoolchildren in South Africa all wear a uniform—a tremendous leveler, making it difficult to distinguish the wealthy kids from those less well off. Here it was different. Students dressed more or less as they pleased, and girls wore new, fashionable clothes almost every day of the week, especially once they were in high school. On our income, we could not possibly compete. Heather's response was to wear the same clothes every day, sometimes defiantly going to school barefoot, and concentrate on her studies. She was a brilliant student, and this alone quickly earned her the respect of her teachers and classmates. With five years of Latin behind her, she was the only student in the Latin class. All four went to Sunday school and youth groups at First United Methodist Church in Palo Alto and formed friendships that have endured over the years. Peggy joined the choir and played in the hand-bell choir with Heather. The choirmaster, Jim Angell, also played the carillon in the Hoover Tower at Stanford, and he frequently took Heather along with him. She was—and is—an accomplished musician, and in addition to the piano and hand-bells, she began playing the carillon.

To afford her as much independence as possible, we bought Peggy a brand-new Volkswagen "Love Bug." It cost only $2,800 and was bright orange. She drove it until the day she died twenty years later, and after her death, we gave it to Tim who was at college in Seattle at the time. She had quickly begun to recover her health and strength and had immersed herself in a myriad of activities at Little House, a senior center in Menlo Park. She took up oil painting, had guitar lessons from a "singing nun," went square dancing, played bingo, and went on occasional bus trips to the casinos in Reno (she was an astute gambler, setting aside no more than $25 to play with and quitting immediately when that $25 was spent; usually her winnings averaged $125). She started playing golf again at the Veterans' Administration nine-hole course in Palo Alto often with Ken Allen, our neighbor up the street, and taking Andrew with her as he got older and became interested in the game.

She even got a little job at the *Country Almanac,* delivering the proofs of advertising copy to customers for their review before the weekly newspaper went to press. This little job later proved important because, without any of us knowing it then, it made her eligible to receive a monthly income from Social Security and from Supplemental Social Security when she finally stopped working. She applied for and received her green card, and on April 20, 1984, ten tears after coming to live with us and ten years, almost to the day, before her death, she became a proud citizen of the United States.

Margaret went back to work, first in the electrocardiogram (EKG) laboratory at Stanford and later as activities director at a major convalescent hospital and skilled nursing facility not far from our home. This latter position eventually led to her being offered a teaching position at a prominent private school, Phillips Brooks, in Sharon Heights (the school was known as "the back door to Stanford") and a complete career change.

But now I must embark on the most difficult piece of writing I have ever attempted—the acknowledgement of the most shameful phase of my entire life. My career at Stanford was flourishing. I was highly regarded as a member of the Memorial Church staff. My courses in biomedical ethics were attracting more and more students. I had begun publishing papers in my field. I was a sought-after speaker and lecturer, locally, nationally, and by 1979, internationally. The chaplaincy department in the hospital had become accepted as integral to patient care, and we were getting more and more referrals from nurses and physicians to counsel and provide comfort to those who were critically or terminally ill.

Some of the women who worked with me as volunteers began to tell me how wonderful they thought I was and how much they were attracted to me. All of this was heady stuff, highly flattering to my swelling ego. I had never made love to a woman other than Margaret. Now I began to behave like a thoughtless, selfish, testosterone-driven teenager. Thrusting aside all moral restraint, I allowed myself to succumb to one female's advances after another and made advances of my own. At first, I tried to keep these affairs secret. Then I became defiantly open about them with Margaret. My angry defensiveness caused her and the children and my Mom the deepest imaginable hurt—the pain of betrayal, humiliation, and rejection. This went on for several years, and I can never apologize profusely enough or ever do enough to make amends.

The crisis came when I finally realized how close I was to losing Margaret. I moved out of the house into a one-room apartment for fourteen months and went into therapy, seeking help from a highly recommended psychologist, Don Ehrmann, on Welch Road. After working intensely with Dr. Ehrmann for about a year, I began to understand myself better and see why I was doing what I had been doing. I was finally ready to begin joint marital counseling with Margaret. We went to see Cleo Ulau together, and within three or four months, we had made sufficient progress for Margaret to allow me to return home and to begin earning her trust and for us to begin rebuilding our marriage—something we continue to work at more than thirty-five years later.

I don't want to go into more detail than this about these years when I went completely off the rails. I take full responsibility for losing my integrity and betraying my wife and family. Now I had the arduous task of working to reclaim it. I want to say again to my family how deeply I regret all the heart-ache I inflicted on them, how sorry I am for the anguish I caused them, and how grateful I am to have been allowed to begin anew as a husband and father.

That difficult confession made, I am able to continue with the main narrative. One important lesson I learned from this was the importance of having a male support group, friends with whom one can unburden oneself of work-related stress without the complications that arise when one's confidants are members of the opposite sex. I had two such friends, both caregivers as I was, with whom I began to meet regularly: John Wax, whom I had known from Memorial Church and was the chief social worker in the Palo Alto Veterans' Administration Health Care System, and Dan Dugan. Dan has a PhD in theology from Vanderbilt. He was a tenured professor of religion at Santa Clara University and had come to me some years before, out of the blue, so to speak, offering himself as a chaplaincy service volunteer a couple of evenings per week. At the time, I was greatly troubled by my own inability to devote the attention I would have liked to the families of patients in the intensive care units who often kept vigil in the ICU waiting areas for days, weeks, or even months on end.

Without being able to offer Dan any guidance or guidelines, I said, "Why don't you hang around the ICU waiting areas and see what you can do to create a support group for families?" Dan took up the challenge and did this magnificently for more than a year. With his easy manner, it did not take him long to create a system whereby the "old-timers"—those with critically ill family members or friends, who had spent extended periods of time outside the ICUs—offered help, encouragement, and support to those newly arrived. The genius of it was enabling families, the "veterans" and the "rookies", to help one another so that the system Dan evolved was not dependent on him alone.

On the strength of this experience at Stanford, Dan applied for and was appointed to a new position at El Camino Community Hospital in Mountain View, the director of a newly established patient and family crisis and bereavement counseling service, largely secular in nature. He resigned his professorship at Santa Clara, and for several years before going on to even bigger things, he ran an outstanding organization very similar to mine at Stanford. John, Dan, and I had much in common. It was enormously helpful to the three of us to share a meal (usually prepared by John but sometimes in a nearby restaurant), discuss the political situation, tell a few jokes, unburden ourselves of our latest hospital horror stories, and turn to one another for counsel and advice. For several years, our informal support group was invaluable for our mental and spiritual well-being. Unfortunately, it came to an end after John died and Dan moved to Chicago as the ethics consultant at Swedish Covenant Hospital. Margaret's and my friendship with Dan and his wife Judy endures and is a cherished part of our life today.

One of the members of the clergy I came to know well after arriving at Stanford was Father John Duryea, a Roman Catholic priest assigned to Saint Ann's Chapel, close to the Stanford campus and serving our Roman Catholic students. John was anything but a typical priest. He held views inspired by Vatican II, perhaps going even further by being open to the ordination of women, the marriage of priests, and social issues such as abortion. He was a veteran of the civil rights movement (as was John Hester who also had marched at Selma). Additionally, he was an experienced backpacker with an encyclopedic knowledge of "the high country," the Sierra Nevada Mountain Range, stretching from Los Angeles to the Canadian Rockies. He knew intimately its flora and fauna and the geology of this magnificent tectonic marvel.[158] John had

---

[158] Margaret and I still have in our garden pieces of petrified wood that we found in the Sierra at 10,000 feet above sea level; since this is a sedimentary phenomenon, its significance is that eons of years ago it would have been at the bottom of the Pacific Ocean.

hiked in the Sierra from the time he was a boy, and without exaggeration, he stated that if he were dropped by parachute anywhere in the mountains, blindfolded, he would know where he was within thirty minutes and would be on his way out to the nearest trailhead. Each summer, he led a small group on a backpacking trip, and in 1976, I joined one of these for the first time—and instantly became one of John's wilderness disciples.

After going backpacking with John once or twice on my own, Margaret joined me and became as addicted as I was. For the next fifteen years, she and I and other backpacking friends, accompanied sometimes by Andrew and always by Tim from the age of six, went on regular backpacking trips up into the Sierra a few times each year. Backpacking also afforded opportunities for occasional spontaneous mountaineering. Frequently, after setting up a campsite in the early afternoon, one or more of us would scale the highest surrounding peak. Other mountains were challenged more deliberately. I climbed Mount Ritter (13,143 feet) in the Minarets and Mount Young (13,177 feet) in King's Canyon National Park (Mount Young is lower than neighboring Mount Whitney at 14,545 feet, but unlike Whitney, there is no trail to the summit, and it is relatively unfrequented).

My friend Fritz Kalhammer (about whom I will say more shortly) and I climbed Mount Reinstein (12,585 feet) also in King's Canyon. This long day was memorable for two reasons. First, we had to hike five miles from our campsite before descending 2,000 feet into a valley. Only then were we able to begin the unrelenting 5,500 feet ascent. Second, not far from the summit and out of a clear blue sky, we were surprised by an electrical storm. The first indication we had of the approaching lightning, thunder, and rain was Fritz having to drop his metal hiking pole because of an electrical shock. Five minutes later, we were sheltering beneath a granite slab from a torrential downpour that lasted no more than ten minutes. Drenched to the skin, we made our way up to the summit and then quickly began the descent back into the valley and the five-mile hike back to our campsite where Margaret was anxiously awaiting us. We had not anticipated the adventure taking the entire day.

My one technical climb was Mount Rainier in Washington State, the highest mountain in the continental United States. After spending a week hiking around the mountain, I attended mountaineering school for two days to learn the techniques of arresting a fall down a steep ice slope in various body positions with nothing more than an ice axe on steep slopes at 7,000 feet.[159] Then on the first day of our ascent, we climbed to Camp Muir at 10,000 feet, and at midnight—after sleeping for only five or six hours—sixteen of us, roped together and with flashlights on our heads, set out on the steep climb to the summit. I was one of four of the sixteen to make it to Columbia Crest, the highest point. The reason for the early start was that we had to begin the descent before 9:00 a.m. Otherwise, once the snow started melting the ice bridges would have been too treacherous to traverse. The year before I climbed Mount Rainier in 1983, eleven climbers had lost their lives in an icefall.

In 1977, John Duryea made a mistake that cost him his position at Saint Ann's—he fell in love with a divorced woman named Eve and asked her to marry him.[160] In due course, he asked me to officiate at their marriage at Saint Ann's, something I felt proud and honored to do. As if calculated to inflict the most pain possible, a letter from the archbishop informing him that he had been excommunicated from the Roman Catholic Church was hand-delivered to him on the day of his and Eve's wedding. However hurtful the letter had been, the church's action in excommunicating him was in many ways liberating for John. Manfred Bahmann, pastor of the University Lutheran Church, immediately offered him the use of the church sanctuary and

---

[159] When climbers are roped together and one falls without being able to arrest his downward plunge he or she could easily drag the others down as well, in the worst case into a crevasse.

[160] John died in Mexico recently, and his wife died soon after him.

fellowship hall on Sunday evenings, and John founded and served the Angelo Roncalli Community for many years. The congregation of ex-Roman Catholics (many divorced, others dismayed by priestly child-abuse) was named after Pope John XXXIII who had convened Vatican II and is regarded as one of the most progressive popes ever. John Duryea was a born pastor and an inspired preacher, and those were in many ways the happiest years of his life.

John Martin was a graduate student in the Department of Religion at Stanford. He worshipped at Mem Chu, and on Sunday evenings, he played the guitar for our student fellowship. He and I loved singing many of the old, familiar songs in harmony. He was also an avid and excellent tennis player. It wasn't long before he persuaded me to take up the game again, and the two of us played singles for several years as often as we could.

Fritz Kalhammer, an electrochemist and physicist at the Electric Power Research Institute in Palo Alto, was another of my tennis partners. He and his wife Barbara attended Memorial Church. The four of us became and remain the best of friends. As mentioned earlier, Fritz frequently joined Margaret and me on our backpacking excursions. Fritz and Barbara later divorced. Barbara remarried and moved to Pennsylvania. Sabine Biedenkopf, a woman Fritz had known fifty years earlier who lived in Düsseldorf after her divorce, became his life partner. For many years they divided their time between Düsseldorf where they have an apartment in a retirement community and Redwood Shores, in the Bay Area where Fritz had bought a condominium after his and Barbara's marriage ended. The time is coming when Fritz will retire from his consulting work, settle permanently back in Germany, and his trips to the United States will become less and less frequent. To that end he has just sold his Redwood Shores property. He has been and is one of my dearest friends. I will miss him enormously. At least we will write to each other and talk from time to time on the telephone, however seldom from now on we are able to meet face-to-face

I met my third tennis partner by accident. One morning, I was riding my bicycle from Stanford Hospital to the old Stanford Children's Hospital.[161] Before the Lucille Packard Children's Hospital was built, Children's was located on a separate campus on the north side of Sand Hill Road. To get from one hospital to the other, one had to ride along Pasteur Drive to Sand Hill Road, crossing Welch Road. Traffic on Pasteur had the right of way. There were stop signs on Welch Road as it intersected Pasteur. From my right, I noticed peripherally a large blue automobile coming up Welch Road toward Pasteur at considerable speed, apparently without slowing down for the stop sign. In fact and most alarmingly, the driver ran through the stop sign just as I entered the intersection. I knew instantly that, if I stayed on my bicycle, the car would crush my legs. I jumped off the bike and onto the hood of the vehicle. I was tossed onto the road, and the car demolished my bicycle. Luckily, my only injury was a massive bruise on my right thigh. I had landed on my side, and a large bunch of keys had popped clear through my right trouser pocket when I hit the tarmac. The driver, Dr. Jim Newell,[162] a gynecologist-obstetrician, was responding to an emergency call from the labor and delivery room and had been too preoccupied to notice the stop sign. Jim could not have been more mortified, apologetic, or solicitous. He had his partner take me to their rooms on Welch Road to make sure I was all right (this is the one and only time I have been on a gynecological examining table!). He bought me a new suit and a new bicycle, and he became my tennis partner. Whenever either of us introduced one or the other to a new acquaintance,

---

[161] My responsibilities as chaplain and ethics consultant included Stanford Children's Hospital as well as the Stanford University Medical Center.

[162] Unfortunately, Jim is now deceased.

our standard line about how we met was "we just happened to run into each other one day."

While on the subject of sport, I should mention that both Margaret and I were runners. In the seventies, we began running half and full marathons. I ran more of these than she did, but we both trained hard. For our twentieth wedding anniversary, we ran a twenty-mile race along the Sacramento River wearing T-shirts we had ordered with the inscription "Twenty Miles for Twenty Years." In all, I ran fifteen marathons—usually in less than three hours.[163]

One of Stanford's benefits provided to faculty and staff was one half of the cost of tuition at Stanford applied to the cost of tuition at any college or university one's children chose to attend. All four of our children were the beneficiaries of this perquisite, Heather being the first.[164] After graduating from Woodside High School, she applied and was admitted to the University of California, Davis, where she majored in nutrition and French in the first of her five degrees. While Andrew was still at high school, Peggy found him a part-time job with Bill Churchill, an architect to whom she delivered copy for newspaper advertisements each week. Andrew enjoyed the work so much that he decided to take up Churchill's profession himself. He was admitted to the California Polytechnic University in San Louis Obispo, graduating in due course with his degree in architecture. Jenny went to California State University, Hayward, where she got her bachelor's degree and teaching credential. Timothy attended the Cornish College of

---

[163] My best time was two hours, fifty-two minutes, in 1986, at the age of fifty-four.

[164] I have written obtained, notarized permission from each of our four children to tell the stories, here, and further on in this narrative, of how they have flourished and made significant contributions to the community since being uprooted from South Africa and replanted in California.

the Arts in Seattle and obtained his bachelor's degree in music performance (guitar).

~

In 1979, after becoming a citizen of the United States, and again in 1980, I accepted invitations from our Berea friend Trefor Jenkins to spend time at the University of the Witwatersrand and other universities in the so-called Bantustan homelands that had been set up by the South African Nationalist government as "separate-but-equal" institutions for higher learning. Trefor wanted to introduce biomedical ethics into their medical school curricula. He planned a weeklong national conference on biomedical ethics each year and invited me as the visiting professor. He asked me stay on after the conference to hold seminars on the subject for medical students in Johannesburg and Durban. Trefor was a professor of medicine and head of the Department of Genetics at the South African Institute for Medical Research and was highly influential in the medical school. In 1979, I went alone. In 1980, I took Timothy, then ten years old, with me. Trefor's initiative succeeded beyond our dreams, and he subsequently invited other American bioethicists to build on the foundations he and I had established.

On the second trip in 1980, I decided to visit my father after my work at Wits was done. He had remarried and was living on the Natal south coast. Tim and I flew from Johannesburg to Durban and were met by my brother Justin and his third wife, Brenda. We stayed overnight with them. I had not seen Justin for many years, and it was a genuinely glad reunion. Justin told me that he had joined Alcoholics Anonymous (AA), had a good job, and had been able to turn his life around. He had recently purchased a new Peugeot diesel and extolled the virtues of diesel over gasoline engines. He and Brenda occupied a beautiful apartment on the seventh floor of a high-rise overlooking Durban Bay and the Indian Ocean.

The day after our arrival, Justin kindly drove Tim and me the hundred miles south to Uvongo where my father and his new wife were living. We arrived at about four o'clock in the afternoon. My eighty-year-old Dad seemed pleased to see me and to meet Tim for the first time, introducing both of us to his wife who appeared to be a pleasant woman. He offered us a beer and had me tell him about the family—something I was delighted to do.

To extend our time together, I invited them out to dinner. They accepted the invitation. Then, not much more than a half an hour after our arrival, Dad's wife burst in on our conversation to say that her little dog had escaped from the backyard and was nowhere to be found. She feared it was probably in danger somewhere on the busy road in front of their home. She was leaving the house to hunt for the dog and wanted Dad to go with her. They did not need Justin's, Timothy's, or my help since we would not know where to search. When they came back empty-handed an hour or two later, we had to leave for Durban without dinner so that Tim and I could catch our return flight to Johannesburg. Reluctantly, we had to say our farewells. That was the last time I ever saw my father.

This story has two sequels—one mortifying and the other tragic. After our return to California, I mailed my father a birthday card for his July 15 birthday. In it, I told him how glad I was that he had been able to meet Timothy for the first time, and that he and I had been able to have such an amicable conversation, brief though it had been. Sadly, a week or two later, I received a bitter, vitriolic reply from him in which he completely disinherited me and castigated me for not addressing the birthday card to him and his wife. I did not reply, and I never heard from him again.

Not long afterward, Jean Young (Winston's ex-wife) called us from Johannesburg with the tragic news that Justin, apparently drunk, had been killed outright in a head-on collision. His wife Brenda had been critically injured and had been admitted to and then later discharged from the nearest hospital. Ten days later, she died after a huge pulmonary embolism lodged in her lung. So 1980 was the year I lost my father, Mom lost one of her three boys, and I lost one of my brothers.

By the mid-1980s, what had started in 1974 as a hybrid appointment with three constituents each paying one-third of my salary, had evolved into three essentially full-time positions. Each of the one-third contributors to my salary expected to be able to command all of my time. In part, this was due to changes in leadership. Bob Alway[165] had been succeeded as dean of the medical school by Clayton Rich and then David Korn. Peter Carpenter had left Stanford and was at the Alza Corporation, a company started by Alex Zafferoni that specialized in slow-release drug delivery systems. He had invited me to join their ethics advisory review board, which is how he and I continued our friendship and stayed in touch.

In the medical school, the teaching of ethics had expanded beyond the two elective courses I had taught initially to a required ethics component in the core curriculum, seminars for residents in practically all of the medical departments, and invited lectures to undergraduates in various university departments—psychology, philosophy, engineering, chemistry, and human biology, for example. Yet the school's one-third contribution to my salary had to be anxiously fought for year after year.

In the hospital, Paul Hoffman had been followed by first one and then a whole succession of more bureaucratic administrators focused on the bottom line and devoid of the vision that had led Paul to lobby for a chaplaincy department in the 1970s. Paul always had an open-door policy as far as I was concerned. I had almost immediate access to him whenever his intervention was

---

[165] Whenever Dean Alway called me on the telephone, he would begin by saying, "This is your heathen friend speaking."

necessary. As an example, I was talking to Beryl Kunzelman[166] in the ICU waiting area one Friday afternoon. Her husband had been admitted to the ICU following coronary artery bypass surgery. Instead of the six-day stay in the hospital originally expected he had hovered between life and death for six weeks. While we were talking, someone from the billing office came up to her and presented her with a bill for $50,000 payable on the following Monday morning.

Mrs. Kunzelman burst into tears and said, "What do they expect me to do—go back to San Leandro and sell our home over the weekend? We simply don't have that kind of money!" Determined to help her, I rose saying I would go to the head of the hospital to talk about this. I went directly to Paul's office. He invited me in at once, and I described what had happened. He was outraged by the callous nature of this incident and picked up the phone, instructing the billing department to back off. He then came with me back to the ICU waiting area to apologize to Mrs. Kunzelman for the insensitivity of the person who had come to her demanding payment, assuring her that she would never again be pressed for money in such an inconsiderate manner. Once Paul left Stanford for Emory, that kind of access to an administrator became impossible. One had to wait at least two months for an appointment. The work (a bottomless pit as I began to think of it) was demanding my time seven days a week, and I was on call twenty-four hours every day.

There were major changes, too, at Memorial Church. After fourteen years as dean, my friend and colleague Robert Hamerton-Kelly resigned to take up a position as senior researcher at the Center for Arms Control, of which Bill Perry was the director and where Rosemary was a research assistant and the office manager. Don Kennedy, who had succeeded Richard Lyman (whom I had come to know well) as president of

---

[166] Both Mr. and Mrs. Kunzelman are now deceased.

the university,[167] appointed a Roman Catholic lay theologian as acting dean while a search was underway for Hamerton-Kelly's successor. The acting dean was new to the university, and not being ordained, was not allowed by his church to celebrate the sacraments. So more work at Mem Chu devolved on me, including doing more of the preaching.[168]

Clearly, something had to give. My salary had increased incrementally over the years, but it was becoming humanly impossible to do justice simultaneously to three essentially full-time areas of responsibility. I decided to relinquish the Chaplaincy Department, handing it on to someone qualified to develop a clinical pastoral education program (which I was not) that would bring one-year chaplaincy residents and interns to the hospital to share the pastoral load. After a national search, the Reverend George Fitzgerald was appointed—and I was free to concentrate on the teaching of biomedical ethics in the medical school and on clinical ethics consultations in the hospital, along with my work at Memorial Church.

Before leaving the brief account of my time as chaplain to the medical center, two stories bear recounting. Harry Humphreys had retired as manager of one of the Lyons Tea Houses in London. He and his wife Alice and their daughter Yvonne (a registered nurse working for the National Health Service, the NHS) had always wanted to travel to California, particularly Yosemite and Big Sur. They arrived in Palo Alto where Yvonne had a friend, a British expatriate, to begin the trip of a lifetime. The day after they landed, Harry had a heart

---

[167] In 1994, I was the recipient of the Stanford Alumni Association's Richard W. Lyman Award.

[168] I typically spent on average of twenty hours preparing a twenty-minute sermon. Much of the preliminary work could be done while I was on my morning run. Once I had an idea of how I was going to interpret and apply the texts appointed to be read on the Sunday I was to preach, I could begin writing. But getting to that point took hours of reading, thinking, and studying.

attack and was admitted to the Stanford Coronary Care Unit. After a week or two, seemingly well on the way to recovery, he had a massive stroke and was transferred to the neurological unit in the care of an excellent but unbelievably opinionated neurologist, Dr. Hanbury, now deceased. There he languished for weeks, not getting any worse and certainly not any better. The cost of his hospitalization steadily climbed, approaching a quarter of a million dollars. Yvonne had been staying with her friend, but Alice refused to leave the hospital. I was able to persuade her to come home with me a couple of times a week to have a warm meal and a hot shower and to leave her washing for us to do. Margaret and I got to know her well. We knew how anxious she was about Harry and the size of his bill. She had a true British horror of and aversion to debt.

I went to Dr. Hanbury to discuss Harry and Alice's situation. They were both in a foreign environment. I told him. Harry enjoyed watching cricket and rugby, not to be seen at all on American television, and knew nothing about baseball or American football. Back in London, they had friends and relatives; here, they were among strangers. Their hospital expenses were weighing on Alice's mind. If I could raise the money, would Dr. Hanbury agree to them flying home? The great man kept me waiting while he pondered his reply. Finally, he gave his permission to do this, providing Harry went on a gurney and was accompanied by one of our physicians and one of our nurses.

I immediately made inquiries about airfares. British Airways quoted me $6,000 to fly them back (Alice and Yvonne had their return tickets). Pan American Airlines (which was still flying in those days before it declared bankruptcy) wanted $10,000—they would have to set up a makeshift onboard-ICU in the first-class section of the aircraft. With this information, I called the editor of the *Palo Alto Times* on Tuesday morning (Palo Alto still had an evening newspaper then), told him of the Humphreys' plight, that we needed a good deal of money to fly them home, and asked if he would publish an article publicizing their need and soliciting donations.

On Tuesday evening, I picked up the newspaper in our driveway and saw that the editor had put this story on the front page. As I walked in our front door, the telephone was ringing. A Stanford professor who wanted to remain anonymous was calling and asked me to meet him at the faculty club for lunch the next day to discuss the Humphreys' predicament. He and I met the next day, and he told me his own family's story. He and his wife and their young daughter had spent a sabbatical year at Oxford University, during which time their little girl was diagnosed with acute myalogenous leukemia. She was treated free of charge for six months by the NHS before she died and was buried at Oxford. He and his wife had always wondered how they could repay the British people for the care they had given her, and this seemed like the perfect opportunity. How much money did I need? I told him what British Airways had quoted me, and he forthwith wrote out a check, telling me to let him know if more was necessary.

When I called British Airways to make the reservation, they backed off. Their excuse was that they had only one gurney, that it was in Singapore, and would not be available in time for the Humphreys' flight home. Plan B, flying on Pan Am, would cost $4,000 more. I called up our donor and explained this latest twist of fate. Without the slightest hesitation, he asked me to meet him again at the faculty club, and over lunch he wrote out another check to cover the extra amount.

The morning Harry left the hospital, the donor agreed to meet him and Alice, who very much wanted to thank him personally. Over tea and cake in the waiting area at the east end of the ICU, the family was able to express its enormous gratitude for his gift and bid farewell to the nursing staff. Harry left Stanford on the gurney, accompanied by Alice, Yvonne, Dr. Tom Feeley (an ICU Fellow), and one of our experienced ICU nurses. Dr. Feeley was able to hand him over to the care of a consultant at Saint Thomas's Hospital in London, where he spent the next two years, before dying of prostate cancer.

On one of our trips through London, Margaret and I were invited by Alice to stay with her. We were able to visit Harry at Saint Thomas. He was in a unit where they still had, and used, iron lungs! The silver lining to this difficult episode was that Stanford was later able to forgive the Humphreys' debt entirely, using funds that became available as a result of the Hill-Burton Act. Such was Alice's sense of indebtedness, however, that each month until she died (in 2013) she would send a small check to Stanford toward the debt she still felt morally bound to repay.

The second, touching story about my years as chaplain to the Stanford Medical Center has to do with a fellow expatriate, a former South African named Michael Eliastam.[169] He was working at the time as an emergency department physician. Michael called me up one day to say that his father, who was visiting him from South Africa, had had a heart attack and was in the hospital. He asked me to drop in to visit his dad, despite the fact that they both were Jewish. I was delighted to do this and went to see Mr. Eliastam senior almost every day he was with us in the hospital. He was a potato farmer from Ermelo in the Transvaal and was a salt-of-the-earth human being. Whenever we were chatting, he would call me Rabbi and sprinkle his part in the conversation with a few Yiddish words. Knowing both German and Hebrew, I could figure out the meaning of most of them and tried to reply in kind. The more I did this, the more Yiddish he spoke. Finally, feeling that I was sailing under false pretenses, I said, "Mr. Eliastam, I have a confession to make. I am not a rabbi. I am merely a Methodist

---

[169] There were several expatriate South Africans on the faculty of the medical school: Michael Eliastam, Ronald Dorfman in the pathology department, and Rob Sladen, a fellow in the intensive care unit. I met Rob's wife Maureen when I was in Bloemfontein and she was visiting her parents in Westminster. Since we all abhorred apartheid, we soon bonded and became close friends.

minister." His reply moved me deeply. "I know that," he said. "But you are *my* Rabbi." We hugged one another. I told him that this was one of the nicest compliments I had ever received.

In 1987, I was promoted to clinical professor in the Department of Medicine, and at the same time Stanford Hospital appointed the first clinical ethics committee, which the medical chief of staff and hospital board asked me to chair. I continued in that capacity until my retirement from Stanford at the end of 2001, and it was one of the most satisfying responsibilities I have had in my life.[170] Right from the beginning we established as a matter of policy that this was to be an open forum. Anyone—patient, family member, nurse, physician, or even medical student—could ask to appear before the committee with an ethical concern. When appropriate, we would deliberate and then, after the meeting, offer a recommendation to the person who had brought the issue to our attention. Often, a member of the committee would be designated to investigate the situation further and then report back to the committee for a final recommendation, either at its next scheduled meeting or at a special meeting. We averaged ten to fifteen consultations a month and were successful in resolving satisfactorily almost all the cases referred to us. Later, I was the principal investigator at Stanford in a multicenter,[171] randomized, controlled study of the effectiveness of ethics consultations funded by the National

---

[170] Other committees I happily served on were the Physician's Well-Being Committee (which helped physicians, residents, and medical students with addiction problems), the General Clinical Research Committee (which reviewed and approved or requested changes in all clinical research protocols at Stanford), and the Animal Welfare Committee (which had oversight of all research at Stanford using animals).

[171] There were six major medical centers involved, in different geographical locations. My friend Dan Dugan, mentioned previously, was the principal investigator at Swedish Covenant Hospital in Chicago and a lead author of the published papers.

Institutes of Health, with Larry Schneiderman as the lead investigator. In articles published in the *Journal of the American Medical Association (JAMA)*,[172] we were able to demonstrate irrefutably first the effectiveness and then the cost savings of ethics interventions.

By 1989, a medical colleague and I had cofounded and then began to codirect the Stanford Center for Biomedical Ethics. Our goals were several. We wanted to consolidate under one umbrella the many biomedical ethics courses being offered throughout the university—for undergraduates, medical students, residents, and postdoctoral students. We planned to extend the number of hours devoted to required instruction in biomedical ethics in the medical school core curriculum. We hoped to integrate biomedical ethics into the life of the entire medical center by offering weekly "brown bag" lunchtime seminars open to students, staff, and faculty, and reach out to the wider university and surrounding communities with quarterly symposia. We intended to bring in fellows and visiting scholars to expand our research endeavors and participate in the growing opportunities for teaching.[173] And we aspired to

---

[172] Schneiderman, Lawrence J., Gilmer, Todd, Tetzel, Holly D., Dugan, Daniel O., Blustein, Jeffrey, Cranford, Ronald, Briggs, Kathleen B., Komatsu, Glen I., Goodman-Crews, Paula, Cohn, Felicia, Young, Ernlé W. D., "Effect of Ethics Consultations on Nonbeneficial Life-Sustaining Treatments in the Intensive Care Setting: A Randomized Controlled Trial." *JAMA,* September 3, 2003—Vol. 290, No. 9, 1166–1172.

Todd Gilmer, Lawrence J. Schneiderman, Holly Tetzel, Jeffrey Blustein, Kathleen Briggs, Felicia Cohn, Ronald Cranford, Daniel Dugan, Glen Komatsu, and Ernlé Young, "The Costs of Nonbeneficial Treatment in the Intensive Care Setting: Ethics consultations can help decide about life-sustaining treatments, which are costly and provide little benefit to dying patients." *Heath Affairs,* Volume 24, Number 4, July/August 2005, 961–971.

[173] Subsequently both Paul Hoffman and Peter Carpenter applied to become and were appointed visiting scholars, each for a year, in the

develop a master's degree and eventually a PhD program in biomedical ethics in the medical school. By the time I retired in 2001, all but the last of these objectives had been abundantly fulfilled. Today, Stanford's is among the premier centers in bioethics in the world.[174]

My new position as hospital ethics consultant afforded me the same privilege I had enjoyed as chaplain, namely that of being exposed at firsthand to ethical issues as raised by nursing and medical staff members, as well as patients and their family members—in all departments of the medical center. With the exception of the fourth, the books I was able to publish were all written, so to speak, from the ground up—not from the realm of theory down.[175]

In the mid-1990s, Memorial Church ceased to fund the portion of my salary to which it had been committed since my recruitment in 1974. The provost of the university had imposed an across-the-board 10 percent reduction in the budget of every university department. Memorial Church was not exempt. The dean informed me that since my work was principally in the medical center, the provost had decided that I was the one staff

---

Center for Biomedical Ethics.

[174] My farewell lecture after retiring from Stanford and as Codirector of the Stanford University Center for Biomedical Ethics is included in appendix 1.

[175] Young EWD. *Societal Provision for the Long-Term Needs of the Mentally and Physically Disabled in Britain and in Sweden, Relative to Decision-Making in Newborn Intensive Care Units* (Monograph). New York: World Rehabilitation Fund, 1984.

Gustaitis R, Young EWD *A Time to Be Born, A Time To Die: Conflicts and Ethics in an Intensive Care Nursery.* Reading, Mass.: Addison-Wesley Publishing Company, June 1986.

Young EWD. *Alpha and Omega: Ethics at the Frontiers of Life and Death.* Reading, Mass.: Addison-Wesley Publishing Company, 1989.

Goldworth A, Silverman WA, Stevenson DK, Young EWD, eds. *Ethics in Perinatology: Issues and Perspectives.* New York: Oxford University Press, 1994.

member to be laid off. Subsequently, a friend of mine, who formerly had been a top university administrator, told me that no provost would ever micro-manage a department's budget. In any case I was now faced with replacing a substantial segment of my salary.

But more than this portion of my income, I had lost a major element in my vocation. From the time J. Clark Gibson pointed me to Isaiah 6—"Who will go for us? Whom shall I send?"—I knew that I had been called to the ministry and that I was good at it, whether sitting with a dying person offering empathy, compassion, support, and strength, or in the pulpit. As a preacher, I knew I had a God-given talent that had been finely honed by forty years of public speaking. There were times in the pulpit when I became utterly oblivious to myself and had the sense of simply being a clear channel for proclaiming a divine message—first to myself and then to my fellow pilgrims.

Preaching at Memorial Church had been particularly exhilarating. The principle of academic freedom trumped doctrinal orthodoxy or denominational considerations.[176] One was at liberty to tackle any topic, however controversial, however provocative. The only requirement was that of academic rigor. And now, apart from occasional appearances in the pulpits of local churches as an invited preacher, this central part of my life was gone.[177]

However, as Mom used to say, one door never closes without another opening. The door that opened was at the Palo Alto Veteran's Administration Medical Center with campuses in

---

[176] Many parish clergy are constrained in the topics they can touch on from the pulpit, particularly when it comes to politics. There is always the threat, as I knew from my experience in Bloemfontein, that those who dislike what is said from the pulpit will leave, taking with them the pledges or actual contributions that often the church can ill afford to lose. At Stanford, the university pays the salaries of the Memorial Church staff.

[177] Samples of my sermons are included in the following chapter.

Palo Alto and Menlo Park (known as the Palo Alto Veterans Administration Health Care System, PAVHCS). Richard (Dick) Maize, MD, was chief of staff. He was exercised about the quantity of nonbeneficial and costly medical care many veterans and/or their families were demanding. He wanted me to revive and chair a moribund ethics committee, offer monthly ethics seminars to resident physicians in the VA system, and serve as ethics consultant to physicians—particularly in the medical and surgical intensive care units. He offered to pay me for my services, and I told him of my need to find one-third of my salary. Without any hesitation, he undertook to underwrite this amount at Stanford through an institutional-personnel arrangement (IPA) and wanted me start immediately. Not only was I provided for but I had been given a new and exciting professional opportunity, which eventually led to me being appointed ethics consultant to the VA Medical Centers in San Francisco and Fresno as well.

The positive benefits notwithstanding, this part-time consultancy began to eat up more and more of my time, and over the years, there were also changes in leadership in all three VA Medical Centers. In Palo Alto, Dick Maize was succeeded by Dr. Frances Conley—the Stanford neurosurgeon who had written *Walking Out on the Boys* after her public feud with a colleague in the Department of Neurosurgery over his alleged sexism. Fran shared Dick's view of the importance of ethics and fully supported all I was doing. However, after her tenure, a psychiatrist did not know and had not met was appointed chief of the medical staff. In our initial meeting a month after he was appointed, he informed me that my services would no longer be required—because of a directive from the Department of Veterans' Affairs in Washington, DC.

The directive—and my subsequently being questioned by the Federal Bureau of Investigation (the FBI)—was in consequence of an article I had submitted to and had been published in the *VA Ethics Newsletter*. In it I had described a case that had come before our ethics committee. These, in brief, were the essential facts of the case. An eighty-five-year-old lady whom I shall call Mrs. Jones,[178] with whom I had previously been acquainted in the course of my work, had asked to see me in my office at the Center. Her eighty-seven-year-old husband had advanced Alzheimer's dementia. He was bedbound and could no longer feed himself. Indeed, he could no longer distinguish food from shaving cream—and he would eat either indiscriminately if it were offered him. He was a heavy man, and little Mrs. Jones could no longer manage his care at home. She sought my advice. I asked her whether Mr. Jones had ever served in the military. She said he had been on active duty in World War II. I immediately called the director of the PAVAHCS hospice, described the situation, and asked him whether he would meet Mrs. Jones with a view to admitting her husband to his unit. He agreed to do this, and in due course, Mr. Jones was admitted to the VA for hospice care (comfort care only).

Some months after his admission, Mrs. Jones asked if she and her son could appear before the ethics committee. I invited them to do so at our next meeting. She told the committee that her husband no longer showed any signs of thirst or hunger and could not at all feed himself, but indiscriminately would swallow whatever was put into his mouth. Her son stated that when he was a young man, he remembered going with his father to visit his paternal grandmother, also Alzheimer's demented, and his father said, "If ever I am reduced to this extent, I would not want to live. Please help me to die." In accordance with Mr. Jones's previously expressed wishes, Mrs. Jones and her son requested that feeding and fluids be withheld from Mr. Jones and that he be kept comfortable until he died.

---

[178] The names of members of this family have been changed to preserve their privacy. Only the son is still alive. I have no idea of his present whereabouts.

Since any decision regarding this request would involve the hospice unit's nursing staff, the committee decided to hold a special meeting in the unit at which the nurses on the morning and afternoon shifts could be present and—after hearing the Jones's petition—provide their feedback. The nurses felt unanimously that they could not do what the family asked, namely withhold food and fluids from Mr. Jones. They suggested that Mrs. Jones should to take her husband home where she would be at liberty to feed him or not. However, as her son pointed out, she was too small and frail herself to manage the care of her much heavier husband, which was why she had wanted him admitted to the VA in the first place. His family did not have space in their small home to accommodate his father in a hospital bed.

The nurses then proposed a compromise solution to the problem. If the family would hire someone to stay each day with the patient in his room, they would be willing to deliver food and water to this sitter with the understanding that he or she would not offer Mr. Jones either unless he showed signs of hunger or thirst. The committee and the family agreed to this arrangement. A sitter was hired. Only very occasionally did his caring companion think that Mr. Jones was thirsty and would then moisten his mouth with water or ice. He was not force-fed, and after three weeks, he died.

In writing this case up for the *VA Ethics Newsletter,* I clearly stated that I presented it, not with any certainty that our ethics committee had arrived at the right decision, but because we wanted to stimulate discussion and seek wider opinion about an important and controversial emerging ethical issue confronting our society. Given the demographics of aging in the United States and the projected increased incidence of Alzheimer's disease in an aging veterans' population, how should requests that food and fluids be withheld from demented patients *in accordance with their previously expressed wishes* be handled? Clearly the administrators in Washington did not want this issue debated. Instead of heeding the message, they fired the messenger.

In this interview in my office at Stanford with two members of the FBI that lasted two or three hours I simply related the facts of the case as I have described them here. They must have been satisfied that I and the committee had acted in good faith and with our contention that feeding and providing fluids for profoundly demented patients unable to eat or drink by themselves were the equivalent of other medical interventions that *could be appropriately withheld or withdrawn in accordance with their previously expressed treatment preferences—whether orally or in writing.* I heard nothing further from them, but my time at the PAVAHCS had come to an abrupt end.

Simultaneously, after the chiefs of staff in Fresno and San Francisco were replaced, their successors were more concerned about coping with the financial crisis brought about by congressional cuts in VA funding than with continuing the ethics programs I had established in these two medical centers. So, after six years as ethics consultant to the PAVAAHCS, and the VAs in Fresno and San Francisco, we parted company. But once again, providence smiled on me. Almost simultaneously with these events, I was promoted to full professor of medicine (biomedical ethics) in the Stanford School of Medicine. My entire salary was now paid by the medical center.

At more or less the same time, Margaret had made a major career change of her own. She had been the activities director at a local convalescent hospital and skilled nursing facility.[179] During her tenure, one of her patients was the elderly mother of Bitsie Root, the principal of the Phillips Brooks School.[180] Margaret had already established a unique program in which

---

[179] The convalescent hospital has since been demolished to make way for a luxury apartment complex.

[180] Bitsie Root unfortunately succumbed to a chronic illness three years ago.

she paired fourth- and fifth-grade children from Phillips Brooks with each of her mentally competent residents. Two children were assigned to each cognitively unimpaired senior. The children visited the residents each week, interviewing them, writing reports about their subjects' lives, reading their essays to those they had interviewed, and generally building important intergenerational relationships that were instructive for the children and a source of tremendous pleasure and stimulus to the elders. While visiting her mother regularly Bitsie had witnessed this program in action and Margaret's compassionate care for all her patients including her own mom. One day she said, "If ever you want a job at Phillips Brooks, I'd be delighted to have you on our early-childhood education faculty." At the time, Margaret merely thanked her and kept the offer in the back of her mind.

Months later, the facility was bought out and taken over by a national motel chain. A new administrator was appointed—one more experienced in hotel management than the care of the frail elderly. He rapidly introduced flashy cosmetic changes that distressed the experienced staff members. One innovation that proved to be the last straw for Margaret was his hiring people to provide valet parking for visitors while refusing to make any provision whatsoever for employing aides to help ambulatory patients out of bed to take them for a short walk each day. In his mind, valet parking was effective as a public relations ploy—and walking ambulatory patients was not a basic component of comprehensive care. Margaret decided that she could no longer work under someone more interested in "window dressing" (as she described it) than the true welfare of the residents. She made an appointment to see Bitsie Root and was hired on the spot for Phillips Brooks' Preschool Department under the leadership of Barbara Dulik. Thus began one of the most satisfying and rewarding chapters in her career.

Margaret immediately enrolled at Canada Community College. Over the next several years, she took all the available courses in early-childhood education as well as in art and creative writing. She became a qualified preschool teacher, and she and Barbara transformed the department, setting the tone and laying the foundation as far as values[181] were concerned for the entire school. Barbara, her husband Bob, and Margaret and I soon became good friends. We helped each other through difficult moments in one another's lives. Their children—Greg (a lawyer), Beth (an NBC broadcaster at the time), and Tom (an architect)—and our children came to know and appreciate each other as well. Barbara and Margaret retired from the school at about the same time. The Duliks moved to San Miguel de Allende, Mexico. We twice went down to San Miguel to visit them in their new homes. Sadly, Barbara collapsed and died in San Miguel on Christmas Day in 2011. Bob moved back to Palo Alto. He remains a close friend, and we see him as often as distance allows.

By that time, our children had become adults and were busily and happily living their own independent lives. During one of her vacations while still an undergraduate at UC Davis, Heather found a summer job in the Food Service Department of the Alza Corporation. Peter Quinby worked in the warehouse, and they fell in love. Heather moved out of the dorms, and they rented a house together. After her graduation from UC Davis, she went to Sacramento City College and graduated as a registered nurse.

At that time (1983), there were more qualified registered nurses in California than there were job openings. So she and Peter moved to Coos Bay, Oregon, where Heather had managed to find employment in the intensive care unit at

---

[181] As Margaret and Barbara observed, these children were extravagantly wealthy in material things, but they were extremely impoverished in terms of values such as kindness, compassion, and concern for those less fortunate than themselves. Barbara and Margaret worked diligently to change this and inculcate the values proclaimed in the school's mission statement.

Memorial Hospital on the night-shift. In 1986, while working as an intensive care nurse in Coos Bay, she earned a BSN degree from Southern Oregon University, Ashland, majoring in public health. In 1985, she and Peter were married at their home in Coos Bay. Rosemary Hamerton-Kelly performed the ceremony, and I walked the bride down the aisle and did the legally required portions of the service. Subsequently, she and Peter moved to Seattle where she earned her master's (1989) and PhD degrees (1991) in gerontology at the University of Washington. This was followed by a highly successful but eye-opening stint in the corporate world. She then returned to academia, joining the faculty of the University of Washington School of Nursing before being recruited by the Oregon Health Sciences University in Portland, and then by her alma mater, the University of California, Davis, where she is associate vice-chancellor for nursing and professor and founding dean of the Betty Irene Moore School of Nursing. She and Peter have homes in Ashland and Davis.

Andrew graduated from California Polytechnic University with a degree in architecture in 1985. He worked for a short time as an intern (a requirement for licensure by the state to practice architecture). He passed his state licensing examinations the following year, and he and Steve Borlik, his roommate at Cal Poly and close friend, then started their own architectural firm in Palo Alto. Almost thirty years later, Young & Borlik, Architects, Inc. is one of the most highly regarded firms in the Bay Area. They recently bought their own office building in Los Altos.[182]

Andrew and his friend from Woodside High School, Dohn

---

[182] For his senior project at Cal Poly, Andrew designed a home on a piece of property Gino (Jenny's future husband) had bought in Emerald Hills, Redwood City. After their marriage, Jenny and Gino built this beautiful home exactly according to the plans drawn up years earlier.

Alexander,[183] jointly invested in a small fixer-upper in Menlo Park. Andrew, with occasional help from Dohn, immediately set to work improving the property and reconfiguring the house—a process that continued for the next twenty years. Along the way, Andrew bought out Dohn's 10 percent share and assumed sole ownership. He also married Dianna Paladini, a clinical psychologist, whom we all came to love. Unfortunately, the marriage did not work out quite as either had expected, and three years later, they divorced. Thankfully, there were no children. In October 1996, Andrew remarried. Mara Green, a landscape architect he had known from their days at Cal Poly, came into our family as Andrew's second wife, and they have two beautiful daughters—Alexandra and Christiana, born in 1999 and 2001 respectively. They have completely remodeled the Menlo Park home, adding a second floor, and have also bought and remodeled a cabin at Twain Harte[184] set in the rolling foothills of Tuolumne County in the Sierra Nevada.

Jenny worked at various temporary jobs after graduating from Woodside High School, including waitressing at restaurants in Menlo Park and Portola Valley. In the early 1980s, she was on duty at the Portola Kitchen when Gino Gasparini—whom she had never met and who is several years older than she—came for dinner with several of his friends. When Jenny presented Gino with the sizeable bill for their meal, he was embarrassed to discover that he had forgotten to bring his billfold with him. He asked Jenny to trust him, promising to repay her the following day—which she did, taking an enormous chance and paying his

---

[183] The fine print of the title to their property included the regulation that no persons other than white were allowed to own property in this section of Menlo Park. Dohn is African-American. Perhaps the authorities in Menlo Park simply ignored this regulation when the two of them bought the property. They had certainly not rescinded it as I saw when Andrew showed me their title deed.

[184] Named for Mark Twain and his fellow author Bret Harte both of whom frequented and wrote in this little town.

bill out of her own pocket. The next day, Gino showed up with the money he owed and presented Jenny with a huge bouquet of red roses. They soon began dating, and not long afterward, they began living together.

Gino had gone to work straight from high school in his father's garbage business, which was later bought out by Browning-Ferris Industries (BFI), steadily moving up from garbage collection into the administration of this large company. Not having had a university education himself, he encouraged Jenny to go to college to get a degree. Jen enrolled in elementary school education classes at California State University, Hayward, graduating four years later with her bachelor's degree and then earning her elementary school-teacher's credential. After a short but stellar career as a fourth grade teacher, she and Gino, having married in 1987, had their first child, Andriana Heather. She was followed in fairly quick succession by Daniel, Michael, and Nicholas. All four children are healthy, athletic, and gifted. They built and moved into their first home in Emerald Hills—the one Andrew had designed while at Cal Poly and which we all worked on during its construction.

Jenny stayed home as a full-time mom while her children were growing up, but once they were in school, she went to work at Young & Borlik, first as a part-time secretary and then as a full-time office manager and project administrator—a position she holds to this day.

After graduating from Cornish College of the Arts, Timothy stayed on in Seattle. He performed regularly in various clubs and bars, supplementing his musical gigs with jobs in construction and eking out a precarious living. Gradually he began to make a name for himself as an electric guitar player. He formed bands of his own and also performed in more established groups such as those led by David Horwitz. He had a brief first marriage to Ana. Then after a time as a bachelor, he married Eryn—having met both women at Cornish. Eryn is an accomplished singer and drummer, and she and Tim frequently perform together. Since the opportunities for musicians are far more numerous in Los Angeles than in the Pacific Northwest, they moved south several years ago. This was a wise decision. Tim taught at the Los Angeles Conservatory of Music, composes and performs music for television shows and films, and is now a paid-up member of the Artistes' Guild, which affords him health care, pension, and other benefits. He performs nationally and internationally. Best of all, he now has a contract with CBS as lead guitarist and musical arranger for the band supporting James Corden's *Late Late Show*.

Tim and Eryn's first child, Levon Psalter Young, was born on October 4, 2014, weighing in at six and a half pounds. After trying for years to get pregnant, then unsuccessfully attempting adoptions first from Ethiopia and then South Africa, they finally had a child of their own. Our seventh grandchild is the only boy to carry forward the name of Young. In Biblical times, the tribe of Levi was designated the custodian of the psalter, the sacred songs. Levon is derived from Levi, and in Armenian, it means *lion*. Psalter is also the name of one of Eryn's admired relatives. Hence, Levon Psalter is the designated "brave custodian of the sacred songs."

To complete this short summary of the lives of our family members, I must finally speak of Peggy. The Peninsula Volunteers had raised money for and then built a subsidized retirement home on Crane Street in Menlo Park named Crane Place, only three minutes away from our home in Atherton. Probably because living with us was difficult at the time my life was in such turmoil because of the extramarital affairs I wrote about earlier, Mom put her name on a waiting list for Crane Place. Four years later, after having lived with us at Camino al Lago for fifteen years, she moved into her own one-bedroom apartment on the fourth floor. In every way, this was an ideal arrangement for her. Her income each month from Social Security and Supplemental Social Security was more than sufficient to pay for her board and lodging, leaving her with enough spending money to meet all her needs. Her apartment was bright and spacious with a lovely view, and was livened by the singing of her budgerigar, Dicky[185]. She bought a secondhand Yamaha keyboard to keep up with her music. She could park her car in the basement and come and go as she pleased, often taking her "old ladies" (fellow residents younger but far less active than she) shopping or to doctors' appointments, playing golf, going to activities at Little House, or coming back to our house almost every day to potter about in the garden or bring us a loaf of freshly baked bread. These were the happiest years of her life.

From Atherton to Woodside

In order not to interrupt these brief summaries of the lives of our family members, I have allowed myself to get ahead of the main narrative. To this, I now return. Toward the end of 1988 and into 1989, three strands in Margaret's and my life converged, which resulted in us moving from the "flats" of Atherton to the coastal (Santa Cruz) mountains and redwoods of unincorporated Woodside.

The first of these was an invitation from Bob Landeen and his wife to have dinner with them over the 1988 Christmas holidays. Bob, a psychiatrist in Woodside, had served on my Chaplaincy Advisory Committee, and we had become good buddies. We would meet perhaps once a month for a lunchtime sandwich and conversation as we walked around the Stanford campus, but we had not been to one another's homes. They lived in the coastal range west of Skyline Boulevard, surrounded by towering redwoods, and looking out over the Pacific Ocean

---

[185] After Mom's death, we gave Dicky to Andriana, then a very young child. Andriana's comment was, "It is so kind of Grandma to lend us Dicky while she's dead."

south of Half Moon Bay. After dinner, we went out onto the deck to admire the view—a brilliant starlit sky above, the vastness of the Pacific Ocean below, and the majestic redwoods surrounding us on three sides. As we drove home that night, Margaret and I said to one another, "This is where we want to live."

Since the children had all left home and Mom was living in Crane Place, there was nothing to keep us in Atherton, especially since while I was still on call seven days a week as ethics consultant I was no longer the on-call chaplain. This made a world of difference. As on-call chaplain, I would have to go in to the hospital often two or three times a night to be with a dying patient or a bereaved family. As on-call ethics consultant, I could make an assessment and offer a recommendation over the telephone, promising to be on the unit first thing the following morning to meet with the principals involved in the case. I no longer had to live five minutes away from the hospital; it was possible to be twenty-five minutes away.

The third strand in our decision followed by sheer serendipity after we decided to prepare 348 Camino al Lago to go on the market. The work we did was extensive, and Andrew's help was invaluable. We replaced the galvanized iron plumbing with copper, installed a new heating furnace, and completely remodeled the two bathrooms and the kitchen. Our neighbor, Bill Bray, was a real estate agent and we engaged him to handle the sale of our home and to look for a house for sale in the coastal range that we might possibly buy. The sale of Camino al Lago took longer than we had anticipated, and what homes were for sale in the coastal range looked east down at the lights of the Bay Area rather than west out over the Pacific Ocean as we had planned. We began to feel discouraged.

Then we had a phone call from Andrew. He was working as an intern with architect John Jang. A draftsman in John's office owned 2.3 acres overlooking Princeton-by-the-Sea, a picturesque fishing village north of Half Moon Bay. He had intended to build on the site, but his wife was pregnant and they had decided it was too remote an area in which to raise a family. He wanted $100,000 for the parcel of land. Were we interested in looking at it? We were intrigued. Andrew, Margaret, the draftsman, and I went up the next day to look at the property. It was on an extremely steep lot between Star Hill Road up above and Tunitas Creek Road down below and beyond Tunitas Creek, stretching six or seven miles to the ocean was the Purissima Creek Open Space District, which meant that nothing could be built between this parcel of land and the ocean. For Margaret and me, it was another experience of instantly recognizing that this was where we wanted to be.

Andrew was confident that we could build on the lot, steep though it was. We wrote out a check for $500 as a good-faith down payment—with two contingencies. One was being able to drill a good well, and the other was finding enough level ground on the property for the 180-foot leach field regulations required for a septic system. We took out a second mortgage and paid the asking price into escrow—subject to our two contingencies being met. In due course, they were. In the first well we drilled, we found water 150 feet down, and to ensure a plentiful water supply, we lowered the well another one-hundred feet. The County of San Mateo approved the location of the septic system's leach field.

We later learned that the draftsman had paid only $40,000 for the property three or four years earlier, but Bill Bray was eventually able to sell our home for $493,000—about eight times what we had paid for it in 1974. After paying off our first and second mortgages on the Atherton home and the contractors who had done the remodeling—Arne and Matt Jorgenson about whom more will be said shortly—that left us more than $300,000 to build our new house. Naively we imagined this would be sufficient.

The next question was who would build the house for us. Without hesitation, Andrew suggested Matt and Arne who had done the remodeling of the Atherton property. Matt had been one of Andrew's roommates at Cal Poly, and for the first three years, they had taken classes together. In the fourth and fifth years, Matt specialized in construction management and Andrew specialized in architecture. Arne, Matt's cousin, was a highly experienced and meticulous contractor. The two of them made an impressive team. We asked them to join us to look at the land we had purchased and asked them whether they could build on this site. Their response was unhesitating: "If Andrew can draw it, we can build it." How about cost plus 10 percent?" I asked. "That's fine with us," they replied. We shook hands on the deal. No papers were ever signed. A handshake was our bond.

From the time we started building in April 1989, Matt would give me an invoice at the end of each month, and I would write him a check for that amount. It was the most amicable and enjoyable experience of our lives. Andrew, Margaret, and I worked alongside Matt and Arne on weekends and our days off. Dohn Alexander, Andrew's school friend, and John Moore (a young Australian from Sydney whom we called "the prawn" because of his size—this in Aussie-speak was the term for shrimp), were hired as laborers cum apprentices. Both learned an enormous amount about construction from Matt and Arne.

Andrew drew up the plans for the "simple" three-bedroom house we had asked for, and what he came up with was hardly simple. He presented us with the drawings for a magnificent, 3,300 square feet, multilevel home that wrapped itself around the contours of the hill. It had three bedrooms—and a huge living room with a twenty-six-foot ceiling, a dining room, a breakfast room, a kitchen, three bathrooms, and a double garage. When we protested at the size of the house, he countered by saying—perfectly correctly—that we could only build once on this site. Further extensions later would be impossible because the foundations were so complicated.

Before proceeding from sketches to working drawings,

Andrew went to the San Mateo County Building Department to ask them whether the Star Hill Road (upper) side of the property or the Tunitas Creek (lower) road was the "front" or the "back." Their ruling, which they stamped and signed on the blueprint showing our parcel of land, was that the front was on Star Hill Road. This was an important decision because it meant that the setback from the road had only to be twenty feet whereas it would have had to be fifty feet were it the back. This made a world of difference to the view since the higher on the property we could build, the better the view. Much to our chagrin, the county reversed this decision after the plans were fully drawn up and were submitted for approval. It cost us another $5,000 and lost us three months to get a variance allowing us to build where they had agreed in the first place. This was another object lesson in the mindlessness (or perhaps the avarice) of bureaucracy.

After selling our Atherton house, we were able to rent a small one-bedroom garden cottage in Palo Alto from a dear ninety-year-old lady, Mrs. Johnson, who lived alone in the main house. We stayed there happily for about a year while our new home was being built. One event in particular stands out.

At three minutes after five on October 17, 1989, Margaret was on her way back from San Francisco with Barbara Dulik where both volunteered every Tuesday at a food bank for persons with HIV/AIDS. I was at my computer in our cottage working on a lecture I was to give at six thirty that evening in Stanford's Continuing Studies Program. I felt the entire brick building begin to shake. I got up from my desk, stood in the doorway, and watched the walls swaying in front of me. I thought I had better save what I was working on, went back to the computer and saved my document, and then returned to stand in the doorway. Cupboards in the kitchen were opening, and glasses and dishes crashed to the floor.

The shaking of the 7.1 Loma Prieta Earthquake went on for at least twenty seconds, although it felt far, far longer than that. When the tremors subsided, my first thought was for Mrs. Johnson. I rushed to her house to see how she was faring. She was in the driveway, staggering down to the house from the mailbox. When I asked her how she was, her reply was amusing: "I thought I was getting a little dizzy," she said. "And then I realized in was an earthquake." She chuckled. "But it wasn't as bad as the quake of 1906!" She had been a six-year-old in 1906 and retained a vivid impression of that major natural disaster and the ensuing destruction of the city by fire. When I accompanied her into her house, we found that all her cupboards had burst open. Smashed glassware and crockery littered the kitchen. Her television set had been shaken off its stand, and the screen had shattered when it fell to the floor. Wherever one looked, there was devastation.

Meanwhile, on Interstate 280, the Junipero Serra freeway, Barbara Dulik and Margaret were on their way home from the food bank in San Francisco. Barbara, who was driving, thought she had blown out a tire and pulled off the road to inspect the car's wheels. Hundreds of other drivers were doing the same thing. Fortunately, the tires and the freeway were undamaged and they continued home uneventfully.

At six fifteen, I went to Stanford to the history building where I was to lecture and saw how extensively the older buildings on the campus had been damaged. There was an electrical power outage. Out of a class of fifty or more students, only two or three showed up. We stood chatting, surveying the dismal scene for fifteen minutes or so, and then when no other students arrived I cancelled the class and we returned home. There were numerous after-shocks with frightening tremors. Since our cottage was an old unreinforced brick structure, Margaret and I got out our sleeping bags and slept in the driveway under the stars. Thousands of Stanford students were doing the same thing, sleeping on the lawns outside the dormitories, many of which had been severely damaged.

Up at Star Hill Road, Matt and Arne were pouring concrete

columns for the foundations of the house. Andrew's design and that of his structural engineer called for a hundred and fifty columns—ninety going twenty feet deep into the ground, and sixty of them (of varying heights, the tallest being twenty-six feet) coming out of the ground—all tied together with grade beams at ground level. Before the beams were attached that joined the tops of the columns they looked like a small forest of trees. Matt and Arne told us that when the earthquake struck the columns simply swayed, as did the redwoods—exactly as they were designed to do. When the house had been completed, the consensus in our neighborhood was that it was the safest place to be in the event of another earthquake.

Mention of the foundations leads me to another important topic—our running out of money to continue the construction and the appearance of our fairy godmother. The extensive foundation work—drilling a hundred and fifty holes twenty feet deep and two, sometimes three feet in diameter, filling them with rebar cages and then concrete, tying them together with grade beams, raising the sixty rebar and concrete columns from grade, and tying them together at the tops of the columns with pressure-treated beams bolted into Simpson joints lodged in the concrete—rapidly consumed the money we had thought would build the entire structure. By the time we had constructed a level playing field from which we could begin raising the house itself, we had almost exhausted our cash reserves. It was then that providence in the person of Anadel Law intervened, enabling us to complete our dream home.[186]

---

[186] After discussing this with members of her family, Anadel has provided written, notarized permission to tell this story. Margaret and I have often referred to her as our "fairy godmother." More accurately, she was our "angella"—a Greek word for messenger, usually translated into English as angel. But an "angellos" (or "angella", the feminine form of the noun) is not a celestial being with wings. She is a living human being who by her life and her deeds is an embodied messenger of God's goodness and loving-kindness.

Anadel was a member of the Ladera Community Church and a Stanford alumna. The previous year, the Ladera Church suddenly had to deal with a crisis. The pastor, whom I knew slightly,[187] made a surprising admission to his congregation that he had become addicted to drugs and was going voluntarily into a yearlong rehabilitation program. This flourishing little community found itself leaderless, and it would take at least a year for another minister to be appointed. At the time I was still on the Memorial Church staff, and Anadel and other prominent laypersons approached me to ask whether I could preach for them whenever I wasn't in the pulpit at Stanford, provide emergency pastoral care to any of their members who were ill or otherwise in need, as well as conduct funerals and a midweek evening Bible study to introduce them to the best of New Testament critical scholarship. After discussing this with the dean, who gave the request his blessing, I agreed to take on these added responsibilities. As best I could, I ministered to the Ladera Community Church for the next ten months until an interim pastor had been appointed—and I did this *gratis,* without asking for any compensation in return.

In the course of these many months at Ladera, I came to know Anadel and her husband Ben Law extremely well. Several of our midweek Bible studies were in their home.[188] In a conversation one evening, Anadel casually mentioned that

---

Roman Catholics refer to a select number of individuals of this caliber as saints. Protestants hold that all believers are called to be "angelloi," those who by the quality of their lives and the compassionate nature of their deeds make the world a better place. In this sense, Anadel Law was our "angella."

[187] To protect his privacy, his name has been withheld. Two years after he left the Ladera Community Church, he died of a drug overdose.

[188] Ladera is a small town between Sharon Heights, a subdivision in Menlo Park to the south and Portola Valley to the north. After earning her teaching credential, Jenny got her first job as a fourth-grade teacher at an exclusive private school in Ladera.

she had a small private foundation and that she had helped two of her friends with construction loans until their houses were complete and they could obtain mortgages. This prompted me to ask her whether she would possibly be willing to do the same for us. She invited me to come with Margaret the next day to have a serious discussion with herself and Ben, a retired lawyer. After telling them of our cash-flow problem, they agreed without hesitation to lend us money at the low bank overnight rate. The arrangement was that I would go to them at the end of each month when Matt and Arne presented us with a bill. Ben would draw up a simple note that we would sign, and they would lend us the money. But for Anadel's help, we could never have completed the house. By the time we had sheet rocked the inside, had attached the exterior siding, and laid the decks (without railings) in place, we had borrowed $300,000 from Anadel. We decided that this was all we could afford and notified Matt and Arne accordingly. We told them that we would do what still needed to be done on weekends and in the evening after I came home from work.

Margaret and I occupied 850 Star Hill Road[189] in July 1990. Since there was a considerable amount of work ahead of us— mainly safety features like railings for the outside decks and the stairs inside the house, and handrails on all the stairs—before we could ask for a final inspection, we did this illegally. Until the final inspection satisfied the county inspectors and they signed off, we could not have occupied the house legitimately or get a mortgage—and until we had a mortgage, we could not repay Anadel the money we had borrowed. So we moved our woodworking machines out of the garage and into the living room and from then until we passed our final inspection in November, we would work hard each night after coming home

---

[189] The house was later renumbered by the county as 230 Star Hill Road.

from Stanford and Phillips Brooks until about midnight and also on weekends. Andrew helped us as often as he could.

One of the fine features of this home was that, long before we began construction, Matt and Arne had built a solar kiln on Arne's property in the Santa Cruz Mountains. The kiln dried out the green beams we were to use to support the ceiling and roof of the house.[190] Now we rip-cut and milled those that had been left over to make the interior bannisters and railings. It was with a huge sigh of relief that by November we passed the final inspection, were able to get our mortgage, repay Anadel with interest, and occupy our home perfectly legally. There was still a substantial amount of work to be done—everything from making the built-in and other furniture, to crafting a beautiful mantel above and bookshelves around the fireplace, and then a customized bar—all according to Andrew's designs. But now this could be done at our leisure without the pressure of our indebtedness.

There is a magnificent postscript to Anadel's generosity. Every year, from Christmas of 1990 until I retired from Stanford at the end of 2001, Anadel would present me with a check for $30,000 for the Stanford Center for Biomedical Ethics. I feel certain that she wanted to give back to Stanford the money we had borrowed from her and then repaid. She and Ben was a truly remarkable couple. Ben died years later, and I was honored to preside over his memorial service in the Ladera Church. Anadel is still wonderfully active at ninety-one years of age, living at the Vi on Sand Hill Road and is an inveterate traveler and an active watercolorist. When we passed our final inspection, she invited us to choose one of her paintings for our new home. We now have it prominently displayed in Talent, Oregon.

Over the years, we steadily improved our property. In

---

[190] Kiln-dried wood is far more expensive than green lumber, but kiln-dried beams do not shrink.

1994, Andrew, Margaret, and I built a four hundred-square-foot workshop below the living room.[191] In 1998, we added a magnificent little art studio for Margaret, which also served as a self-contained apartment for guests, with a double-glazed glass roof on the side facing the ocean. This little gem was filled with light by day, and at night, one could lie in bed (a futon) and look up at the trees and the stars. By that time, Margaret had retired from Phillips Brooks. She was a fine watercolorist—taking classes at Canada College, Little House, and then in Redwood City—and graced our home and the homes of our family members and many of our friends with her paintings. She also became an active and committed volunteer at the Opportunity Center in Palo Alto,[192] working each week in the "clothes closet," distributing clothing to the homeless.

I end this chapter with sadness comingled with gratitude: sadness, because on April 19, 1994, on Easter Monday, Peggy died; gratitude, because she died as she (or any of us) would have wished. She had driven up to our home in her little VW "bug" on Easter for Sunday dinner (as she did every week), and Tim had driven down from Seattle. Andrew and Dianna were with us as well. We had a lovely family gathering. Mom had played nine holes of golf the day before and was feeling fatigued. She talked of giving up golf "because impatient people were constantly pushing me from behind." Margaret suggested

---

[191] When Matt and Arne poured the columns that supported the living room and the parking turnaround, they were farsighted enough to insert bolts at exactly the right height into the wet concrete so that later support beams for the workshop floor and the deck and stairs leading down to it could be easily attached to the columns.

[192] The Opportunity Center is a multi-story building designed to provide temporary housing and comprehensive services to the growing number of homeless people in the Bay Area. The money for the project was raised by the Methodist, Presbyterian, Congregational, and Episcopalian churches. Its full-time staff members are paid from a budget funded by several charitable foundations, but it is heavily reliant on volunteers for many of its services.

that rather than give up the game, she should simply wave through those behind her and sit down and rest until they were far enough on for her to resume play. Mom said she would think about it. Tim was leaving after our midday meal to drive nonstop back to Seattle, a journey that would take him fifteen hours. We asked him to call us when he got there to assure us he had returned safely, and Peggy wanted us to phone her as soon as we heard from Tim—no matter what time it was. We were relieved when Tim called us at about 2:30 a.m. on Monday, as was Mom when we contacted her immediately afterward.

Margaret faithfully called Mom at about seven o'clock every morning before going off to work to be sure she was all right. On April 19, Peggy's telephone rang and rang without any reply. We assumed Mom had gone out to breakfast or had taken one of her "old ladies" to an appointment with a doctor. Margaret left for Phillips Brooks, and I said I would keep calling throughout the morning—which I did, without any reply. About mid-morning, our telephone rang. The manager of Crane Place was on the line: "Mr. Young, you had better come down to Crane Place immediately." "Is my Mom dead?" I asked. Evading my question, she repeated, "You need to come down immediately." This short exchange and the tone of her voice was enough to tell me that my Mom had died, and after calling Margaret at school, I left at once for Crane Place.

When I arrived at Mom's apartment, two Menlo Park police officers were already there. The curtain between the little living room and her bedroom was drawn. I asked permission to go through to the bedroom to see my Mom. They refused. The coroner was on her way, and until she arrived, no one was allowed to enter the bedroom.[193] I retorted that Mom had

---

[193] The law in California decrees that unless the deceased has seen a physician at least three weeks before death occurs, it automatically becomes a "coroner's case" to rule out any possibility that death is by unnatural causes.

seen her physician, Dr. Wally Bortz, at the Palo Alto clinic the week before, and I put through a call to him telling him what had happened and asking him to assure the police that he would certify the cause of Mom's death. This he did. Still, the police were adamant. The coroner was on her way, and until she arrived, I could not enter Mom's bedroom. When the coroner finally entered the apartment, I put her in touch with Dr. Bortz. Dr. Bortz assured her that he had seen my mother the previous week and spoke of her chronic heart condition. This satisfied the coroner, and she left at once with the police. Finally I was able to see Mom.

Peggy looked unbelievably beautiful. She was lying on her side. Her left arm was beneath her head, and she had an expression of the utmost serenity on her old—now amazingly young—face. An empty teacup was on the nightstand next to her bed. Evidently, after we had called her to tell her that Tim had arrived safely in Seattle she got up and made herself a cup of tea. After drinking her tea, she had gone back to sleep and had never woken up—this side of eternity.

Margaret and Andrew soon arrived, and we all spent time with her and spoke to her of what was in our hearts before calling the Neptune Society to remove and prepare her body for cremation. Heather, Jenny, and Timothy arrived later. Weeks earlier, as if intuiting her own imminent death, Mom had brought with her when she came for Sunday dinner an article she had cut out of the local paper describing a man who had made his own coffin. She asked me whether I would make her coffin. I reminded her that she had always wanted to be cremated and said that instead of a coffin I would make a beautiful hardwood box to contain her ashes. We picked the spot on our property where we would inter them. When we were building the house, we often brought a picnic lunch and spread the tablecloth on the stump of a redwood tree that had been hollowed out by fire decades before. Into this hollowed-out stump, I carved a niche into which the box with Mom's ashes fit. To cover the niche we had an engraved copper plate made with the words "Margaret Jane Young (Peggy), May 18, 1904–April 5, 1994".

We held a memorial service at Crane Place the Sunday afternoon after Mom died so that her friends there and in Menlo Park could attend. Our whole family was present. We later flew Winston out from Ireland, and after his arrival, we held a second simple service around the redwood stump with our whole family and Mom's and our closest friends in attendance. Winston and I interred her ashes in the box I had made and bolted the copper plate over the niche.[194]

We gave everything in Mom's banking accounts to Winston, and after staying with us for a couple of weeks, he returned to Dublin. That was the last time I saw my brother. We spoke on the phone occasionally. His job, rebuilding highly complicated color-printing machines over a period of six months or more, took him from one city to another but paid well. Eventually, he was able to buy a home in a new development on the outskirts of Dublin overlooking a river. And it was there that he had a massive heart attack and died. Gavin, his oldest son, called us with the sad news and handled all the funeral arrangements.

---

[194] When we left Woodside for Oregon, we unbolted the copper plate and removed Mom's ashes, bringing them up to be reinterred somewhere on our new property.

PART 5

Endings

10

From Woodside, California, to Talent, Oregon

By 2001, I had decided to retire from Stanford and as Codirector of the Stanford University Center for Biomedical Ethics. It was not because I had even begun to tire of the work. There were two chief reasons. One was that my hearing had begun markedly to deteriorate,[195] which made it increasingly difficult to engage in seminar discussions—a format I had always excelled in—and in the question-and-answer sessions that invariably followed public lectures. Despite explaining my hearing deficit to my students or audiences and asking them to speak clearly and distinctly, I had trouble following the drift of their arguments or the thrust of their questions. The other reason was that I had tired of the political infighting that seems to be an inevitable feature of academic life, and was beginning to pollute the atmosphere of the Center.

I asked myself, "What am I going to retire to?" I always believed that one had to keep active and involved—even in retirement. So what were the projects I wanted to occupy the final years of my life? Three answers quickly sprung to mind.

---

[195] I went partially and then almost entirely deaf largely because of working with woodworking machinery and pounding nails during the construction of our Woodside home without ear protection.

One was to devote more time to woodworking, my lifelong hobby and avocation. Next, I looked forward to reading what I wanted to rather than what I had to in order to stay abreast of literature in my field. And the third was to return to the piano because I envisioned myself having time to practice—a luxury I had not been able to fit into my crowded schedule during my full-time career. I also felt I owed it to Peggy for having stopped taking piano lessons from her as a child who didn't want to practice. I will say more about each of these goals in due course, but first I must describe another serendipitous opportunity that presented itself along the road I have traveled.

From Stanford University to NASA Ames Research Center

The National Aeronautics and Space Administration (NASA) has ten field centers in the United States in addition to the administrative headquarters in Washington DC: Ames (research), Armstrong (flight research), Glenn (research), Goddard (space flight), the Jet Propulsion Laboratory [JPL] (space flight), Johnson (space), Kennedy (space), Langley (research), Marshall (space flight), and Stennis (space). These ten centers provide leadership for and execution of NASA's mission. The oldest is Ames Research Center at Moffett Field[196] in Mountain View, California. It was founded in 1939 as a laboratory for the National Advisory Committee on Aviation (NACA). In 1958, with the advent of the space age, NACA metamorphosed into NASA.

In the late 1990s, I had been invited to conduct an all-day seminar for the members of the Human Research Institutional Review Board (HRIRB) at the NASA Ames Research Center. Dr. Ralph Pelligra was both the chair of the HRIRB and the

---

[196] Moffett Field was originally a naval air force base and later a coast guard air station. During World War II, a gigantic hangar was built to house and service dirigibles; it is now an historical monument.

research center's medical monitor. At medical grand rounds at El Camino Medical Center, he had heard me lecture on ethical issues in research with human participants, and he wanted me to explore this topic more fully with the members of his board. I was pleased to do this and spent a delightful day at Ames interacting with the HRIRB, which included some of NASA's most distinguished scientists, and thought no more of it.

In August 2001, five months before the date I had set for my retirement, I received an unexpected telephone call from Dr. Stephanie Langhoff, chief scientist at NASA Ames Research Center, asking whether we could meet to discuss a position she wanted to offer me at Ames. A few days later, we met for lunch. Dr. Langhoff (who had been in the seminar I had offered at Ames years earlier) outlined the job offer. A group of external auditors had recently reviewed all research done at Ames with human participants, and the Director of the center had just received the comprehensive report of their findings. This came to be known as the Brookshire Report. The principal recommendation of the Brookshire Report was that a new position be created with independent oversight over the entire research enterprise at Ames. The Director had acted promptly in establishing an Office for the Protection of Research Participants (OPRP), provided funding for the chief of OPRP, who would report directly to him, and had asked the chief scientist to conduct a search for an ethicist to fill this part-time position. Stephanie's invitation to our luncheon meeting was to follow up on the Director's request

Stephanie informed me that, since I was not a civil servant and—because of congressional budget cuts—there were no available billets for any more civil servants at Ames. She went on to provide a detailed outline of the work I would be doing. I would be an ethics specialist employed on a contractual basis. Twenty hours a week had been allotted for the chief, OPRP, to hire an assistant to serve as the office administrator, and I would be welcome to select this person myself. I would be free to set my own hours. I would have my own office and another for the administrative assistant. My primary duties would be to oversee all research done at Ames with human volunteer participants and to provide research ethics instruction to scientists and staff at Ames as well as to members of the HRIRB. Additionally, it would be up to me to provide an annual report to the NASA Administrator in Washington, D.C. in which I would have to describe all the human research that had been done at Ames during the year, any untoward incidents or complications, and my own educational activities in ethics.

Was I interested in the position as she presented it? I was impressed with Dr. Langhoff as a person, and the job offer was something I could only have dreamed of. Years earlier, at Stanford, I had introduced a required course for all doctoral and postdoctoral students on "the responsible conduct of science"[197] for which I had continued to immerse myself in the ethical issues of research with human participants. I felt fully prepared for this new assignment.

So after receiving Margaret's endorsement, I enthusiastically accepted the Ames job offer, undertaking to start work on February 1, 2002 (the day following the date I had set for my retirement from Stanford). This answered in large part the question of what I was going to retire to. Dr. Stephanie Langhoff and I subsequently became firm friends and close colleagues.

Before returning to the subject of the piano, I should summarize my twelve years at Ames. Five months later, after my farewell public lecture at Stanford,[198] I started work at NASA Ames, as agreed, on February 1, 2001. To set up the Office for the Protection of Research Participants, I recruited

---

[197] Two years later, the National Institutes of Health made courses such as the one I had been offering mandatory for all doctoral and postdoctoral students in the sciences at every institution in receipt of federal funding throughout the country.

[198] See "My Swan Song" in appendix 1.

Elaine Timm whom I had known as a congregant at Memorial Church. She had spent much of her working life at Roche, the pharmaceutical company, and had a strong background in pharmaceutical research. She was retired and lived only five minutes away from Moffett Field.

Elaine was excited to be offered this part-time opportunity and responsibility, and readily accepted the position. She and I soon saw that research at Ames was abysmally disorganized and began a process of remedying this. There was no proper filing system, and we had to create one. Research protocols were often missing or lost, and we had to ensure that, once submitted to our office, the originals never left it. When we started working there, we observed at the monthly meetings of the HRIRB that the members had no clear idea what they were supposed to vote on and were expected to do this without having been able to read full descriptions of the proposed research projects.

We introduced an entirely new system. All research had already been classified in the Common Rule[199] either as "minimal risk" (defined loosely as risks no greater than those encountered in the course of everyday life) or "greater-than-minimum risk." For each minimum risk protocol, I prepared a one-page summary, describing the purpose of the research and how it would be conducted, as well as my assessment of the probability and magnitude of harm to participants as weighed against the likely benefits of the research for them personally (typically there were none) and for society generally. The

---

[199] Health and Human Services (HHS) regulations, 45 CFR part 46, include four subparts: subpart A, also known as the Federal Policy or the "Common Rule"; subpart B, additional protections for pregnant women, human fetuses, and neonates; subpart C, additional protections for prisoners; and subpart D, additional protections for children.

summary also indicated whether or not I had given the research an expedited approval.[200]

Elaine included these one-page summaries in the agenda that was circulated before each meeting to give board members ample time to consider them. Greater-than-minimal-risk protocols could not receive an expedited approval, so full copies of these proposed studies were also sent out to board members ahead of time so that in addition to the factors described above the board would also be asked to evaluate their scientific merit. At subsequent meetings of the HRIRB, all the members were prepared and ready to discuss each protocol and vote intelligently on both categories of research. These documents were confidential and after each of our meetings were collected and sent to the shredding machine.

As the name National Aeronautics and Space Agency announces, all research at any of the field centers around the country is focused on improving the safety and efficiency of the national and international air transport system, on space exploration, or as at Ames, on both. At Ames, most of our minimum-risk research had to do with aeronautics. The far fewer greater-than-minimum-risk studies with human volunteers involving either our G20 centrifuge or the Vertical Motion Simulator (VMS) were designed to elucidate and contribute to the solution of problems associated with the exploration of space.

The chair of the HRIRB, as medical monitor, was actively involved during most if not all of these centrifuge or VMS studies, and he and I jointly conducted the informed consent process in which investigators apprised volunteer participants of the purpose of the research, the foreseeable risks and benefits, and how they would be taken care of and compensated

---

[200] In terms of NASA's regulations, members of the HRIRB could ratify an expedited protocol approval, whether given by the chair, or me, his designee, but they could not reverse our decision.

in the event of anything going wrong. I would also observe participants once they were actually involved in studies on the centrifuge or the VMS.

In the course of my work as chief, I came to know personally most of our leading scientists, including Baruch (Barry) Bloomberg with whom I had been friendly while on sabbatical at Oxford in 1985 (we often hiked in the Cotswolds' together). Barry had won the Nobel Prize in Medicine for identifying the Hepatitis A and B viruses.[201] I would visit their laboratories better to understand and also to monitor the studies they were conducting. This exposed me constantly to areas of science I had not previously encountered. This was one of the things that made my new position so stimulating and interesting.

Another of my responsibilities was to provide ongoing research ethics education to members of the board and to our principal investigators. In addition to half-day seminars two or three times a year, which were open to all scientists at Ames, I prepared a fifteen-minute talk each month for members of the board on a topic of contemporary interest in the area of research ethics. Again, I would provide a one-page summary-outline of the presentation, with background readings. These would be sent out with the agenda for each upcoming meeting, enabling the members to study and think about the topic beforehand and come prepared to discuss it. These proved so popular that I could hardly begin my ethics talk each month before the discussion started, often going on long after the allotted time. The chief scientist was particularly enthusiastic about this innovation, having done considerable work in business ethics in the course of earning her MBA, a degree she was awarded after her PhD.[202]

---

[201] Barry died during my time at Ames. His death was a tremendous loss to science in general and Ames Research Center in particular.

[202] We developed an OPRP NASA web-site, and copies of my ethics talks were posted on this site each month.

What I thought would be a part-time job lasting a year or two turned into something far bigger and more rewarding than I could possibly have imagined back in 2000. After twelve years, more and more of the oversight of the studies conducted at Ames was left to me. I could time my commute from Woodside to Mountain View and then back to avoid the morning and evening rush hour traffic. Elaine proved to be an invaluable assistant, and she, Dee O'Hara, a nurse who was responsible for ordering and keeping current the drugs used at Ames to stock the crash cart always available to the medical monitor, and I were congenial coworkers and friends.

Looking back, it is gratifying to be able to state unequivocally that the objectives set forth in the Brookshire report had been accomplished. Because the chair, the chief scientist, and the chief had been able to work together closely and collaboratively with, yet independently of, one another, research with human volunteer participants had been established on a sound ethical footing with unquestionable integrity.

———

During these twelve years, Margaret and I had time for playing and practicing the piano. This part of my story unfolded as follows. Mark Dalrymple was and still is Stanford's chief sound engineer. Mark, his wife Julie, Margaret, and I had known each other and been friends from the day I began my ministry at Memorial Church. At that time Mark had been a full-time PhD student in geology with a prime interest in seismology and worked part-time as a sound engineer. He eventually withdrew from graduate school to devote himself entirely to sound engineering.

In addition to doing the sound for Memorial Church, Mark set up the amplification and recording equipment for every live performance in each of Stanford's auditoriums. He must have listened to thousands of musicians in the course of his career. I figured that if anyone could recommend a good music teacher, it would be him, and I asked for his advice. Unhesitatingly, he told me that the best piano teacher in the Bay Area was Jodi Gandolfi, PhD. She had been on the faculty of the Music Department at Stanford and was giving private lessons at her home in Menlo Park.

I called Jodi and asked whether I could meet with her to discuss her facilitating my return to the piano by accepting me as a student, mentioning that Mark had given me her name. She readily agreed. The day I went to meet her, I took with me the Methodist hymnal and a book of Scott Joplin's compositions. I had been using the hymnal and one or two of Joplin's pieces to try to relearn to read music. I told Jodi about taking lessons from my Mom as a child and then stopping because I disliked having to practice, of playing the piano by ear under Uncle Tom's tutelage, and of wanting to be able to play some of the music that I loved (Haydn, Mozart, Beethoven, Debussy, and Chopin were among my favorite composers) whose compositions I couldn't possibly play by ear. I confessed to wanting to do this not only for myself—and also for Mom.

Jodi listened attentively. She invited me to play something. And then she asked, "Will you practice?" I promised her that I would. She and I—and soon afterward, she and Margaret as well—then began musical journeys that continue to this day. Jodi is a rare and remarkable human being. She is a consummate musician—composer, arranger, teacher, and performer—whether as soloist, accompanist, or member of an ensemble. As a teacher, she meets her students where they are musically and gently challenges them to move forward, neither so slowly as to allow boredom to set in nor so quickly as to frustrate or discourage. She creates an environment in which beginners or intermediate-level players participate in recitals along with advanced and semiprofessional students yet always feel supported and affirmed. She exposes her students to the classical repertoire and to new and novel musical genres. She is particularly interested in bringing to the fore the music of African-American composers and has spent countless hours in the Library of Congress doing research into this much-neglected but amazingly fertile field. She is a fiercely liberal Democrat, as are we.

A piano lesson with Jodi often begins with a stimulating conversation about current affairs in which we mutually lament the latest Tea Party or right-wing bigotry. She hosts regular recitals in which her students play whatever they have been working on, and these are followed by a social hour where the fortunate members of this little musical community get to know one another and share one another's joys and sorrows. Jodi records these recitals and provides her students with a compact disc of each. These make it possible for one to measure one's progress. Her husband, Walter Mooney, is a distinguished seismologist working for the US Geological Survey and an excellent videographer. He and Mark Dalrymple, who records the sound, produce DVDs of many of Jodi's performances—whether with the Peninsula Women's Chorus, the Picasso Ensemble, or the African-American Music Initiative. In short, Jodi became our music teacher, mentor, and beloved friend.

Why did we decide to retire and move away from the Bay Area? There were several reasons. One was that the house in Woodside, which Andrew had designed and we all had helped build, where Margaret and I had lived in happily for twenty-four years, was demanding more and more of our time in maintenance and was becoming too large for our needs. Another was the increase in bicycle traffic from the flats as we called them up into the hills where we lived—particularly on weekends.

This was a preferred route for cyclists because of the challenge presented by King's Mountain Road steadily climbing up to Skyline Boulevard, continuing on west as Tunitas Creek Road going directly to the coast, and then south along the coastal roads until returning once more uphill to the Bay Area through La Honda. They had begun riding in packs, and one could hardly go around a corner without being confronted with twenty or more riders all bunched together on the wrong side of the road. This became increasingly not only a nuisance but also hazardous. A third reason was that our children and grandchildren all had their own lives, and we were seeing less and less of them. We anticipated seeing as much of them in Southern Oregon as we did in the Bay Area.

Southern Oregon was where we decided to re-locate. Heather and Peter owned a house in Ashland on five acres, and we had been up several times over the years to visit and stay with them. Life was—and is—slower here. There were rich cultural opportunities, with the Oregon Shakespeare Festival, the Britt Music Festival, a symphony orchestra, a chamber music series, and a choral ensemble all emanating from the University of Southern Oregon in Ashland.[203] It was a small town with a real sense of community, and it was extremely progressive politically.

We readied our home for the market and began the process of selling it in the summer of 2012. Simultaneously, I gave notice at Ames that, once the house sold, we would be leaving for Oregon. I wanted the Director to have ample time to begin a search for someone to succeed me. It was important that my successor should be able to build and expand on the foundations Elaine and I had laid.

We had expected our home to sell quickly, but as time went by, and summer gave way to the onset of winter (not an ideal time to have a house on the market) we became more and more discouraged. Sunday after Sunday, Margaret and I left home with a picnic basket so that our real estate agents could invite

---

[203] There is also an Ashland professional symphony orchestra or band that provides six free outdoor concerts in Lithia Park every summer. In terms of an article in the city charter drawn up more than a century ago, funding for this band is a city council responsibility.

potential buyers to an open house. And Sunday after Sunday, we would come back to find that while there had been many visitors, none proved to be seriously interested in buying. The twenty-five-minute drive from the flats up into the hills partly explained it. The resourcefulness required in the hills to keep a house going when there are power outages and other crises— minor where help from plumbers or electricians is only minutes away but more serious unless the homeowner can handle them without such assistance— must also have influenced several potential buyers. And for the younger, urbanized set, life in the hills must have seemed isolated and dull. For us, it was infinitely rich and varied. We had relished being far removed from the noisy crowd.

Whatever the explanation, it was not until February 8, 2013, that we received our first and only offer—after reducing the price. We countered, slightly increasing the price offered, and our home was sold. Coincidentally, the man who bought Ukuthula (a Zulu word meaning "peace within", the name we had given to our home) and his wife had lived in another house designed by Andrew. They were undergoing a divorce. His wife (whom we never met) was to occupy that home so that their two children could continue their schooling in the flats. And he wanted a place to call his own where he could have his children with him at weekends. Andrew's signature style of architecture at once appealed to him.

As part of the sale, we asked to be allowed to stay in our house for another month after escrow closed, for two months in all, while we hunted for a new dwelling in Southern Oregon. We had not begun our search in earnest until we knew we had cash in hand from the sale of our house. While our Woodside home was still on the market, we spent Christmas of 2012 with Heather and Peter in Ashland. They put us in touch with the real estate agent who had found them the home they had bought several years earlier.

We met with her to tell her something about ourselves and

the criteria we had for a new abode: space for our grand piano, Margaret's watercolor painting, and a good-sized woodshop; it must be on one level and smaller than our Woodside home; it must not be so close to neighbors that noise from either the piano or the woodshop could disturb them; it must not be too far away from physicians' offices, clinics, and hospitals; it had to be fairly close to the cultural activities we saw ourselves participating in; and it must either have or have space for vegetable and flower gardens. We told her that, until Ukuthula had been sold, we could not make a firm offer on anything she might show us and that our meeting was preliminary at this point. She took us to a few of the houses that she had available, more to see how they matched what we had in mind than anything else. Only one of them truly appealed to us, but it was terribly overpriced. However, it did give her and us a mental picture of what we were looking for.

Once the Woodside house sold, Margaret and I again went up to Ashland to meet with our realtor. We were now prepared to begin making serious offers. We stayed in a motel (Heather was in Davis, and we wanted to be close to town so that all day Saturday and Sunday could be spent house-hunting). That Friday evening, looking for somewhere to eat, we saw in one of the local papers an advertisement for Arbor House, a family-owned-and-run restaurant in Talent and decided to try it. Talent is approximately five miles north of Ashland and is in a bucolic rural and predominately agricultural area. Dinner at Arbor House was magnificent, and we were entranced by the little village of Talent. It even had its own theater, the Camelot.

We saw five or six houses the next day, nearly all in Ashland, but the last was in Talent.[204] It was five minutes from

---

[204] At one time, Talent was known as Wagner's Creek. In 1876, Aaron Patton Talent bought Jacob Wagner's land, which he had used primarily to harvest logs for cutting into lumber in his own sawmill. A. P. Talent, the new owner, applied for a post office to serve the

the village itself in an area of rolling hills, surrounded by vineyards, peach and apple orchards, stud farms, and even a llama-breeding ranch. The house belonged to a couple who had recently divorced. She is a landscape architect and had a done a spectacular job of landscaping her garden and vegetable patch. Her office was on the top floor of a detached octagonal room with picture windows on every side. It was large enough to accommodate our grand piano and provide space for an exercise machine and for Margaret to paint. Below it was a huge double garage that her ex-husband had used as the workshop where he restored old cars and trucks.

The house had three bedrooms and a living room with a fine Norwegian wood-burning stove that opened out into a kitchen and dining room. It sat on two and a half acres, had two peach and two pear trees, a fig tree, and the most glorious views of the Rogue Valley below and the hills beyond. We thought we had found what we wanted, but before making an offer, we wanted Andrew the architect and Heather and Peter who are extremely knowledgeable about housing in Ashland and its environs to see it. When they did the next day they all confirmed our feeling that this was the right home for us. We made an offer.

The homeowners wanted more. We offered more, and the deal was done. Escrow on both homes, the one in Woodside and the one in Talent, closed on March 9, 2013, and as we had to vacate the Woodside house by April 8, we arranged to be able to move into the home in Talent the following day. That last month in the home we had lived in with such pleasure for twenty-four years was hectic. We engaged a moving company (Shamrock), told them what we would do and what we wanted them to do, and began the process of sifting, sorting, winnowing down, and packing our possessions.

Gino arranged for us to have a debris box into which

---

people of Wagner's Creek. The approved application named the new post office Talent.

anything to be discarded could be dumped and we worked nonstop to get ready for the move, wanting to leave the home we were to vacate in pristine condition. The Shamrock people came to pack and collect what we ourselves had put into boxes on Sunday, April 7. I went to work at NASA for the last time on Monday, April 8, and then I went home to help Margaret with the last-minute cleaning of the house and packing of our truck.[205]

We left California on Tuesday, April 9, in our 1993 Nissan pickup with the bed of the truck filled with items we would need immediately and our little eight-week old puppy, Tuppy[206], a Lhasa-Ohna I had given Margaret as an early birthday present, and arrived in Talent that evening at five. The former owners of the house graciously met us with flowers, a hamper, and a couple of bottles of wine. After drinking to our health and happiness in our new home, they handed over the keys. Before they left, they urged us to get a large dog to keep deer out of the garden and raccoons out of the koi pond. The next morning, the Shamrock movers arrived at eight o'clock sharp. I found a doughnut shop five minutes away and came back with a few dozen freshly baked donuts for the workers. With apparent and astonishing ease, they offloaded dozens of boxes more or less

---

[205] We had given our BMW Z3 to Timothy, with only 75,000 original miles on the odometer and sold our Honda Accord hybrid to Andrew, who had a similar vehicle with considerably more mileage on the odometer, for whatever price he got for his. This left us with our 1993 Nissan pickup—a vehicle we still have with only 80,000 original miles on the odometer.

[206] Tuppy was the name of the first dog Margaret had, equally small. We now call him our "healing dog". When I was unable to walk and in a wheelchair he would sit on my lap every day and sleep on my stomach every night until I recovered. He did the same for me, and then for Margaret, after our shoulder surgeries. The warmth of his little body against ours was tremendously comforting and certainly contributed to our mental well-being and, who knows, to our physical recoveries as well.

into the rooms where we wanted to unpack the contents later. They installed the piano in the studio and my power tools in the workshop, and they were done by noon.

We went to the animal shelter to inquire about a boxer needing adoption. Our first dog, Bess, the beautiful brindle boxer given to us by Viv and Thea Harris as a wedding present, had watched over us in our first home in Rynfield. We loved the breed. Our first dog in Woodside was also a brindle boxer we named Jess. And we fancied a boxer for our first home in Oregon.

The shelter had closed for the day, but one of the volunteers told us that there was a boxer-mastiff up for adoption. If we came early the following morning, she said, we could be among the first to see him. After that, we picked up the new Volkswagen Touareg six-cylinder, turbo-charged diesel, which we had ordered and paid for earlier.[207]

We were at the animal shelter bright and early on Thursday and were taken to see Max, the boxer-mastiff. The sad-looking dog, another beautiful brindle, cowered in a corner of his cage, obviously frightened. We were told that his previous owner had been unable to handle him, and we suspect that he had been abused. I took him outside the enclosed kennel area for a short walk. He perked up immediately. We felt fond of him at once.

We filled out all the paperwork and paid the fee charged by the shelter and for his license and took him home as the fourth member of our little Oregon family. Several immediate challenges awaited us. Obviously, unpacking our fifty or so boxes was among the first. This process, by the way, is not yet complete almost four years later. Building ourselves some new furniture was a fairly urgent imperative. Much of the furniture

---

[207] One of the advantages of making major purchases in Oregon is that the state has no sales tax. By previously paying for the vehicle in cash and waiting to take possession of it until we arrived and were able to prove to the DMV that we were Oregon residents, we saved several thousand dollars.

we had made in Woodside, including our unique bed, had been built-in because of the unusual angles of many of the rooms in our old house. These pieces, representing years of work, had to be left where they were and now replaced.

A third priority was finding a piano teacher. A more diffuse fourth was getting to know our new environs and neighbors. And a fifth was finding a dentist and primary physician. We began the unpacking with necessities and decided that pictures and photographs could wait until we knew our new home better and had a surer sense of where we wanted to hang them. The previous owner had asked us to keep her bed in the main bedroom until she could find a place for it in the house she had yet to find. We wanted our own bed as soon as possible, and our furniture making began with this important item.

I had always half-jokingly referred to my hobby as 'Young's Woodworking". When we were told that the best place in the Ashland-Medford area for hardwoods was Beavertooth Oak, the clerk asked for the name of my company and whether I would like to open a cash account. I said, "Young's Woodworking", and "Yes, I would like to have a cash account." Ever since then I have been given the pick of the finest hardwoods at wholesale prices and have become one of their regular customers. Once the bed, complete with underneath drawers, was finished, a chest of drawers, an entertainment center in the living room for our television and stereo equipment, and chairs and small tables followed.

Shortly after arriving in Talent we found an excellent piano teacher who lives half-an-hour away in Ashland. Kate Culbertson is thoroughly well acquainted with the overall music scene in the Rogue Valley and is technically proficient. However, after four years as her students we have stopped having lessons with her. We hoped to find someone closer to home to study with, equally well-qualified and nearer to where we live—saving us an hour of travel-time each week. I think I have found such a teacher in Pat Daly; Margaret will presently start taking lessons with his wife, Margie. They live five minutes from our home. In any event, we are determined to continue our stimulating musical journey

It didn't take long to find our bearings in our new area. We had several construction projects in the offing and needed a general contractor to do the work—an enlarged deck outside our bedroom where we envisioned having a hot tub, a carport for our two vehicles now that I had commandeered the double garage for my woodshop, and a bathroom for the octagonal studio where we had installed the piano, and where Margaret had her artist's table and I my desk and computer. Our realtor put us in touch with Garth Evey, whom we soon discovered was indeed a first-rate craftsman, thoroughly reliable, and unbelievably reasonable in his charges. Garth did the construction we needed, and he introduced us to the area with the intimate knowledge of a long-time Oregonian. Most of all, he became a friend.

As for our neighbors, we discovered that—with two exceptions—they were slow to warm to strangers. Yvonne Reynolds, a former nurse, and Roger Kitchen, who worked in a lumber mill, live next door and have become congenial acquaintances. Ken and Linda Lund who live above us have become dear friends.

And there is a humorous story to be told about our next-door neighbors on the side of the house opposite Yvonne. Before and since the incident I am about to relate, the most they had ever done was wave to us when they passed us on the road up to our house. Almost as soon as we had Max, I had begun routinely taking him for a three- or four-mile walk each morning. In the spring after we arrived, this was highly pleasurable.

Once spring gave way to summer, bringing with it temperatures above a hundred degrees Fahrenheit for days on end and with wild-fires all around us filling the air with smoke, our walk became more grueling. One such morning, the temperature was 105 degrees, and the air was thick with smoke from dozens of fires in the surrounding hills which had been sparked by dry lightning strikes. I was walking Max back up to our gate when this neighbor stopped his huge truck, rolled down the window, and yelled at me, "You're an animal!" Taken aback and wondering what I could possibly have done to offend him, I asked, "I am?" "Yes," he shouted. "You're an animal!" With that, he stretched out his fist to hit mine, rolled up his window, and drove off.

When next I saw Heather, still puzzling over this incident, I asked what it meant. She burst out laughing. In Oregon, she told me, the highest praise anyone can offer is to call you an animal. This was our neighbor's way of expressing his admiration for someone crazy enough to walk his dog when the conditions were so bad! Other than that, he has not spoken a word to either of us since.

We have a superb dentist right here in Talent, recommended by our friends Gary and Coralie Farnham. Finding a physician we trusted and respected had to wait until some unfortunate medical issues arose. This is the time to describe these briefly.

One of Jodi's projects in the Bay Area has been to offer a benefit concert each year for the Eastside Preparatory College in East Palo Alto. In all the years we lived in the Bay Area, the city of East Palo Alto, separated from Palo Alto proper by highway 101, was as poverty stricken, crime ridden, and educationally deprived as Palo Alto proper was affluent, safe, and home to some of the finest schools and one of the top universities in the nation. It was the only town where working-class African-American and Hispanic families could find affordable housing. It offered few opportunities for young people other than membership in one or other of the gangs engaged in drug trafficking and associated crime.

Then, around the turn of the twenty-first century, a Stanford graduate student in education decided to start a preparatory college in East Palo Alto to afford its young people better options. With the help of some of the Silicon Valley entrepreneurs he had come to know at Stanford, he founded the Eastside Preparatory College, and after graduating from Stanford with his PhD, he continued as its first principal. What this visionary educator has accomplished is altogether extraordinary. The school has a beautiful campus with modern buildings and a splendid auditorium. There are now dormitories for two hundred boarding students. Most importantly, the school has a 100 percent graduation rate, its students have a 100 percent rate of acceptance into four-year colleges, and these students have a 100 percent graduation rate from college! African-American and Hispanic students at Eastside now have opportunities open to them never before dreamed possible in East Palo Alto.

For the last three or four years we were with Jodi, she and her advanced students put on a benefit concert at the end of January to raise money for the school. Her research in the Library of Congress led to the discovery of previously forgotten or neglected African-American composers whose work she and her students and ensemble perform. She commissions new music from young African-American composers. And for the past four or five years, she has been able to fly out from New York Valerie Capers, a blind jazz pianist, composer, and professor of music, and John Robinson, her consort, a bass player, clarinetist, and virtuoso on the recorder, to perform at the concerts.

Margaret and I have been staunch supporters of what has since become the African-American Composers Initiative, a nonprofit organization devoted to discovering and performing music by African-American composers. In January 2014, we drove down to the Bay Area, resolved not to miss the annual concert at Eastside.

Driving home after a short stay in the Bay Area, I noticed a dark shadow in the right-hand lower corner of my right eye. The shadow persisted. As soon as we got back, I called the office of Bill Epstein, the ophthalmologist I had been seeing since we arrived in Talent (he had been recommended by Michael

Gaynon, my trusted ophthalmologist in the Bay Area for many years). Bill urged me to come in to see him at once, which he did as soon as I arrived. He immediately diagnosed a detached retina, put a call through to Jeff Rinkoff the retinologist with whom he works closely and in whom he had the utmost confidence, and scheduled me for surgery the next day. This turned out to be the first of four eye surgeries I was to have in 2014, all under general anesthetic: on February 6 (retinal reattachment), March 20 (retinal reattachment with a partial buckle), April 22 (cataract removal and placement of new lens), and April 29 (retinal reattachment with a complete buckle).

Between them, Bill Epstein and Jeff Rinkoff saved my right eye, yet my vision in it is still poorer than any of us had hoped. Fortunately, I have 20/20 vision in my left eye, and my brain is learning to compensate for what I don't have by enhancing what I do have. Despite this, I am able to read—and do so, widely and voraciously. But worse was to follow.

Less than a week after the fourth eye surgery, on Monday, May 5, I went to our bathroom to change an adhesive bandage on my right knee. I had my leg up on the countertop and suddenly lost my balance. I fell to the floor like the proverbial felled log. As I hit the floor, I heard bones snap. I called for Margaret before losing consciousness. It later became evident that Margaret, with the help of Jean Smythe who was visiting us from South Africa, actually saved my life. I was wedged at an awkward angle against the door. She called 911, and she and Jean held my head up to keep me as comfortable as possible until the ambulance arrived. The paramedics took me to Asante Hospital in Medford. I spent much of the night in the emergency room having x-rays and other tests, only later being taken to the orthopedic floor. By that time, Heather had driven up from Davis, and as will become apparent, I owe my life to her as much as to Margaret and Jean.

The orthopedist did not see me until I had been in the hospital for twenty-four hours. He informed us that the fall had shattered my pelvis, and there was no one in the Ashland-Medford area skilled enough to undertake the complex task of rebuilding it. I would have to go either to Portland or Seattle to get the surgical help I needed. Instead, Heather wanted me admitted to the University of California Medical Center at Davis. She advised the local orthopedist what to enter into my chart in order to meet the Medicare criteria for transfer from Medford to Davis. The transfer was anything but simple. Because of my recent retinal reattachment, I could not go more than five hundred feet above or below the altitude in Ashland where the surgery had been performed. This made transportation by ambulance impossible because of the Siskiyou Summit pass at about four thousand feet on the main interstate (I-5), the only direct route south.

Margaret and I had to be flown to Davis in a pressurized Mercy Flight aircraft.[208] All this was arranged for Wednesday, May 7, and Heather was back in Davis to meet us, having driven down with Jean earlier in the day. After more x-rays and an MRI scan, Jon Eastman, a young orthopedic surgeon and one of the few on the West Coast specializing in pelvic fractures, informed me he would be operating early the next day, Thursday, May 8.

The operation would take thirteen hours, but it was in the first two hours that the life-saving miracle (I use the word deliberately and advisedly) was revealed. I have been on Coumadin, a blood thinner, for many years because of atrial fibrillation. When I fell in our bathroom, a shard of bone from my fractured pelvis penetrated the iliac artery. Despite being on a blood thinner, a clot the size of a fist formed around the severed artery, staunching the bleeding from Monday evening until Thursday morning.

When Jon Eastman opened up my belly, the clot gave way.

---

[208] The Mercy Flight cost more than $18,000. Thankfully, because of the way Heather had encouraged the orthopedist to word his entry into my chart, Medicare met this expense.

I immediately lost two liters of blood. A vascular surgeon, John Anderson, had to be called into the operating room. He took two hours to repair the artery before Jon could begin his work, which lasted for the next eleven hours. The miracle that saved my life had several components. Margaret holding up my head with Jean's help until the paramedics arrived allowed that clot to form. The pressure from the blood loss inside my belly must have contained the clot for three-and-a-half days. By Heather arranging for me to go to UC Davis Medical center, I had the best possible team of surgeons, particularly Jon Eastman and John Anderson. And by getting to Davis swiftly by air rather than slowly by a devious route down the coast, something Heather made sure of in her instructions to the local orthopedist, I was in the operating room before the clot gave way and I bled to death.

There is one additional fact. When I saw Jon Eastman a year later, he told me there are two standard ways of performing the operation he had done on me. One is to go in from the side through an arthroscopic opening. The other, his personally preferred way, is to make an incision completely across the abdomen and access the pelvis from the front. Had he gone in from the side, he said, he would not have seen the clot and I could have bled to death later. By going in from the front, the clot gave way at the start of the operation—and the vascular surgeon was called in.[209]

How can I ever adequately express my gratitude to Margaret, Jean, Heather, Jon, and John? Beside everything else she had done, Heather's position as vice-chancellor for health sciences at UC Davis made it possible for her to ensure that I had VIP treatment: the best hospital room imaginable and the finest nursing and medical care one could wish for. Two weeks after admission, once I had learned to transfer from my bed to a

---

[209] I have included Dr. Eastman's postoperative x-rays of my repaired pelvis in appendix 2.

wheelchair and use a walker, I was discharged in a wheelchair. Heather and Peter drove Margaret and me home by the coastal route (to avoid an abrupt change of altitude), taking two days to get back. Jean flew back to South Africa from the Bay Area. For two months, I was instructed not to bear any weight on my legs. With Margaret's help, I had to learn to walk again. Progress was perforce slow. We found a beautiful little park, Colver Park, five minutes from home with a flat, quarter of a mile track around the perimeter. Each day, we would go there for a few steps with the walker, then a few more, then, after I had begun physical therapy, a few steps sideways. I began to take steps in opposite directions—forward and then backward, then further sideways, left and right. Eventually, a cane replaced the walker. I exchanged the walker for my Nordic ski-walking poles. Soon I was walking a mile a day, then two miles, then three miles, and then four. In my darkest days in the hospital, I had wondered whether I would ever walk again—and now I was back to normal!

Jon Eastman, to whom I reported regularly, was as ecstatic as we were. Finally, no longer needing my arms to bear my weight, I was able have the sixth and final surgery of 2014. When I fell on May 5 and shattered my pelvis I had also severely torn the muscles of my left shoulder. Now I could have the rotator cuff repair that had been postponed for so long.

The best shoulder surgeon in Southern Oregon is Hal (Scooter) Townsend. His schedule is so fully booked that it is almost impossible to get an appointment with him. But here again, a guardian angel was watching over me—and this brings me back to describing how we found our primary physician. When I had my eye surgeries, I had the same anesthesiologist for three of them. Before the third, while being prepared for the operation, I asked this physician, with whom I now had a relationship, whether he could recommend a good internist since I was dissatisfied with the two I had had brief dealings with.

Unhesitatingly, he gave me the name of Robert Yamane, who had recently moved to Ashland from Cottage Hospital in Santa Barbara. Both Margaret and I had met with Yamane, liked him instinctively, and became his patients. It turned out that he and Hal Townsend had known each other from the time they were eleven years old. They had been undergraduates together at Stanford. After graduating in engineering, Hal went to medical school at Harvard and then went back to Stanford for his residency training in orthopedics. Robert did it the other way round. After his undergraduate work in engineering at Stanford he went on to Stanford Medical School, and then to Harvard to do his residency training in internal medicine. As soon as I mentioned to him that I wanted Hal to do my shoulder, but that I would have to wait a very long time for an appointment, he told me not to worry. He would have a word with his friend. Sure enough, within a few days, I had an appointment.[210]

Hal looked at the MRI images taken at UC Davis and put me into his schedule for surgery on August 22. He told us that because the tear was so severe and I had had to wait so long, he couldn't promise a perfect result. What he could promise, he told us, was to do his best and to treat us the way he treated his own family. He also insisted that my left arm be immobilized in a sling for eight weeks after the operation. Only then could I begin passive/assist physical therapy (PT), eventually moving on to active PT.

Heather and Andrew came up to be with Margaret for the surgery, which lasted three hours. Hal was cautiously optimistic about the result. And now, more than two years later, I have strength and a good range of motion in this arm up to shoulder height. Above shoulder height (reaching up to a high shelf, for

---

[210] At the time, the chair of the Department of Orthopedic Surgery was Eugene Carragee, who had been one of my bioethics students and whose marriage I had performed. Hal had been one of his residents.

example), I am aware of deficits. But I am able to play the piano again, use all my hand and power tools in the woodshop, and have been completely free of pain.

Not to be outdone, Margaret followed me into Hal's operating room for the same rotator cuff surgery fifteen months later. In the summer of 2015, she was going down our driveway to the lane leading up to our house to pick some of the blackberries that grow there in profusion. On the way down, she slipped on some gravel, put out her right arm to break her fall, and tore all three muscle groups in her right shoulder. Hal operated on her shoulder on October 27, 2015. Again, Andrew and Heather were there with me in the waiting area outside the recovery room.

When the operation was completed, Hal came out to speak to us. He was extremely pleased with what he had been able to do. The ligaments were still tightly bundled (unlike mine, which were badly frayed), and he was able to snare them and then attach them to little titanium anchors he had screwed into her shoulder bone. She had to undergo the same postoperative regimen as I had: eight weeks with the arm immobilized in a sling, then passive/assist therapy, gradually moving on to active therapy. Hal, Margaret, her physical therapist, and I are confident that in time she will have a full recovery. In a way, it was fortunate that her accident occurred when it did, after returning from our vacation in Alaska.

Once my surgeries were behind me and my physical therapy for the shoulder was well advanced, we decided to treat ourselves to a cruise at the end of May. It was Margaret's reward for caring for me for so long, so diligently, and with such devotion. We had never been to Alaska and decided to cruise the Inland Passage from Fairbanks to Vancouver. It was the most relaxing trip and the most interesting experience imaginable. We flew into Fairbanks and then traveled the scenic railroad route to McKinley National Park. We later took a bus to Denali National Park.

We signed up for several land excursions and also took a

flight in a de Havilland Otter (which takes eight passengers) around Mount Denali and onto the Ruth Glacier at 8,000 feet. The Ruth Glacier is the first of three camps for those attempting to climb Denali (the others are at 13,000 feet and 18,000 feet). On the glacier, we met some of those making the attempt, including one young climber from Argentina. Although lower than Mount Everest (29,029 feet), Mount Denali (20,323 feet) is one of the most formidable mountains in the world to challenge climbers. It creates its own weather, which can change rapidly from complete to zero visibility, and has claimed many, many lives. Two weeks after returning home, we were shocked and saddened to learn that two newly retired schoolteachers from Medford had taken a flight similar to ours, also in a de Havilland Otter, and that the plane had crashed into the face of cliff in a deep gorge, killing all nine on board, including the pilot.

After four or five days on land, we embarked on our small cruise ship at Whittier (we had selected the smallest of the cruise ships because the larger vessels cannot get in as close to the face of the glaciers that roll down to the sea). The cruise was luxurious. We had our own balcony with constant views of mountains, glaciers, and icebergs. The food left nothing to be desired, and this was especially important for Margaret who had been providing us with three meals a day as well as caring for me for the previous year.

There were several land tours we took at the ports we stopped in for a day—the most spectacular was our hike up to the face of the Mendenhall Glacier, unfortunately receding at the rate of a couple of miles per decade as a consequence of global warming. And there were onboard lectures, one of them by Libby Riddles, the first woman dog musher to win Alaska's Iditarod, a thousand-mile dogsled race. Libby brought two of her huskies with her. These unexpectedly small animals can run fifty miles a day pulling a sled. It costs her $30,000 a year just to feed her team of thirty dogs, and lecturing on land and at sea helps meet this expense.

We arrived at Vancouver a week after leaving Whittier, completely rejuvenated and ready for whatever life would bring (little knowing then that it would be Margaret's surgery in four months' time). With that now behind us, we are hoping that living in Talent will settle into some semblance of normality. Our days are full. Doing our exercises and walking takes two or three hours. The piano claims another hour or two. We try to put in a few hours each day in the woodshop, working on projects for others now that almost all our own needs for furniture have been satisfied. And Margaret is getting back to her painting after a long hiatus. We love reading. We have season tickets for the symphony, the chamber music concert series, and the Oregon Shakespeare Festival. We go occasionally to hear the Ashland Band and the Repertory Singers, as well as attending our local Camelot Theatre. And there are still many places on this wondrous planet that we want to explore and to which we want to travel. The coast of Oregon, with its rivers, forests, and mountains, beckons us.

In 2016, we cruised around the French Caribbean islands of Dominique and Guadeloupe with Andrew, Mara, Alex, and Christi, as the six passengers on a fifty-seven-foot catamaran.[211] In May of this year, we spent two weeks in the United Kingdom with Ken and Deanne, exploring the Isle of Lewis and Harris in the Outer Hebrides where they have bought a crofter's cottage in Crossbost, overlooking a beautiful loch that opens out to the Mizzen, the sometimes treacherously stormy sea between Scotland and the Outer Hebrides. Crossbost is twenty minutes away from the largest town in the Hebrides, Stornaway, where there is a National Health Service (NHS) hospital as well as two supermarkets and other shops that supply the small island with all necessities.

Although we miss our friends and family in the Bay Area,

---

[211] These, and others in the Virgin Islands, were utterly devastated this year by hurricanes Irma and Maria.

we see many of them fairly regularly. Our dearest friends—among them the de Busks, the Fienes, Iris Litt and Dale Garrell, Mary Ann Carmack and Rod Derbyshire, Peter and Jane Carpenter, Mason and Wendy Willrich, Judy and Dan Dugan, Fritz and Sabine, Kathy and Gary Fisher, and Bob Dulik—as well as all our children and grandchildren—have been to see us, sometimes staying in our home for a day or two. Once we are completely restored physically, we hope to travel more frequently down to the Bay Area to visit them or to Los Angeles to be with our youngest grandchild, leaving Max and Tuppy in one or the other of two excellent kennels close to our home.

When Margaret and I made the move to Talent, many of our contemporaries were contemplating moving into retirement homes. This is not something either of us is attracted to. For as long as we have each other, we want to live independently. We said to ourselves when we arrived in Talent that if we had ten good years here we'd count ourselves blessed. We've now had almost five, and despite the fact that they have not been easy, we haven't once had second thoughts about living where we are. The setbacks we have experienced made us aware of the need to get help—gardeners to do much of the yard work and house cleaners to keep the house spruce—and we have been fortunate in finding good, decent people to take over these chores from us.

None of us knows what the future will bring. The lesson we have both learned (or relearned) is the importance of living in the present, making each moment count. For each moment is a gift, never to be taken for granted, least of all squandered by living in the past or in the future rather than the here and now. If and when the day ever comes when we no longer feel able to live autonomously, we'll cross that bridge when we come to it and make the requisite adjustment. Until then, we feel most fortunate to be where we are, and we are thankful to the One who has watched over us all our days and never let us go or let us down.

I have entitled this final part of my memoir "Endings" and, of course, the ultimate ending any of us faces is death. I feel obliged therefore to say something about Margaret's and my thoughts and feelings on this topic, which we discuss with some frequency. In speaking for us both, I feel it is true to say that neither of us fears death, *per se*. Indeed, our experience with death, such as it has been, inclines us to the view that death itself may be the last great experience of life, the prelude to new life in an eternal realm with God and with those we have known, loved, and lost—and many we have not. It takes too much hard work to become the persons we are for it all to end with death. In Plato's *Apology,* Socrates's final words to his followers before his own death express our own view:

> Let us reflect in another way, and we shall see that there is great reason to hope that death is a good for one of two things—either death is a state of nothingness and utter unconsciousness, or, as men say, there is a change and migration of the soul from this world to another. Now if you suppose there is no consciousness, but a sleep like the sleep of him who is undisturbed even by dreams, death will be an unspeakable gain. For if a person were to select the night in which his sleep was undisturbed even by dreams, and were to compare this with the other days and nights of his life, and then were to tell us how many days and nights he had passed in the course of his life better and more pleasantly than this one, I think that any man … even the Great King will not find many such days or nights, when compared with the others. Now if death be of such a nature, I say that to die is gain; for

eternity is then only a single night. But if death is a journey to another place, and there, as men say, all the dead abide, what good, O my friends and judges can be greater than this? If indeed when the pilgrim arrives in the world below, he is delivered from the professors of justice in this world, and finds the true judges who are said to give judgment there, Minos and Rhadamanthus, and Aeacus and Triptolemus, and other sons of God who were righteous in their own life, that pilgrimage will be worth making. What would a man not give if he might converse with Orpheus and Musacus and Hesido and Homer? [And, we might add, Leonardo and Rembrandt, and Bach and Brahms, Darwin and Einstein, Tillich and Barth?][212]

If we do not fear death, what we do fear is that one of us will have to leave the other behind—alone. Neither of us could live where we do now on our own and enjoy the independence and privacy we cherish. Whether Margaret or I are the first to die, the other will have to make a tremendously difficult transition to a completely different way of life. But if endings also hold the promise of new beginnings, we trust that our innate resilience and the emotional support of our children, grandchildren, and cherished friends will enable the survivor to move on bravely to that next phase of life here on earth.

---

[212] *Plato, Selected Dialogues, Apology,* the translation of Benjamin Jowett. The Franklin Library, Franklin Center, Pennsylvania, 23–24.

11

Looking Back with Wonder and Gratitude

Frequently in my years as a professor and clinical ethics consultant, one or other of my Stanford students would ask wistfully, "How does one get to do what you do?" I would tell them that when I was their age I couldn't possibly have known what I was going to be doing when their paths crossed mine, let alone have formulated any plan to end up doing it. My only advice to them was, "Do what whatever it is you are doing *right now* to the very best of your ability. Do it with all your heart. Do it with passion and joy. Be ready to walk fearlessly through whatever next door may open to you. And remember, especially, that whenever one door slams shut, another always opens."

Margaret and I often marvel at the twisting road our lives have taken. Who could have predicted that a young man from peri-urban Bedfordview and a young woman from suburban Parktown, Johannesburg, would end up at one of the finest universities in the world and live in such desirable parts of the planet as the Bay Area and where we are now in south-western Oregon? Who could have foreseen that our children would go on to do the amazing things they have done with their lives?

I summarized briefly each of our children's careers in a previous chapter and will not repeat what I wrote there except to say a few words about each to bring their stories up to date.

Heather has had a stellar career in nursing, specializing in gerontology.[213]

Andrew's and his partner Steve's architectural firm, Young and Borlik, has been practicing in the Bay Area for more than three decades and has earned a reputation second to none with clients from around the country and from overseas.[214]

---

[213] After earning her PhD at the University of Washington, she worked for some years in the private sector as the chief executive officer of ERA Care, an organization dedicated to building and running retirement communities for the elderly. Deciding to get back into academia, she accepted a professorship at the University of Washington, and then was offered a professorship at the Oregon Health Sciences University with responsibility for rural health. This allowed her to live in Ashland with Peter and to work both at the University of Southern Oregon where she had an office as well as in Portland to which she commuted for a week or more each month and where she lived in a rented a condominium and had her primary office. During this time she was elected a Fellow of the American Academy of Nursing, a signal honor. Then there followed possibly the most brilliant phase in her life's work until now. The Betty and Gordon Moore Foundation had given the University of California, Davis, a grant of $100 million to establish a school of nursing. When she asked what we thought about her applying for the founding deanship of the new school, Margaret and I were among Heather's many friends and colleagues who urged her to do this. The point we made was that if she truly wanted to make a difference for good in her chosen field, this was the opportunity of a lifetime. She went ahead and applied. After an international search, Heather was offered and accepted the deanship, and with it the responsibility of founding a new school—something she has done with the utmost distinction. After eight years, the school is already among the top 25 percent of nursing schools in the nation, and Heather's reputation as a leader, an educator, a pioneer in the field of gerontology and a force to be reckoned with in healthcare in the United States and around the world has grown. Further, even larger opportunities are already beckoning.

[214] They have weathered downturns in the economy as well as the major recession of 2007–9 and have become stronger as many other architects have gone under. Their firm is highly regarded

Andrew's and Mara's two girls, Alex and Christi, the one a graduate of and the other a junior at Menlo-Atherton High School, have developed into young women beautiful in every way: vivacious, gregarious, athletic, extremely bright, and most of all, humble, compassionate, civic-minded, and committed to improving the lot of those less fortunate than themselves. Alex entered Southern Oregon University's Honors College, here in Ashland, in the fall of 2017.

For many years, Jenny has been office manager and financial officer at Young and Borlik in charge of payroll, billing, accounts receivable, and at the same time making sure that the firm's various projects are proceeding on schedule and that every one of their employees is kept busy. She and Gino's children, now adults, have done extremely well for themselves. Andriana, Daniel, and Nicholas have each earned their master's degrees. Andriana is employed by a lighting company in Arizona, getting a taste of the real world; Daniel has just earned his teacher's credential, following in his mother's early footsteps as an elementary school teacher; Nicholas (the youngest) is serving an internship at a major construction company in order to fulfill the state of California's requirement for certification as an architectural engineer; and Michael has shown a remarkable aptitude for working with heavy equipment and is licensed to drive eighteen-wheeler tractor-trailer big

---

by contractors, building departments of cities in the Bay Area, and clients alike. At any one time, they have close to one hundred projects actively under way. They have purchased their own office building, a new structure in Los Altos. And with all this, Andrew and Mara make time to serve their community—coaching soccer teams, working to raise money for the schools his girls have attended, and—in Mara's case—designing and then, with volunteer help, building a lovely little drought-proof park on a piece of property belonging to the utility company PG&E adjacent to their home that previously was a dumping ground for neighborhood junk.

rigs, something he is doing for a garbage company. He is highly gifted and has a bright future.

For decades, Timothy struggled hard to make ends meet as a professional musician. For him, as he cheerfully says, it was never either a feast or a famine; it was merely a snack or a famine. And then, two years ago, his fortunes changed for the better. First of all, his wife Eryn became pregnant. They had given up all hope of having a child of their own. Their two serious attempts at adoption, though costly in terms of the money they had to spend and the ordeal of being interrogated by social workers and adoption agencies, came to naught. Much to the delight of the whole family and principally themselves, little Levon Psalter was born on October 4, 2014. He has begun pre-school at the French School even as I write and will remain there through high school. Already, he is speaking a little French. By the time he leaves school he will be completely bilingual.

The other possibly life-changing event for them both, briefly mentioned earlier, is that Timothy now has a contract with the Columbia Broadcasting System (CBS) as lead guitarist and musical arranger in a new band that backs up CBS's *Late, Late, Show.* Early in 2014, CBS hired British comedian James Corden to host this show. Corden negotiated with CBS to have his own band, something that the show did not have previously. Once CBS agreed, Corden asked his friend, Reggie Watts, a vocalist, to form the ensemble. The first person Reggie called was Timothy. He and Tim had been students and friends together at the Cornish College of the Arts in Seattle twenty-five years earlier and had maintained their friendship over the years. So now, for the first time in his career, Timothy has financial security,

It is doubtful whether any of our children or grandchildren would be doing all this or would have become who they are had we been allowed to stay in South Africa. In 1994, when Nelson Mandela became prime minister of the new rainbow nation, the country seemed to have infinite promise. Unfortunately, Mandela's successors in high office have shattered that dream. Corruption, self-serving, and a callous disregard for the well-being of South Africa's majority, whose lot the African National Congress Party was supposedly committed to improving, have left the country impoverished, the infrastructure devastated, with soaring rates of unemployment and crime, and the currency drastically devalued.

Those with skills are emigrating at the same time as Syrian and north-African refugees are seeking better lives in Europe and in the United States. They have difficulty finding a welcome in any developed country and often have to do menial rather than skilled work when they are accepted as immigrants—as one of my cousins is doing in Australia. In South Africa, he was general manager of a large printing company. He and his wife once were well off, living in one of the most exclusive areas in Johannesburg's northern suburbs. Now, in Brisbane, they are working as housecleaners to make ends meet.

We look back on the circumstances that brought us to this land of opportunity in the early 1970s with inexpressible gratitude and wonder. How blessed we, our children, and our grandchildren have been because the door to living in California opened just as the door to staying in South Africa closed.

Profound theological questions lie beneath the surface of the language used in the above short paragraph. I write of feeling blessed, and this raises the question "By whom?" I express feelings of gratitude and wonder. Again, this begs the questions, "Gratitude to whom? Of whom am I in awe? And what or who moves me to a sense of wonder?" Perhaps I can offer our children and grandchildren no greater gift than an honest description of the spiritual convictions that have sustained me throughout my life's unpredictable journey. So here, in summary, is what I believe.

Over the years, my religious beliefs have undergone radical changes, yet at a profoundly deep level, my core convictions have remained unaltered. I am as committed to and passionate about social justice and as opposed to racial and religious bigotry as I was more than sixty years ago. Both Margaret and I are staunch members of the progressive wing of the Democratic Party. I am as disturbed by the widening gap between those with wealth and those who live in poverty here in the United States as I was in South Africa.[215] Trained as a biblical scholar and as a theologian, I abhor a literalist approach to the Scriptures as well as Christian dogmatism and imperialism. That is to say, I am convinced that the historical-critical approach to reading and understanding the sixty-six books that make up the canonical library we know as the Bible is the only way to make sense of them. Each was written in a definite historical context, and each addresses issues contemporary at a particular time and place, important for the spiritual and moral understanding of those to whom they were addressed. Only as these contexts and historical backgrounds are studied can the message of each book be appreciated and applied to ourselves.

King-James-Version literalism, by which I mean taking a four hundred-year-old English translation as the absolute Word of God—rather than any one of the myriad variant readings in the original Hebrew or Greek manuscripts or fragments— is too simplistic to be given credence. What I referred to as Christian dogmatism and imperialism is equally abhorrent. Bob Hamerton-Kelly used to talk scornfully about evangelical Christians with a capital K, who proclaim their dogmas as the final Word of God and wish to impose them on all-comers. Those who resist, of course, are deemed nonbelievers, doomed to end up in hell because only those who believe as they do will be "saved." I couldn't agree with them less or with Bob more.

So if these foundational convictions have not changed, what has?

---

[215] Whenever I bought a new jacket and went out and saw people in rags outside the store, I felt guilty.

My understanding of what it means to serve God has been enlarged. All of my spiritual mentors, J. B. Webb, J. Clark Gibson, and William Sangster, to name three, reinforced my naïve notion that the only call from God was to the ordained ministry. I no longer believe this. Scientists can be and are called to serve God through the pursuit of truth and knowledge. Artists can be and are called to serve God in creating music, literature, drama, or sculpture. Physicians can be and are called to serve God through the art and science of medicine. In fact, if I had to do it all over again, I think I would have gone into medicine and not the ministry.

My years as chaplain to the Stanford Medical Center taught me many things, among them the need to meet and respect patients where they are spiritually and to condense my own beliefs into the simplest formula I can. Patients confronting serious, critical, or life-threatening medical issues may or may not be "Christian" or even religious. Some may belong to other faith traditions—Buddhism, Hinduism, Islam, or Judaism. Others may be agnostic or avowedly atheistic, but all must grapple with life's ultimate questions. Being with and respecting them means keeping an open mind and attempting to appreciate where they are coming from without making any judgments, spoken or unspoken. And distilling my own beliefs into a simply communicable form is necessary because frequently, after telling me what they do or do not believe, patients or their family members would ask me to tell them about my own beliefs.

So what do I believe? I will state three core convictions that have guided me throughout the long years of my life and that have not changed.

The first is that I believe in God without even beginning to know all that those three letters mean. Perhaps Alcoholics Anonymous is right to speak of a Higher Power rather than any particular God. This Higher Power moves me to gratitude and wonder. I glimpse the face of God through the telescope and the microscope, through the exquisite beauty and complexity of the universe of which our galaxy is part and of universes beyond it; and of the breathtaking detail and power in a desert flower, a butterfly's wing, or a strand of DNA. I glimpse the face of God in the faces of ordinary human beings who have lived extraordinary lives—lives of heroic struggle on behalf of the downtrodden and oppressed; lives of boundless compassion for those in need; lives of integrity, goodness, and truth; lives of those who left the world better because they inhabited our planet. And most of all, I glimpse the face of God in the visage of Jesus, the Jewish Rabbi, the carpenter's Son, the One who exhorted us to love God with all our being and our neighbor as we love ourselves. In his teaching, in the deeds that exemplify his teaching, and in his suffering with, and for, and because of us, I find myself in touch with the divine. This fully human one contains as much divinity as can be poured into a mortal being—and more than my little mind is able to encompass.

In his profound yet apparently simple little book, *The Way of All the Earth: Experiments in Truth and Religion,*[216] John S. Dunne offers an analogy that captures perfectly the view of God I have just expressed.

Dag Hammarskjold ... on his outer journey was Secretary General of the United Nations, while on his inner journey, as his spiritual diary attests, he was a Christian. The Meditation Room which he designed at the United Nations Building and the short leaflet he wrote for visitors reveal the connection between the two journeys, the inner and the outer, as he saw it. "We all have within us," he begins, "a center of stillness surrounded by silence." Then he goes on to reflect on the scene in the Meditation Room, a shaft of light striking a block of iron ore which looks like an empty altar "not because there is no God, not because it is an altar to an unknown God, but because it is dedicated to a God [humans] worship under many

---

[216] University of Notre Dame Press, 1972.

names and in many forms." ... "There is an ancient saying," he concludes, "that the sense of a vessel is not in its shell but in its void. So it is with this room. It is for those who come here to fill the void with what they may find in their center of stillness."[217]

In my outer journey in the medical school, to a certain extent as chaplain to the Stanford Medical Center, and at NASA, I practiced Dietrich Bonhoeffer's posture of anonymous Christianity. I tried by my life to demonstrate what it means to live as a Christian, not necessarily with words—unless asked specifically about my core convictions. But in my inner life, and in my preaching at Memorial Church, I could speak of him who filled the void in my private center of stillness. And this is the God whom I have come to know most surely through the life, suffering, death, and teaching of Jesus, the Jewish Rabbi of Nazareth.

A second core conviction is that the three cardinal virtues of faith, hope, and love summarize the essence of spiritual obligation and duty. Faith is not the same as belief, though it includes an element of belief. Essentially, faith has to do with trust, with entrusting oneself and one's cares and concerns into the hands of the God one believes to be the ultimate source of all being. Belief is theoretical. Faith is practical. It is a moment-by-moment entrusting of oneself, one's loved ones, one's world, into the keeping of the divine. Hope is not the same as optimism, though optimism can result in an optimistic glass-half-full rather than half-empty attitude toward life (which I have always had). Hope holds that God alone has the final word in human affairs and that the destiny of individuals and of nations is beyond human control but is ultimately determined by a divine purpose, and that that purpose is good. Hope can confront even death unafraid because life is stronger than death, light is more powerful than darkness. And love: a love that is mightier than whatever attempts to extinguish it. Love begins

---

[217] 131.

with the love of God for us. We love because God first loved us. Our love is but a response to that infinitely wider, deeper, and greater love. In the words of the old hymn: "Love so amazing, so divine, demands my soul, my life, my all." And as already touched upon, this entails loving God with one's entire being, loving oneself without qualification since this is how God loves us, each one, and then loving one's neighbor unconditionally as oneself. Obviously, embodying these virtues of faith, hope, and love is the work of a lifetime. It is not accomplished without daily effort and the grace of God that constantly picks us up after falling down, sets us on our feet again, and empowers us to begin anew.

The third element in my credo is trust in the providence of God. Grandma expressed this simply in the notion that no door ever slams shut without another gently opening. By providence, I do not mean divine intervention. It is difficult for me to believe in an interventionist God for one simple reason: if God were to intervene to save *me* from a fatal automobile accident in which others perished, why was there no intervention to save *them*? Rather than providence interpreted as divine intervention in human affairs, I understand it as humans actively aligning themselves with the divine purpose. It was that divine purpose, working through Margaret, Jean Smythe, Heather, Jon Eastman, and John Anderson, that saved my life after I fell and shattered my pelvis. It was at work through Bob Hamerton-Kelly and the search committee at Stanford that brought us from Bloemfontein to California. It was at work through Anadel and Ben Law in making it possible for us to complete the building of our Woodside home. And to go even further back, it was at work through Margaret's insisting that I should find and speak to Bishop W. Kenneth Pope to ask him to help me with a job offer, essential for our getting green cards, which allowed us to enter the United States as permanent residents and later to return after we had to leave South Africa. Providence requires human agency as well as an overarching divine purpose. So my gratitude and wonder have two foci: I am grateful to and in awe of the divine purpose that has been the unseen but overarching reality in my life; and I am thankful to all those who have nudged me, or pushed me, into aligning my own will with His, thus shaping who I am and leading me to where I am.

So my final and deepest word of gratitude is reserved for my family: for Margaret, my beloved wife for fifty-eight years and for our children and grandchildren whom I love until the end of counting and back. To them and to those friends who have walked beside me on this amazing, unpredictable journey, I owe a debt of thanks I can never possibly repay.

In conclusion, I will end this chapter with the three last sermons I preached on consecutive Sundays at Memorial Church after ministering for more than twenty-one years to this unique congregation of students, faculty, university staff, alumni, and interested members of the Bay Area community. In many ways, they are a summation of the essential core convictions by which I have tried to live and of which I have written.

Faith and Reason

I will begin on a personal note. I became a Methodist almost entirely by accident. As a child, I had been raised Roman Catholic, in accordance with a promise my Roman Catholic father had made when he married my Episcopalian mother. Catholicism never meant much to me. At the time, the services were all in Latin and involved long periods of kneeling. When my back didn't feel like it was going to break, I was bored to tears. After I had received my first Holy Communion at the age of seven, my father's duty was done, and I was free. After that, I didn't go to church much, except maybe at Christmas and Easter, when I went with my mom to her Episcopalian services.

When I was nineteen, I decided to take voice lessons and was advised that the best singing teacher in Johannesburg was a man named Rupert Stoutt. I later learned that Rupert was also the organist and choir director of the Methodist Central Church. Before long, he had invited me to sing in his choir. That's when I became exposed to a form of Christianity that, for the first time, made sense to me. The minister of Methodist Central Church was Dr. J. B. Webb. He was a giant of the pulpit, a graduate of Oxford University, who combined a profound faith in God with a concern to make faith intelligible to thinking people. He also combined his love for God with a passion for social justice. This led me to say to myself: "If this is what Christianity is all about, count me in." That's how I became a Methodist; that's how I met the young woman who would eventually become my wife; and that's how I took the first step that later led to offering myself for the ministry. J. B. Webb became one of my mentors, a model of someone who held faith and reason together, in constant, creative tension.

I did not know it at the time, but this was true, also, of Methodism's founder, John Wesley. Wesley was an Oxford don. The "Methodists" were a group of Oxford faculty and students, members of the Church of England, who were serious about their faith. Wesley brought them together for daily Communion, prayer, and Bible study in the original Greek. They were nicknamed "Methodists" (which they later adopted as descriptive of their new spiritual movement) at that great university because they pursued their spiritual goals so methodically. The model of faith in constant, creative tension with reason exemplified by J. B. Webb and the early Methodists has always been crucial to my own Christian self-understanding.

I will speak of this form of the relationship between faith and reason at greater length later. But, first, two other, diametrically opposite ways in which faith relates to reason require a brief mention. In the one, faith supersedes reason; in the other, faith is subordinated to reason.

In the cults and sects, most obviously, but also in fundamentalist Christian circles, faith typically supersedes reason. Faith is taken to mean uncritical assent to a set of propositions authoritatively declared by the leader or leaders of the cult, sect, or group. These propositions may or may not derive from the Bible. When they do, it is always the leader's interpretation of the Bible that has to be accepted. Ordinary members are not encouraged to think for themselves. To the contrary, the cults lead those who join them to believe that their previous way of thinking about life and the world was completely misguided. So first they have to be *deprogrammed* before they can be *reprogrammed* to think and believe as their leaders want them to. This requires a deliberate suspension of the critical faculty. Reason is to be set aside. All that matters is faith—in the sense of believing utterly everything one is told.

In a masterful little book the French philosopher Etienne Gilson described people in this category as those "according to whom Revelation had long been given ... as a substitute for all other knowledge, including science, ethics, and metaphysics. Ever since the very origin of Christianity up to our own days, there have always been such extremists in theology. Reduced to its essentials, their position is very simple; since God has spoken to us, it is no longer necessary for us to think."[218]

This view of the relationship between faith and reason is inadequate in several ways. First, it conveniently fails to emphasize that we are to love the Lord our God "with all our heart, with all our soul, with all our *mind,* and with all our strength."[219] Loving God with all our mind is as much a duty as trusting God with all our might. Questioning and probing have their place in the religious life as much as believing. As Tennyson put it: "There lies more faith in honest doubt, Believe me, than in half the creeds."[220] Second, it allows people

---

[218] Etienne Gilson, *Reason and Revelation in the Middle Ages.* New York: Charles Scribner's Sons, 1938, 5f.

[219] Mark 12:29–30.

[220] Alfred, Lord Tennyson, *In Memoriam,* cviii.

to be manipulated by those who assume the prerogative of doing their thinking for them. Remember how eight hundred followers of the Reverend Jim Jones permitted themselves to become so brain-washed that they drank Kool-Aid laced with cyanide when he ordered them to? And, third, this view of religion, far from enabling people to realize their full potential, ultimately retards and stunts their development as persons. It is an infantile, rather than an adult, form of spirituality. It holds people back, whereas authentic Christianity should carry us forward into fullness of being.

At the opposite extreme, and perhaps in reaction to this type of Christianity, there are those who would subordinate faith entirely to reason. If Tertullian, Tatian, and their followers asserted the primacy of faith, modern rationalists retaliated by proclaiming the primacy of reason. By the end of the thirteenth century, rationalism was steadily gaining ground in Europe. Some of the rationalists' propositions (quoted by Gilson) are that "there is no higher life than philosophical life," that "there are no wisdoms in the world except those of the philosophers," or that "nothing should be believed, save only that which is self-evident, or can be deduced from self-evident propositions."[221] The Renaissance and the period in history known as the Enlightenment further elevated to a fine art skepticism of anything that could not be demonstrated rationally. The supreme subordination of faith to reason occurred in the twentieth century in the writings of A. J. Ayer, who made the claim that only those propositions capable of empirical verification could be regarded as true. Ironically, Ayer failed to recognize that this assertion is not itself capable of empirical verification and, therefore, on his own terms, must be false.

Those who dismiss faith by holding that reason alone can lead us to truth are as mistaken as those who make the opposite

---

[221] *Ibid.,* 64.

claim. To start with, they ignore the fact that even in that most rational of human endeavors, the pursuit of science, there is usually a hunch, an insight, or an intuition, which the scientist trusts and then proceeds to test and possibly corroborate by empirical observation and rational inquiry. That is to say, faith is ingredient to the scientific enterprise. Further, to assert that reason alone can lead us to truth is to ignore other areas of human activity that men and women in every generation have experienced as profoundly real: for example, the experiences of falling in love (how can this be explained rationally?), of being moved to the core of one's being by a requiem, a cantata, a symphony, or a sonnet, or of becoming aware through a totally non-rational but undeniably powerful dream of an important area in one's life where work needs urgently to be done? Love, music, dreams, poetry, paintings, dreams, and meditation are all ways of encountering what is true and what is real that are almost entirely independent of reason.

And, thirdly, there is something arrogant and even presumptuous in the conceit that our little minds, with finite rationality, will ever be able fully to encompass and contain the majesty and the mystery of God. God is greater, and higher, and holier, and more wonderful, and more awful than anything we can ever think or think to know. As the prophet Isaiah put it: "For my thoughts are not your thoughts, nor are your ways my ways ... For as the heavens are higher than the earth, so are my ways higher than your ways and my thoughts than your thoughts."[222]

This brings me back to where I began. For me, the only tenable form of the relationship between faith and reason is one where both are held together, constantly, in creative tension. Without faith to inform it, reason is sterile and one-dimensional. Without reason to illumine it, faith is superficial and degenerates quickly into credulity.

---

[222] Isaiah 55:8–9.

I have to define more precisely what I understand by faith. Usually, it is thought of in terms of belief, of assent to certain propositions. In my view, this is only a very small part of faith. The much more important component is that of entrusting oneself to God on the basis of one's beliefs. Let me offer a simple illustration. I may believe that the water in a swimming pool will support my weight and that I need not drown when surrounded by it. But that belief means nothing until I dare to jump into the swimming pool, entrusting myself to the water. In this sense, faith is an indispensable element in the spiritual life. We have to dare to entrust ourselves to God on the basis of what we have come to believe about God's nature and purpose; we have to find the courage to dare to live on the basis of these beliefs.

Reason has a crucial role in formulating and refining these beliefs. Reason enables me to look critically, not only at the Bible, but at the way authority figures interpret it. Reason requires me to look equally critically at church teaching and tradition. This is not blasphemous. On the contrary, if I am attempting to love God with all my mind as well as with all my might, it is an expression of my piety, of my deep commitment to the one who is above and beyond my loftiest aspirations and my highest thoughts. And that critical look enables me, in part, to sort out what in the Scriptures and in church teaching and tradition is time-bound and culturally conditioned and to separate it from that which is timeless and universal. In this, sense, reason makes belief more well-informed.

So there is this endless dialectic, this perpetual dance, between faith and reason. Reason enables me to refine and reformulate my beliefs. I entrust my life to God, that is to say, I dare to live on the basis of these beliefs. Then I reflect back critically on where this has taken me and on what has happened to me and the work of refining and reformulating my beliefs begins all over again. And that, in turn, leads to new ventures in entrusting and living.

I have described myself from this pulpit, more than once,

as a Christian agnostic. That is to say, there are some things I know. But there is also so much that I do not know. I have more questions than answers. I know a good deal about God's love for me and about what God requires of me because of Jesus Christ, his life and ministry, his death and resurrection, as these have become real to me through my critical reading of the Scriptures and of the church's teaching and tradition. And the things I know, I am committed to. This is the meaning of faith, in the deeper sense of entrusting. But there are also extensive areas where my knowledge is partial or incomplete. And there are some things about which I know nothing at all. Here I have to struggle on the basis of reason alone, in the belief that reason itself is God-given and can be used of God to lead me forward into a deeper and deeper understanding of life and its mysteries. And always there is the humbling realization that some of these mysteries will remain until I no longer see through a glass, darkly, but face to face.

"Love the Lord your God with all your heart, with all your soul, with all your mind, and with all your strength." Don't allow your faith to supersede reason, or your faith to be subordinated to reason. Hold faith and reason together in constant, creative tension. This is what we owe to God. This is what we owe to ourselves. This is what we owe to our mentors. This is what we owe to one another.

Love and Justice

In my sermon last Sunday, I mentioned that one of my early mentors was a Methodist minister by the name of J. B. Webb. Not only did Dr. Webb lead me to see the importance of holding faith and reason together, in constant, creative tension; he also inspired in me a passionate commitment to social justice. The theologian who later had the most profound influence on me in this area was Reinhold Niebuhr. I never had the good fortune to meet him personally. Yet I think I read everything

Niebuhr wrote. Today's sermon title is the same as that given to a compilation of several of his shorter writings.[223]

In the arena of social ethics, Reinhold Niebuhr opened my eyes to two salient truths—the inadequacy of exhortations to love as a basis for social policy and the necessity of concentrating first on working for social justice. I will expound on these two points at some length. Then, in closing, I will suggest that justice eventually requires love for its completion and fulfillment.

Niebuhr never tired of pointing out the insufficiency of exhortations to love as the foundation for a social ethic. The liberal pulpit, in particular, came in for relentless criticism from him. Up to a point, liberalism had been a healthy reaction to an evangelical pietism that concentrated solely on convicting individuals of sins such as drunkenness, adultery, debauchery, and violations of the Sabbath, bringing them to repentance, and offering them a new life in Jesus. This peculiarly American form of Christianity had (and to a large extent still has) no noticeable social conscience. Liberals sought to remedy this by proclaiming a social gospel. Commendable though this was, the attempt was doomed to failure because liberals simply applied the commandment that we love one another to social relations, that is, to the relationships between groups, whether economic or ethnic. And, as Niebuhr pointed out with devastating logic, love as a foundation for social ethics was invariably deficient— for at least two principal reasons.

The first is that groups are powerfully motivated by self-interest. However selfless individuals may be in their dealings with others, one on one, as members of groups, we are driven by collective self-interest. "Whatever may be possible for individuals," Niebuhr wrote, "we see no possibility of a group voluntarily divesting itself of its special privileges in society.

---

[223] Reinhold Niebuhr, *Love and Justice: Selections from the Shorter Writings.* Edited by D. B. Robertson. New York: Meridian Books, The World Publishing Company, 1967.

Nor do we see a possibility of pure disinterestedness and the spirit of forgiveness on the part of an underprivileged group shaming a dominant group into an attitude of social justice."[224] Men have been telling women how much they love them for thousands of years. But, collectively, men were and are a privileged group in society relative to women. It was only when the feminist movement began to pressure men to face up to this and to accord women equal rights in the workplace and in the home that this started to change—and the changes really have only just begun. The point is that it took more than exhortations to (or even expressions of) love to overcome men's collective self-interest; it required pressure. Exactly the same could be said of the civil rights struggle. However decent individual whites may have been in their dealings with persons of color, whites, collectively, were and are a privileged group in society relative to other groups. Exhortations to love did not and do not change this. The power of collective self-interest was and is too great. Overcoming the collective self-interest of whites required pressure—the pressure of protest and the sanctions of civil rights legislation.

A second reason why urging people to love one another is insufficient as a basis for a social ethic is that it assumes that Christianity is the dominant religion in society, and that all members of society, therefore, will be equally amenable to injunctions to obey the commandment to love. This assumption is patently incorrect—more so, perhaps, in our time, than in the decades immediately following World War II when Niebuhr's was the most eloquent theological voice in the United States. Today, our society is increasingly secular and pluralistic. Christianity is one religion among many, and it is certainly no longer dominant. However much the members of Christian churches may be willing to heed exhortations from the pulpit to love one another (and this itself is questionable), the vast

---

[224] *Ibid.,* 34.

majority in society is not listening. Even those who are listening are paying attention only up to a point. They tune out when the call to love others comes into conflict with self-love. If one has to choose between paying one's mortgage and supporting the homeless, one's mortgage inevitably will take precedence.

To the extent that we have become complacent in thinking that merely telling people to love one another is enough to fulfill the Gospel demand for social justice, we are little different from those whom Jesus denounced in Matthew's Gospel: "Woe to you, scribes and Pharisees, hypocrites! You tithe mint, dill, and cumin; and have neglected the weightier matters of the Law: justice, mercy, and faith. It is these you ought to have practiced without neglecting the others."[225]

Because exhortations to love were and are inadequate as a basis for social ethics—for at least these two reasons—Niebuhr elevated working for social justice to the top priority for Christians. Concentrating on justice rather than love allowed Christians to form powerful alliances with people of other faiths, or of no faith. Certainly, this was an impressive feature of the civil rights struggle: priests, rabbis, pastors, humanists, and atheists joining hands in a common cause, that of working for a society in which, more truly, there would be justice and liberty for all.

And Niebuhr's voice provided impetus to this struggle. He wrote: "Every realistic system of justice must assume the continued power of self-interest, particularly of collective self-interest. It must furthermore assume that this power will express itself illegitimately as well as legitimately. It must therefore be prepared to resist illegitimate self-interest, even among the best [people] and the most just nations. A simple Christian moralism counsels [people] to be unselfish. A profounder Christian faith

---

[225] Matthew 23:23.

must encourage [people] to create systems of justice which will save society and themselves from their own selfishness."[226]

Broadly speaking, creating these systems of justice requires compensation for past (and present) injustices, as well as an evenhanded allocation of social goods. That is to say, justice has to be thought of in compensatory terms, as well as distributively.

Distributive justice insists that social goods be allocated equitably, without reference to ethnicity, religion, gender, or—as we would add in our time—sexual preference. It is the notion of fairness, applied to the way in which the benefits and services of society are apportioned. This is not without its problems. For example, does the man awaiting a second transplant whose liver disease has been caused by alcoholism have the same right to a donor organ as the woman whose liver disease was caused by a viral infection still on the waiting list for a first transplant? Does a convicted felon or an undocumented immigrant have the same claim to high-technology, high-cost medical care in this country as a law-abiding citizen?

Compensatory justice gives rise to affirmative action programs. Because past discrimination put so many present members of society at a competitive disadvantage, the injustices of the past must be compensated for now by giving preferential treatment to those who have been held back historically. But the backlash against the notion of compensatory justice has become an inflammatory political issue. It raises the ugly specter of reverse discrimination. The tough question is: How long must the present generation continue to pay for what previous generations did not do or would not do? There is no easy answer to this question. Can thirty years, or even a hundred years, make up for centuries of slavery and oppression? Perhaps it might be said that, at least until there is a level playing field, compensatory justice is a necessary component of any social ethic. But that raises a further question: Is the fact

---

[226] *Ibid.*, 28.

the playing field still is not level due to past discrimination or to present social policies? Which is the more important cause of social inequality: the fact that present tax structures and welfare programs make it likely that only 40 percent of African American children will have a father present to them as they grow up, for example, or the manifest injustices of the past?

Problematic as they are, the twin concepts of distributive and compensatory justice are more realistic as a basis for social policy than preachments from the pulpit exhorting people to love one another. Until the playing field is more or less level, neither the victims nor the perpetrators of injustice are in any position to meet and own one another as fellow human beings, as children of the one God, and thus to find one another in love. The first priority, then, in social ethics, is to follow the lead of the prophet Isaiah: "Is not this the fast that I choose: to loose the bonds of injustice, to undo the thongs of the yoke, to let the oppressed go free, and to break every yoke?"[227]

This brings me to the final suggestion I want to offer. It is only when justice (distributively understood as well as in terms of compensation) is being achieved, however imperfectly, that love can be invoked to complete and fulfill the process. Until both the beneficiaries and the victims of injustice have been jolted, respectively, out of their complacency and their sense of impotence, calling on them to love one another is both premature and unrealistic. Only when the playing field has been more or less leveled, is it possible to find one another as fellow human beings, as children of the one God and to begin to care for and about each other with genuine compassion and empathy. And, when the possibility is realized, love immediately takes us way beyond the strict requirements of justice into a realm of pure grace.

I was vividly reminded of this in July, 1995, when I returned, with Margaret, to the "new" South Africa. I had not been back

---

[227] Isaiah 58:6.

for sixteen years. One morning I walked past the school which Margaret had attended as a child, and where Heather, our older daughter, had gone after her. When I used to walk Heather down to school from our home each morning, it was a school for whites only. When I walked past this same school last July as a visitor, one could see immediately the difference that the Mandela era had ushered in. Now, the children, all wearing the same navy blue uniforms, were of every color in the rainbow. It was playtime when I walked by, and I stood transfixed at the sight of these little boys and girls—black and white and brown—all playing together, jostling, chasing, hugging, embracing, wrestling one another, with utter indifference to the color of one another's skin. I stood there and cried. I had been given a glimpse of what heaven will be like. I thought to myself, *These little kids will grow up completely unconscious of ethnicity and color. They will be one people, citizens of the same nation, and children of the one God.* But that would never have been possible had not the barriers separating one group from another been torn down in response to demands from within the country and from around the world, for social justice. Nor would it have happened had not affirmative action programs been in place, beginning to make amends—in some small measure—for the manifold injustices of the past four hundred years.

The relationship between love and justice is one in which justice has to come first. Only when the pressures of public opinion and the sanctions of the law are creating equality of opportunity, for women as well as men, for ethnic minorities as well as for the dominant white majority, for people who are marginalized by their HIV status or their sexual preference as well as for those in society's mainstream, is it appropriate to begin to call upon these groups, as well as the individuals that comprise them, to love one another: to forgive each other, to accept each other, and to affirm each other as fellow sisters and brothers, as children of the one God, as joint heirs of the gift of life. And when that happens, the miracle of God's redeeming grace and transforming love is repeated anew.

Grace and Gratitude

Grace and gratitude. In these two words, we have the quintessential summation of what Christianity is all about. As Karl Barth put it: "Grace and gratitude belong together like heaven and earth. Grace evokes gratitude like the voice an echo. Gratitude follows grace like thunder lightning."[228] It is more than coincidental that in the Greek, the two words are remarkably similar: *charis* is the word for grace, *eucharistia* the word for gratitude. The Eucharist or Holy Communion is essentially a celebration of thanksgiving for the grace of God.

What is the meaning of this word *grace*? What are the implications of human gratitude either not following grace like thunder lightning; or of grace evoking gratitude like the voice an echo, respectively? These are the questions I shall attempt to address.

Grace is a gift. In Biblical thought, the word is shorthand for the sheer, unmerited generosity and unbounded goodness of God. In the Hebrew Scriptures, God's grace is depicted with terms like *loving-kindness* and *steadfast love*. Creation is an expression of God's loving-kindness; it is God's lavish, even extravagant, benevolence that brings the world into being and gives life to all that is. The covenant God makes with Israel is an affirmation of God's steadfast love. There is a difference between a covenant and a contract. A contract is entered into between equals. A covenant is struck between those who are, in almost every respect, unequal. When God, who is transcendent, initiates a special relationship with the Hebrew people and promises to watch over them faithfully and with

---

[228] Karl Barth, *Church Dogmatics,* IV.1 New York: Charles Scribner's Sons, 1956, 41.

compassion, this is an act of utter magnanimity: "Let me sing for my beloved my love-song concerning his vineyard ... on a very fertile hill. He dug it and cleared it of stones, and planted it with choice vines; he built a watchtower in the midst of it, and hewed out a wine vat in it; he expected it to yield grapes, but it yielded wild grapes."[229] This is Isaiah's poetic description of the gracious covenant God made with a fallible people, Israel. And the exodus, God's deliverance of the Israelites from their oppression in Egypt, and God's leading them, under Moses, toward a land of promise, is again a demonstration of grace, evidence of God's steadfast love, a sign of God's unfailing loving-kindness.

When we turn to the New Testament, the main and characteristic use of the word *grace* is with reference to God's redemptive love, which is always active to heal our brokenness and is ever seeking to bring us back into right relationships with ourselves, with one another, and with God. This gracious word of redemptive and transforming love is spoken to us most eloquently in the person of Jesus Christ: in his birth, his life among us, his ministry and teaching, his death, and his resurrection.

There is a passage in the letter to the Ephesians that captures this perfectly: "You were dead through the trespasses and sins in which you once lived, following the course of this world ... But God, who is rich in mercy, out of the great love with which he loved us even when we were dead through our trespasses, made us alive together with Christ—by grace you have been saved."[230] Jesus's healings, such as his curing the ten men with leprosy (Luke 17:11–19), are a revelation of God's grace. In the ancient world, lepers were feared and shunned. To embrace them, as Jesus did, was an action both unexpected and culturally unacceptable. Jesus's reaching out to the ill and the

---

[229] Isaiah 5:1–2.
[230] Ephesians 2:1–2, 4–5.

infirm are all magnanimous gestures of undeserved kindliness and astonishing goodwill.

In both the Hebrew Scriptures and the New Testament, then, God's grace always expresses itself in acts of surprising goodness and surpassing generosity: in creation, in establishing the covenant, in liberating the Israelites from bondage and leading them toward freedom in a land of promise, and in coming to dwell among us in the person of Jesus of Nazareth, in order that we might have new life, abundant life, life in all its fullness. Not even our intransigence and stubbornness will finally be able to cut us off from the grace of God. Paul put it thus in the letter to the Romans: "I am convinced that neither death, nor life, nor angels, nor rulers, nor things present, nor things to come, nor powers, nor height, nor death, nor anything else in all creation, will be able to separate us from the love of God in Christ Jesus our Lord."[231]

What happens if the human response to grace is not gratitude, but ingratitude? If the two belong together, with gratitude intended to follow grace like thunder lightning, what if, instead of walking toward God and then more closely with God in response to grace, human beings accept the gift but coldly walk away from the Giver? The answer to this question given by Karl Barth, the greatest Reformed theologian of the twentieth-century, is that, essentially, ingratitude is sin. Paul Tillich, considered by many to be the most profound if not the most influential theologian of the twentieth century, thought of sin in terms of alienation. Reinhold Niebuhr, the premier American theologian of the twentieth century, defined sin as pride, on the one hand, and concupiscence, a constant reaching for more— more sex, more material possessions, and more power— on the other. Barth alone sees sin in terms of ingratitude: "Radically and basically all sin is simply ingratitude—[human beings'] refusal of the one but necessary thing which is proper to and

---

[231] Romans 8:38–39.

required of [those] with whom God has graciously entered into covenant."[232]

God looked to Israel, the beloved vineyard, to yield grapes, "but it yielded wild grapes."[233] Jesus healed ten men with leprosy. Only one of them, "when he saw that he was healed, turned back praising God with a loud voice. He prostrated himself at Jesus's feet and thanked him. And he was a Samaritan. Then Jesus asked, 'Were not ten made clean? But the other nine, where are they? Was none of them found to return and give praise to God except this foreigner'?"[234] The response of Israel and of the nine lepers in this story is incommensurate with the gift they have been given. Instead of being drawn closer to God in thankfulness, they walk away with utter indifference. And this, says Barth, is what the Bible means by sin.

To the extent that you and I live our lives independently of God, wrapped up in the illusion of our own self-sufficiency, taking lightly or for granted the astonishing gifts we have been given, including the gift of life itself, and the offer of new life in God, we are sinners. We are no different from the nine who accepted the miracle of being healed and then casually walked off, or from the chosen people, God's vineyard, who, instead of bearing fruit, yielded wild grapes. But the truly astonishing thing about grace is that God's reaction to our ingratitude and our indifference is not to write us off, nor simply to let us walk away into the darkness, but to follow after us with a love that will not let us go and that will never be satisfied until we are back where we belong. The nineteenth-century poet, Francis Thompson, caught this exactly in his poem "The Hound of Heaven":

I fled Him, down the nights and down the days;

---

[232] *Ibid.*, 41–2.

[233] Isaiah 5:2.

[234] Luke 17:17–18.

I fled Him down the arches of the years;
I fled Him, down the labarynthine ways
Of my own mind; and in the mist of tears
I hid from him, and under running laughter.
But with unhurrying chase,
And unperturbed pace,
Deliberate speed, majestic instancy,
The beat—and a Voice beat
More instant than the Feet—
"All things betray thee, who betrayest Me."[235]

Even for Thompson, the homeless opium addict, there came a time when he could run no longer and allowed God's grace to claim him—or perhaps we should say, to reclaim him. Finally, he permitted grace to evoke in him a sense of gratitude, like the voice an echo. This, surely, has been true in our lives as well. Its implications are worth emphasizing in response to our third question, and they are these: *gratitude*, the one word human beings are called by God to utter in response to the grace with which God speaks to us, like an echo to the voice, is the only proper foundation for both spiritual and moral endeavor.

There is an anxious type of spirituality which operates on the following mistaken premise: if only I do enough for God; if only I pray harder, read the Bible more diligently, go to church more often, or serve others more sacrificially, then God will accept me and I will find peace. This premise is mistaken because it ignores the fact that God has already accepted me as God has accepted you. It forgets that the default mode of God's posture toward us is that of grace; and that whatever we do for God—whether in terms of praying, or reading the Bible, or going to church, or serving one another, is simply a response, a way of saying thank you. A spirituality operating from this

---

[235] Francis Thomson, *The Hound of Heaven*. Nicholson & Lee, editors. *The Oxford Book of English Mystical Verse*, 1917.

premise is free of anxiety. It is spontaneous and joyful. It is more like a love affair than indentured servitude.

Exactly the same is true in the moral life. There is an anxious morality which functions in the belief that keeping the commandments, playing by the rules, observing the various moral norms and codes of ethics governing our personal and professional lives, is a means to earning God's favor. But this also puts the cart before the horse. We don't have to earn God's favor. We are not on approval. All that God asks of us is that we show forth our thanks. The moral life is the way in which we do this. Behaving decently, treating others fairly, and maintaining our own integrity in all our dealings and doings are simply ways of expressing gratitude. Anxiety has no place in this moral framework. Whatever we do, we do gladly—not in order to be approved and accepted, but to say thank you because we are already accepted, unconditionally and absolutely.

It was by God's grace that I was given the opportunity to come to Stanford Medical Center and to Memorial Church at the end of 1973—when our family left South Africa and we had nowhere to go. It was by God's grace that, my own many serious mistakes notwithstanding, I have been used by God to touch the lives of others for good in this place. As I leave you my predominant feeling is one of gratitude: gratitude, above all, to God for the myriad ways in which my family and I have been blessed since we came to California. But gratitude as well to you and those many people through whom God's grace has been mediated to us. I hope to spend the rest of my life, both spiritually and morally, giving thanks.

Appendix 1

Farewell Public Lecture at Stanford—Swan Song—
December, 2001

Bioethics at Stanford: Retrospective and Prospective

Tom and Larry, I deeply appreciate your kind words. Thank you for them and for your colleagueship over the years; Anne Footer, and your team of helpers from our office, thank you so very much for your hard work in organizing and orchestrating this event. I also thank the members of my family and my friends, not only for coming tonight, but for supporting, encouraging, critiquing, and advising me over the years. Long may the ties that bind us endure!

Tonight I will be telling a story, a story that has really only just begun. Certainly, the full tale has yet to be told. In this story, there are many characters. Some of them will be named; others will not. Some of them are present here tonight; others aren't. To each of them, I owe a debt of gratitude, as does the university and medical center. For they all have played a role in the story of bioethics at Stanford—and some of them will continue to play their part long after I have left the scene.

The story begins sometime in 1973, when three people— Paul Hoffman, CEO and president of Stanford Hospital, Peter Carpenter, vice president of the medical school, and Robert Hamerton-Kelly, dean of Memorial Church—had the vision to create a new position in the medical center. The person appointed to this position would be asked to begin the teaching of biomedical ethics in the medical school, develop a chaplaincy program in the hospital, and serve as associate dean of Memorial Church. Bob Hamerton-Kelly and I had been classmates at Rhodes University back in the 1950s. He had come back to South Africa in 1973 to visit his mother in Bloemfontein, where I was the superintendent minister of the Methodist Church, responsible for the care of some forty-two thousand Methodists—some of them white, some of them so-called colored, and most of whom were black. I was moving in these three different worlds and was extremely active in the struggle against apartheid. Bob saw firsthand some of the work I was doing. Later that year, we decided to leave South Africa. I had been tipped off that I was about to be banned (placed under house arrest, without the benefit of a trial). We were heading back to the United States since we all had permanent resident status. When Bob heard of this, he immediately suggested that I apply for the new position and come to Stanford in an acting capacity while the search to fill the position was conducted.

As you can imagine, Margaret and I were elated by this offer. We arrived here in January 1974 (with four suitcases and our two younger children, Jenny and Timothy—the older two, Heather and Andrew, joined us later at the beginning of the new school year) and began work. At the time, if I remember, the salary I received was $14,000. In April, the search was concluded and I was formally appointed as chaplain to the Stanford Medical Center.

Academically, I was given a home in the Department of Family, Community, and Preventive Medicine, of which Count Gibson was the chair. In Count, I had a staunch ally in the long struggle to integrate bioethics into the medical school curriculum.

My training had been in theological ethics. Because of resistance to apartheid I was primarily interested in social and political ethics. I now had to apply ethical theory to a brand-new field. In order to begin to know what I was dealing with and talking about, I plunged into my own medical education—taking the gross anatomy course (which at that time extended over three quarters, three afternoons a week), auditing as many lectures as I possibly could in the medical school, and going into the operating room to observe procedures like open-heart surgery. My first course was offered in the spring of 1974. Bill Mobley and Bill Hurlbut were two of the medical students in the class. Both have gone on to have distinguished careers—Bill Mobley as chair of the department of neurology, and Bill Hurlbut as one of primary instructors in ethics in the department of human biology who has just been appointed to the President's Council on Bioethics. At the time, I think we were the second medical school in the country to offer a course in biomedical ethics.

Simultaneously, Ron Ariagno and others of us began regular early morning meetings in the division of neonatology to try to figure out ethical guidelines for treating extremely low-weight, very premature infants. These meetings continued for many years. In the era of Baby Doe, the framers of proposed regulation visited Stanford, saw what we were doing, and began to require that there be ethics committees in hospitals around the country.

Father John Hester joined me in the chaplaincy service (as it then was named—it later became a department) early in the summer of 1974, and together, we began to meet the spiritual needs of patients, family members, and staff in this medical center. John has been a valued colleague ever since and continues to be an incredibly dedicated spiritual caregiver in the hospital. I soon found that serving as chaplain was an invaluable adjunct to teaching biomedical ethics. As chaplain, I would move across all the specialties in medicine in a single week in a way no specialist physician was able to do: from obstetrics/gynecology to emergency medicine, from pediatrics to geriatrics, from the critical care setting to psychiatry, from oncology to orthopedics, from anesthesia to surgery. In each of these areas, I was involved in difficult cases that I could later draw upon in teaching, thus enabling me to expose the students to material from the real world.

Gradually, we began to offer more courses in bioethics in the medical school, attracting not only medical students but also undergraduates and graduate students from other departments. Slowly, the chaplaincy service grew in strength and numbers. And Memorial Church afforded me and many of my colleagues a spiritual home and base from which to operate.

Then, in the late 1970s and early 1980s, a number of new developments took place. One was the arrival back at Stanford of Tom, who had done his residency training at the Peter Brent Brigham Hospital in Boston. Tom and I teamed up in the intensive care unit in 1977 or 1978. His philosophy of intensive care was bold and refreshing. Tom believed that the job of the intensivist was "to salvage the salvageable, and to enable the dying to have a good death." This resonated precisely with my own view that when life could no longer be extended with meaning, then dying should not be prolonged by technological means. Together, we began to make a difference in the way end of life decisions were made in the intensive care unit.

At about that time, I also became increasingly aware that the people who most need exposure to biomedical ethics were not the medical students so much as the residents. Residents are on the front line, and have heavy responsibilities, little authority, and, at least in the beginning, no experience. I began working more and more with residents, offering bioethics seminars in the intensive care unit, in pediatrics, in anesthesia, in obstetrics/gynecology, in internal medicine, and eventually even in surgery!

The third development was the appointment in 1983 by Larry Crowley, then dean of the medical school and vice president of the university, of the first medical center ethics committee with Tom as chair. This committee had on it scholars from every major department in the medical school and from across the university. We concentrated on developing position papers on important biomedical ethical topics. Three of these papers were published in the *New England Journal of Medicine*. It was not until 1987 that the first hospital ethics committee was appointed, with me as chair. This was a medical staff subcommittee that focused on clinical ethics consultations, policy development, and bioethics education within the hospital. Margaret Eaton has recently taken over as my successor in chairing this outstanding committee. I can't think of any person better able to assume this responsibility.

Early in 1989, Tom and I decided that bioethics at Stanford had grown to such an extent that we needed to establish a Center for Biomedical Ethics. Until we had raised about $530,000 from private donors, the dean of the medical school wasn't receptive to the idea, but with cash in hand we were granted permission—not only by the dean but also by the provost and president of the university—to launch our new endeavor. Some of those who gave us financial support in the beginning and since then are in this audience tonight. I know that they would be embarrassed to be named, so I shall simply thank them, most sincerely. In order to devote myself more fully to the Center and to the activities we brought under the Center's umbrella, I stepped down as chaplain to the medical center, and George Fitzgerald took over. He has continued to build a strong Chaplaincy Department, one that is now an important national resource for training those called to hospital ministry. Linda Judd came over from the Chaplaincy Department to join me, becoming our first office manager and laying the foundations for our present infrastructure. By the time she accepted a position elsewhere in the university about a year ago, she and I had worked together for twenty-three years. Tom and I also formed a steering committee for the Center, comprised of distinguished scholars from the university as a whole, including Kenneth Arrow, Victor Fuchs, Susan Okin, David Stevenson, Linda Giudice, and Hank Greely, the current chair.

In its early days, the Center concentrated on consolidating the teaching of biomedical ethics—in the medical school, with residents, in the medical center through the monthly noon seminar series, and in the wider community through this quarterly symposium series, and on clinical ethical work. Bill Stubing, of the Greenwall Foundation, kept us going with a three-year operating budget grant, which he wisely made conditional on the dean eventually picking up some of the cost of keeping the center going. This later happened. But our research program needed to be strengthened. In 1995, we were able to recruit an executive director, and she has dynamically built up the center's research program. This, in turn, has brought in research associates and fellows, and gave rise to the Program in Genomics, Ethics, and Society. This program allowed us to organize three major conferences and publish important papers on ethical issues in genetic testing for breast cancer and Alzheimer's disease.

The Center has been able to attract a growing number of senior research associates and postdoctoral fellows. On display in the lobby are several posters summarizing the center's current areas of research as well as our undertakings individually. The principal investigators will be available during the reception to talk with you about their work.

An increasing number visiting scholars from around the world and around the country, including both Paul Hoffman and Peter Carpenter, has further helped build a national and international community of scholars associated with the center.

That brings the story up to the present day. The center is responsible for all bioethics education in the medical center, for all the clinical ethics consultations in Stanford Hospital and Clinics, for film production under the leadership of Maren Monsen (there is a video in the lobby featuring stills from Maren Monsen and Julia Haslett's upcoming documentary, *Worlds Apart,* an educational film exploring the impact that culture has on medical decision-making), for CD-ROM development by Sally Tobin, who has an interactive display in the lobby about the genetic revolution in medical care, and for the important research projects I mentioned a moment ago. We have an administrative staff of four, headed up by Anne Footer, our assistant director, and more than a score of faculty, research associates, and visiting scholars. We have about 2,300 square feet of office space and are continuing to grow rapidly, not only in size, but also in influence around the country and around the world.

That completes the retrospective part of this story of bioethics at Stanford. But as I said in the beginning, the story is still unfolding and will continue to unfold—I trust—for the remainder of this century, and beyond. This brings me to the prospective part. This segment of the story will be briefer. In it, I will sketch my vision for bioethics at Stanford as we look forward.

The challenges and opportunities presented to those in the field of bioethics today are truly staggering. They arise because of several interdependent factors: the constant development and deployment of new technologies; the changing economics of health care in the United States and the pressures economics is exerting on practicing physicians and nurses, as well as health care institutions; the way the law in its many guises—case law, regulation, and legislation—is evolving; the advent of new diseases such as HIV/AIDS and the potential resurgence of old diseases like smallpox in the hands of bioterrorists; and also the major demographic shifts that are occurring in our society, particularly in terms of the aging of America and our increased ethnic, cultural, and religious diversity.

Let me offer as an example a case referred to our hospital ethics committee, with which Margaret Eaton and Tom Fiene, both members of the committee, will be familiar. An incarcerated felon, convicted of murder, and sentenced to life without possibility of parole, was sent to Stanford for evaluation for liver transplantation. His liver had been destroyed, in the words of the medical director of the facility where he is incarcerated, because he had used "every possible substance imaginable, both legal and illegal." While in the penitentiary, he "found religion," turned his life around, gained some education, and then became a technical assistant in the facility's infirmary. The question, referred to us, was: When there is a dire shortage of livers for transplantation—of every one who receives a new liver, eleven on the waiting list will die for lack of suitable donors—ought convicted felons (or illegal immigrants, for that matter) be eligible to receive such a scare and costly resource?

In our analysis of this ethical issue, two considerations were in tension. On the one hand, we did not want considerations of "social worth" to figure in the allocation process. After all, who is of more social worth—the plumber or the physician, the poet or the politician? Trying to decide on this basis entails making subjective value judgments, with no objective way of settling the issue. On the other hand, we did not feel it ethically fair that medically indigent citizens—typically, the working poor who are ineligible for publicly funded programs like MediCal or Medicare, yet who do not earn enough money to be able to purchase private health insurance—should be unable to receive a life-saving therapy that could be made available either to felons or illegal immigrants. This was a concern about distributive justice.

What would you do? I won't make the question easier by telling you what we did at the time, except to say that our long-term recommendation was that there be a debate at the public policy level between the state legislature, the California Department of Corrections, and the public in general, about what felons and illegal immigrants ought to be entitled to in the way of high-technology, exotic, and very costly medical interventions. There is much that it is possible to do. But what ought we to do? That was the question. Needless to say, neither the Department of Corrections nor the state legislature has shown much inclination to confront this issue publicly.

Looking ahead, it is possible that new technological developments will ease ethical quandaries such as this, but at the same time substitute new questions for old. For example, if it proves possible genetically to engineer pig livers and other organs so that they will be histocompatible (that is, not subject to rejection by the body's immune system), this should alleviate the dire shortage of donor organs. However, the major concern with xenotransplantation has to do with organisms found in animals but not in humans that could cross the species barrier and wreak havoc in the human population, as HIV seems probably to have done—crossing the species barrier from nonhuman primates to humans. To address this problem, will there be those who will think of offering pig livers first of all to convicted felons—just to make sure that the rest of us are safe?

Or, looking even further forward, if it becomes possible to produce histocompatible hepatocytes from embryonic stem cells, obviating the need for donor organs and requiring only the transplantation of these new liver cells in a way similar to bone marrow transplantation, will the criterion for access to this new therapy be that of being able to pay for something that will inevitably be highly expensive? This will raise the old issue of distributive justice in a new guise.

These are the sorts of questions that do and will occupy those in the exciting field of bioethics. What is needed if we are to be equal to these challenges and opportunities?

First and foremost, the Center needs an endowment, as the Markkula Center in Applied Ethics has at Santa Clara University. If any of you in the audience would like the Center to be named after you, then please provide us with the money we need to be more independent from the medical school's budgetary constraints and less dependent on grants and gifts from foundations! An endowment would give us a permanent place in the life of this institution. At present, we are very much in a survival mode.

Second, we will need more faculty members. We will need

more people for teaching, for clinical ethics, and for research. Let's take these areas, one at a time.

A strategic goal for the Center, at the time of its inception, was that of being instrumental in creating a master's degree in bioethics here at Stanford, and eventually a PhD in bioethics as well. This would enable medical students who took an extra year or two to graduate with both an MD and either a master's or a PhD degree in bioethics. It would also allow undergraduates who wanted an advanced degree in bioethics to earn one here rather than at one or other of the other leading universities in the country—most of which now offer graduate degrees in bioethics. We have not realized this goal. This is partly because we do not have enough faculty members to teach and advise graduate students, and there are two reasons for that. One is that academic billets are scarcer than hen's teeth. The other is that even if we had the billets, we don't have the funding to hire anybody. In addition to an endowment for the center, we need endowed chairs in bioethics. But in the meantime, we need to integrate bioethics more completely into the medical school curriculum. The shape and form of the curriculum is currently being discussed. Whatever finally emerges, bioethics needs to be an integral component of medical education at every stage of the students' experience—from the first year through the fourth or fifth years of medical school, in the preclinical years and in the clinical rotations. Again, seizing this opportunity at all adequately will require additional personnel. And that takes us back to the issues of billets and funding.

Similarly, we need at least one full-time clinical ethicist in the hospital. We need ethicists who have the time to do daily rounds with the medical staff on each patient in each of our acute and critical care units, raising ethical aspects of patient care along with the predominantly and necessary medical concerns. At present, except for the medical-surgical ICU where we have interdisciplinary rounds twice a week, we are largely reactive rather than proactive. That is, we respond to requests for ethics consultations rather than identifying ethical issues beforehand, addressing these as early as possible—which is the only way truly to improve the quality of patient care.

In keeping with the mission of the university and the medical school, research in the field of bioethics has to become an even more pivotal component of the Center's life and work. When I look back and see how much we have accomplished with so little since our executive director joined us, I am amazed and proud. But we have only begun to scratch the surface. There is so much more important research needed on ethical issues in genetics, in geriatrics, in stem cell research and regenerative medicine, into ethnic and cultural beliefs and values as these are expressed in the health care setting, in biotechnology, in neurology, in medical informatics. The list goes on and on. Doing this work will require personnel. Keeping top researchers will require that they have opportunities for career development and advancement within the medical school in terms of tenure track positions. Making these two statements is easy. Translating what has been said into reality will take years and years of hard work and generous financial support.

I could go on, but I think I have said enough. My final word is one of gratitude. Gratitude for having been privileged to be part of a church community, a chaplaincy department, a medical school, and a Center that have been so important in the lives of so many people over the years; gratitude to all who have played a role in the story of bioethics at Stanford; gratitude to those who have taught me so much—patients, students, colleagues, critics, and friends. Above all, I am grateful to God—the giver of every good gift. Thank you for being here tonight and for being part of this story—retrospectively and prospectively. May what is yet to be accomplished eclipse everything we have so far been able to do!

Appendix 2

X-rays of My Pelvic Reconstruction Performed
by Dr. Jon Eastman at the University of
California, Davis, Medical Center
May 8, 2014

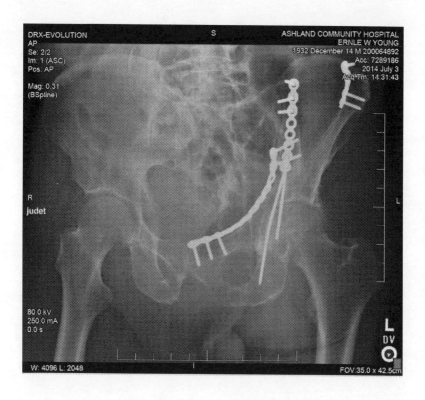

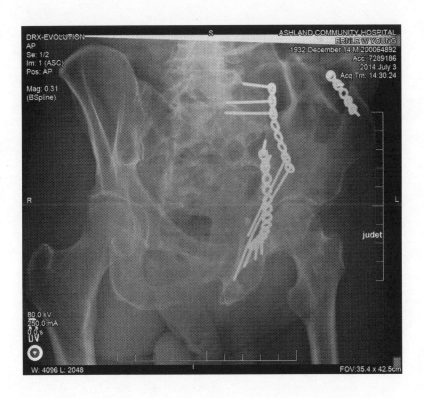

Printed in the United States
By Bookmasters